D0385119

Praise for
STRANGE BEAUTIFUL MUSIC

"I have known Joe since I was 12 years old, and every time Joe puts his fingers on a guitar what comes out sounds like inspired music, even if it's just a finger exercise. He created and branded a niche with his own voice and in so doing he wielded an entire genre, and he continues to do so with no excuses. He paved the way for many others!"

—STEVE VAI

"Joe Satriani's my favorite guitar player."

—SAMMY HAGAR

"Joe Satriani is in and surf's up, y'all! It's all about the wickedness of the wave and when the sand is shakin', you know Satch be earthquakin', makin' loud of his superbly satisfying signature sound. And when I say surf, think, 'The Silver Surfer' who stands out . . . shiny and showy . . . instant connectivity with Satch when his chome-plated silver 6-string thing is strap'd up, ready to slang, bang, and tang-the-tang. Ya' gotta dig on some Joe, now. A pleasantry in the purest with performance and power to please the most particularly picky of palettes. Jang on with Joe Satch, Brothers and Sisters. Surf's up."

—BILLY F. GIBBONS

"After all the times I had been on stages with Joe, been on the side of stages watching and listening to Joe, and all the times I have been in the audience cheering for Joe, I continue to have no idea how Joe does what he does. How does he do it? In 52 years of playing with others in public, very few have given me the personal and professional support that Joe has. It is exceptionally rare that a player of this standard is also this generous."

—ROBERT FRIPP

STRANGE BEAUTIFUL MUSIC

STRANGE BEAUTIFUL MUSIC

A Musical Memoir

JOE SATRIANI

AND JAKE BROWN

Foreword by Brian May

BenBella Books, Inc.
Dallas, TX

BenBella Books, Inc.
10300 N. Central Expressway, Suite #530
Dallas, TX 75231
www.benbellabooks.com
Send feedback to feedback@benbellabooks.com.

Printed in the United States of America
10 9 8 7 6 5 4 3 2 1

Library of Congress Cataloging-in-Publication Data

Satriani, Joe.
Strange beautiful music : a musical memoir / by Joe Satriani and Jake Brown.
pages cm
Includes bibliographical references and index.
ISBN 978-1-939529-64-0 (trade cloth : alk. paper)—ISBN 978-1-939529-65-7 (electronic) 1. Satriani, Joe. 2. Rock musicians—United States—Biography. 3. Guitarists—United States—Biography. I. Brown, Jake. II. Title.
ML419.S227A3 2014
782.42166092—dc23
[B] 2014000811

Editing by Erin Kelley
Copyediting by James Fraleigh
Proofreading by Cape Cod Compositors, Inc. and Laura Cherkas
Cover design by Ty Nowicki
Cover photo by Chapman Baehler
Text design and composition by Silver Feather Design
Printed by Bang Printing

Distributed by Perseus Distribution | www.perseusdistribution.com

To place orders through Perseus Distribution:
Tel: (800) 343-4499 | Fax: (800) 351-5073
E-mail: orderentry@perseusbooks.com

I would like to dedicate this book to the visitor from outer space who saw fit one night so many years ago, out on a distant lonely road, to beam me up to his spaceship, teach me how to play electric guitar, and return me to Earth, just to see what would happen next. Seriously now . . . This book is dedicated to all my wonderful fans around the world.

—JOE SATRIANI

This book is dedicated to my beautiful fiancée, Carrie Brock (Brown by the time this book is in stores!), for being so patient with my creative process and so loving to me personally throughout the journey that was writing this book.

—JAKE BROWN

Contents

Foreword

Queen used to work in Munich a lot, in a studio called Musicland, well known for its output of rock recordings. Our producer/engineer was called Mack—who notably made a song called "Crazy Little Thing Called Love" into a record in a matter of hours (with a little help from Freddie and us boys). One day Mack phoned me up and said, "I'm working with a young lad called Joe Satriani, who is an admirer of your playing. He wants me to send you the material we're working on so you can hear it." Just a young lad. Well, that first Satriani album arrived in the form of a cassette tape, and it's now one of my most treasured possessions. The content, as you all know, was spectacular, and the Man Who Surfed with the Alien has never looked back since.

A few years later, I was the musical director of a one-night stand in a set of shows in Seville, Spain, called Guitar Legends. Ours was the Rock Night. It was an amazing opportunity to put a set of brilliant guitarists together on one stage—including Steve Vai, Joe Walsh, Nuno Bettencourt, and, of course, Joe. I asked Paul Rodgers to come and galvanize us all—a smart choice, as it worked out; no matter how technically adept a guitarist is, I have never met one who didn't rate playing "All Right Now" with Paul as one of the great moments of his life! We all turned up for early rehearsals, so we were actually able to work together to make some unique collaborations. Joe was already a mighty star by that time, but he and his band jumped at the offer of going on first. I remember wondering if I was mad allowing this to happen, but I was backstage watching a TV monitor when Joe hit the stage smack on the dot of showtime, live on Spanish national TV. It was one of the most spine-chilling moments I can ever remember. It was as if the TV screen caught fire.

I'm proud to say that Joe became a great friend and we have played together a few times over the years. He's one of the most modest men I have ever met, and always makes me feel like I'm special, but I never get over the feeling of awe standing next to him on a stage. Joe has refined his own style of playing to a point where he's forever up there in the stratosphere of excellence that is reached by very few musicians. His technique is flawless, dazzling, and peppered with so many special bits of magic that few can even try to emulate. But over and above his technical skills, Joe has a burning passion in his playing that clinches his mastery and makes him one of the great guitar heroes of all time.

Among all the fireworks, Joe never lost his earthy edge. One of my great delights recently was playing the debut Chickenfoot album for the first time. I just couldn't stop smiling all the way through—especially in "Sexy Little Thing"; hearing Joe get back to ground level and lay down a riff as part of a great big hard-rock band outing was, to me, the greatest joy. I keep it in my car as the best pick-me-up I know for when I feel down. Yeeeeouch!

—**Brian May**
June 2013

CHAPTER 1 ★★

The Hendrix Experience

Jimi Hendrix was my biggest influence growing up, and on September 18, 1970, the day that Jimi died, I was crushed, for reasons I can't fully explain. It's impossible to go back in my mind to that moment as a teenager. Even now I can't quite say what happened in my head, but I know that because he died, I decided to become a guitar player. That moment of decision was immediate and profound. It changed my life and everything about me.

That same day, I quit the football team and announced to my coach that I was going to become a musician. At home that night, I told my family I had decided what I was going to do with my life: be a *Professional Guitar Player*.

After all the dust settled at the dinner table, my sister Carol offered to donate her first paycheck from working as an art teacher at the local high school to buy me an electric guitar, which speaks to the extremely supportive and musically inclined family I came from.

When I was growing up, my mom would spin classical music records as we played, with the intent of educating us, but the music she and my dad listened to was jazz. Mom would play the most popular classics, so we heard Mozart, Beethoven, Wagner, Puccini—all the usual suspects. Then we would hear Miles Davis and John Coltrane, all the way to Dave Brubeck and, later on, Stanley Turrentine and Freddie Hubbard when the seventies began. She was also a big Wes Montgomery fan (I think she had all his records), so we listened to him, too. My dad was a bit more big band–ish, but he listened to all styles of music throughout his life. He would tell me great stories about going to see all the great swing bands for a nickel as a kid growing up in New York City. He said he'd walk into these places, and it would be free half the time—you could get a beer for a nickel and watch the greatest big bands of all time. When my parents hosted parties they would spin all kinds of music and dance to all of it. They were both very open-minded and progressive in their appreciation of music.

Me at 15 with my first electric, a Hagstrom III
PHOTO BY SATRIANI FAMILY ARCHIVES

Being the youngest kid in the house, I grew up listening to what my older sisters and brother listened to, so that's how I heard early rock 'n' roll, Motown, and all the pop music that was around. Then, during the mid-sixties, when rock really started to become a thing, they brought that home, and as a little kid I was exposed to all of it. In 1966, when the first straight-ahead rock albums were being released by the bands who used to play pop, I was on the verge of turning ten, and being ten years old in the mid-sixties was a lot younger than being ten years old today. There was no Internet or anything like it, so my only new-music influences were what was on the radio and the music my siblings were bringing home.

I think the first time I connected with music was when we were on a summer vacation up in Vermont, and my sisters were going to a dance. So they let me stand inside the door of the dance hall for, like, half a minute, and I'm maybe eight or nine years old, and when I heard this band playing "(I Can't Get No) Satisfaction," by the Rolling Stones, it was a life-changing moment. It was the best-feeling and best-sounding thing I'd ever experienced in my life. That feeling never left me.

I think when I started to see the Beatles and the Stones on *The Ed Sullivan Show*, that sort of awakened my desire to play drums, so that's how I started out on drums. There was a piano in the house that my mom played jazz standards on. My three sisters struggled unsuccessfully with piano lessons, but my brother and I were somehow given a free pass—we never had to suffer through that. I think they had just given up on forcing us to take music lessons. Once I started playing drums at nine, I took lessons for a year or so, but that was really my whole musical education at that point. I was basically left to my own devices.

I remember quite clearly the first time I heard Jimi Hendrix, the Who, Led Zeppelin—these were the bands that my sisters were listening to. Their boyfriends would bring albums over, and they would get a kick out of the fact that I, just this little kid, had an appetite for this new music. I guess they thought it was cool, so they would say, "Hey, look at this, Jimi Hendrix, when he plays this part"—I think it was on *Electric Ladyland*—"no one knows how he does it." I'd listen to it obsessively. As my sisters would stop listening to their old 45s and LPs, they would pass them on to me. I also inherited a portable record player, the little suitcase kind. I would go to a quiet corner of the house, plug it into an outlet, put on the records, and listen to them constantly. So I assume my family witnessed this—me, just hanging out with the record player, listening to records over and over again and not playing with my toys while the music was on. I would just sit there staring at the record player and the LP jackets.

The conflict early on with that was that every time I would try to participate in making my own music, it was a bit of a failure. I couldn't play the piano as well as my mother; I could never get my brain around the left-hand/right-hand thing. Then I had my year of drum lessons, but I reached a wall where I recognized that I wasn't really progressing. So then I moved on to guitar, which was also a struggle, but I saw hope because I made these small, incremental steps forward every time I would play. I'd love to say that in 1970 I knew I was going to be an amazing guitar player, but I think it was more of a desire than a confirmation of any talent I recognized in myself.

My older sister Marian was a folk guitarist, so as a kid I got to hear her play, write songs, and even perform at her high school. Her acoustic guitar was the first one I started playing—she told me that I could play it whenever I wanted. She also showed me the chord chart she had in her guitar case, and explained it to me by telling me to just put my fingers where the dots were and to follow the numbers. That was it. She was very encouraging and just left me alone with the guitar, so I taught myself the first basic ten or twenty chords based on that chart. The next step came when a friend of mine told me about a guy he knew who could teach me barre chords. So I went over to this kid's house and he wrote them out on a piece of loose-leaf paper. I took them home and taught myself how to play those chords.

By that point, my parents had decided that if I was determined to play the guitar, I was going to have to take lessons. They were not adverse to one of their kids becoming a musician, because they knew that it could be done, that not everyone needed to go the conservative route of getting a college degree in order to survive. But they did have a hard-knock attitude toward it, sort of like, "If you're gonna do it, you're gonna do it." So I took three lessons from a guy in town. He was the epitome of what you would call a square guy who was quickly being left behind by the current generation. He looked square, he played square, and he was teaching guitar as a secondary thing while he studied to become a chiropractor. So after three lessons where he tried to teach me to read the sheet music to "Jingle Bells" while I was bringing him Jimi Hendrix's first album, asking to learn "Purple Haze," we parted ways.

For the next three years, I just taught myself. My parents had no interest in spending a lot of money on a guitar (especially since I'd just washed out on the drums!), so, with my sister Carol's offer to buy me my first electric, I was on my way. There was this white Hagstrom guitar at a local music store that looked like Jimi's—I was so naïve at the time that I didn't even really know what a Fender Stratocaster was!—and it was only $125, so I thought it would do. Once I got home and sat down with it for the first time, I quickly realized it was a completely different animal from my sister's acoustic. The art of electric rock guitar is really learning how to play all over the neck. I quickly started to realize how difficult it was to get the sound right, too, because I didn't have an amp back then. This was due to the understandable fact that there was no way my parents were going to buy me an amplifier just yet, because they were waiting to see if I was going to progress musically and stick with the guitar.

As a substitute, I managed to fashion my first guitar amp out of this old Wollensak reel-to-reel tape recorder my parents had at home. I don't know how I figured out that I could plug my guitar into it, but it made a cool little amp. I also found the only way I could hear the sound come out of its small, built-in speaker was to put on a reel of tape and push the RECORD button. So by the nature of the process, after I would play for fifteen minutes, I could listen back to what I had just played.

This discovery had a very big impact on me. It was really funny how it worked out, because once I started listening to myself play, I remember thinking how horrible I sounded, so I started to work on trying to "sound" good. The tape recorder also had a function that allowed you to play on top of what you had just recorded, essentially giving me my first exposure to multitrack recording. Once I discovered that, it also helped me work out this idea of playing solos on top of a rhythm, so that was what I did for about six months or so. After listening to me work like that for a few months, my dad broke down and bought me a small Univox amplifier. I'd turn it up to 10 and it sounded all distorted and I remember feeling like I was in heaven! My first effects pedal was an Electro-Harmonix Big Muff Pie fuzz box that I bought through the mail after seeing an advertisement in *Circus* magazine, and it was the biggest, fattest fuzz ever created. This was the first of many pedals to come.

It was very confusing when I first played with these pedals because I had no idea how to use them, or how to make myself sound like Hendrix! There was no YouTube back then to instantly instruct you on how to set things up, or on what sounds you could get out of a new piece of gear—you were pretty much on your own. After starting with the Big Muff, the next thing I got was a Maestro Phaser unit with the three buttons on it, and then the MXR, another phaser unit, and then a wah-wah pedal showed up eventually. I really didn't have a whole bunch of pedals back then. I was still trying to get my amps—which were small—to sound really big, and so I would turn them all the way up. Besides the Univox, I eventually used a few small Fender amps that I would borrow from friends. I wish I still had those amps from the early days . . .

CHAPTER 2 ★★

High School Confidential

Almost as soon as I got that Univox amp and my electric guitar, I started playing with some older guys in school. I was in a few no-name, no-gig bands before I joined a group called Mihchuacan. This was a band of guys who were a year or two ahead of me in high school. I'm not even sure how I got in the band, but somehow I wound up playing with these guys.

I learned A LOT from the guitar player, John Riccio, who could not only play a lot of different styles of music, jam, and improvise, but he could also play rock very well, either with a pick or by Travis picking. He was a very versatile player, and I was not; I was just a straight-ahead electric guitar player who used a pick. We had a lot of great times playing together, just the two of us, as he would instruct me with the band's material before we got together with the whole band for practice.

I remember the first show I ever did was a high school dance in the gym. I had extreme butterflies, so to help with that, I brought my Hendrix candle to the show. It was a very small, empty bottle of cheap champagne with a multicolored candle stuck in it. I would burn this candle and several candles like it every time I practiced. It was like a confidence booster to get me in touch with the spirit of Hendrix, to increase my talent, I guess. I don't know what I was thinking at the time—I just wanted some Hendrix mojo. So I brought it to the gig, and we played on these little risers that the school had provided for us. I was kind of in the middle by the drums. I remember feeling exhilarated the first time I stepped onstage to perform before a real rock 'n' roll crowd, but at the same time, I had my back turned to the audience, and I was petrified. I remember thinking it was the greatest thing ever, even though I don't think I really faced the audience throughout the whole performance!

After that, I went from being a kid on the football team to being a kid who just wanted to play music all the time. At the time I must have been responding to Jimi's pure genius, tempered with his sound, which was completely unconventional. In other words, he sounded like a virtuoso who never practiced a day in his life. He just sounded like a totally natural guitar player. Of course, years later, I'd learn that wasn't the case. I toured with Billy Cox, Hendrix's bass player, who told me that Hendrix practiced all day long. He said, "You hear those silly stories about someone sleeping with a guitar, that's the way he did it. He always had the guitar on, he was always working on his rhythm-and-blues guitar playing. That was his love, and he would practice it over and over again. He wouldn't practice scales; he would practice rhythm."

Once I'd caught the fever, I became obsessed with practicing, to the point that I was relentless about it: I had to do it every weekday, and then on the weekends. When I got to be sixteen and seventeen, I would stretch it longer when the summers came. I would just stay in and practice all day long. My friends would always call me on a Saturday night, asking, "Where are you?" or saying, "We're going to this big party," and I would say, "I'll meet you there after eleven. I'm busy practicing." I had to prove to myself that I could play as well as I had the day before, as well or better.

As I continued to grow more and more into myself as a guitar player, I started playing with a group called Tarsus, which featured Tom Garr on drums, Steve Muller on bass, and Danny Calvagna on vocals. Pete Maher replaced Tom on drums when Tom went to college, and we added a second vocalist, Paul Lancaster. It was a lot of fun. I did a lot of growing up through crazy rock 'n' roll experiences, the kind you have when you're young and in a band!

Steve Vai: Joe and I went to high school together. He was three or four years older than me, so his social group was very different from mine. He was part of the older cool kids. When you're twelve years old, a sixteen-year-old that plays the guitar can seem like a god. But there was no mistaking that he was very well known in our school and town as a great guitar player. He was the only one in our town, or many surrounding towns, who could really play. He was in a very cool band called Tarsus and they did rock covers from Led Zeppelin. I was in a band with the younger brother of the singer who was in Joe's band. We tried to emulate them in every way—we even named our band "Susrat," which is Tarsus backward.

Joe was different from anyone else in our school. He exuded a cool that permeated the vicinity he was in. He had the longest hair of anyone and everything he did or said just seemed cool to us. We all looked up to him and talked about him all the time. We would wait in the hallways that we knew he was going to pass through just to say hi to him. My standard presentation was a nervous smile, a little wave of my hand, and a "Hi, Joe." Any elicited response from him was fetishized and discussed among our group.

It was really great having someone like that in our fold that we could worship. I mean, this was a guy who could actually play the solo to Led Zeppelin's "Heartbreaker"! Although I was listening to guys like Jimmy Page, Jimi Hendrix, and Ritchie Blackmore while growing up, in all honesty, I thought Joe was better than any of them. I couldn't figure out how someone who was living in my town, who was sitting in front of me, could be so good. Better than my so-called heroes. Joe was my hero. Even when I was becoming successful with folks like Zappa and Roth, I would talk to the press about this guy who was leagues above us all. I thought that if the idea of a person becoming successful was based on their talent, then Joe would be an icon one day. I discovered this to be true

> because I can count on one crippled hand the number of people I have felt this way about, and Joe is one of them.

As soon as I started playing high school dances, kids started to ask me to give them guitar lessons. So when I was still fifteen, I started giving guitar lessons in my bedroom! My parents thought it was the greatest thing ever, mostly because it gave me money to buy my own guitar strings. It was mostly kids, but I had a few grown-up students as well. That's where I wound up teaching Steve Vai, and that's how we started our long friendship.

> **Steve Vai:** There's no way to quantify the importance my lessons with Joe had for me. From the first time I ever laid eyes on a guitar I was enamored with it. I never felt I was good enough to own one or play it, perhaps because of self-esteem issues. Finally, when I was thirteen years old, I got ahold of a guitar but never told anyone I played it. A friend of mine who lived a few houses down was taking lessons from Joe and he gave me Joe's number. Joe's a great teacher for many reasons, firstly because he could really play! He knew all the cool songs that I wanted to learn and his rock playing sounded authentic. Every time he touched the guitar something musical came out. He had a vast understanding of music theory and how it could apply to the guitar, and was very strict and demanded that I understand and memorize any theory he taught me.

When you're a teacher, you realize that you have to clearly encapsulate some unrelated technical ideas that you take for granted and understand and put them into words so someone else will understand them. That process crystallizes the lesson not only for the student, but for the teacher as well. So, I found the process of having to organize my thoughts about music helped me crystallize them for myself, and maybe understand them just a little more.

I got a kick out of sitting across from a thirteen-year-old Steve

Vai and realizing, "This kid is going to be playing better than me." I knew it, I just instinctively knew it. One thing was for sure: When I suddenly saw talent in front of me, like I did with Steve just innocently playing, it instantly made sense to me that there was no other way to be a teacher than to simply surrender everything that you knew. It was amazing to watch him take something that I figured out maybe just months ago, and watch him learn it and come back and play it better than I could. I thought, "Well then, if you're a teacher, you have to do it, surrender everything you know." You're bound by some sort of moral compass to do it that way.

Steve Vai: He set an amazingly high standard and pulled me up to it. I'm sure he gave freely to all of his students. He was a selfless teacher, meaning he gave you everything he had. But most importantly he inspired you to find yourself within it. He taught me to think independently and to find my own voice on the instrument. He always seemed to have a warehouse of information that never stopped flowing. He was very effective when teaching things such as form, style, exercises, scales, chords, theory, and so forth, because he was an example. I was able to see with my own eyes that what he was teaching he had mastered. That's the richest kind of inspiration. Along with that, he did not skimp on the academics. I was a subpar student in school and struggled terribly to comprehend and retain anything I learned in academic studies, but when Joe told me to learn something I committed it to memory unconditionally. It's amazing what you are capable of doing when someone you deeply respect has great expectations of you.

There was no time more exciting than 4:00 P.M. Thursday afternoons when I would walk across town to his house and sit in his room for my lesson. Even his room was the coolest. He had rock 'n' roll posters covering every wall, a stack of exceptional records, amplifiers, guitars—the works. My lessons were the most important thing in my life. They were treasures. They were my escape from some of the personal challenges I was going through. My lessons were my sanctuary and were all I cared about and focused on. My entire goal in life at the time was to make sure that Joe would approve of how I learned and grew from the previous week's lesson. Just being in his room was glorious. There's a psychological exercise that people do if they are experiencing a difficult time in their life. They focus on a "happy place," a time or place in their life where they felt safe, content, happy, and secure. For me, one of those places is Joe's teenage bedroom and my guitar lessons.

CHAPTER 3 ★★

Learning Curves

During this time, when I was sixteen and seventeen, I would turn on the radio and be mesmerized by what I was hearing. But every time I played the guitar, even though I loved it, there was always that frustration of wishing I could play better. I think for every musician, that's a daily reality where, if you're lucky, you can say, "Wow, I am a little better today than yesterday. I *do* remember this. I'm not in the dark with this concept." Even with that, I always ended every session thinking, "I wish I was better—maybe tomorrow."

Back then, influences were flying at me from all sides of the music spectrum. Growing up in the seventies exposed me to a crazy variety of musical styles. The radio was playing the Beatles; Led Zeppelin; America; Steve Miller; Steely Dan; Crosby, Stills & Nash; the Stones; Queen; Humble Pie; all that classic rock. So from 1970 to 1974, my formative years of learning how to play electric guitar while in high school, I heard all that music, everything from James Taylor through Black Sabbath, and I loved all of it. So I kept thinking, "I want to be able to play acoustic like James Taylor; I want to be able to make this dark, incredible music like Tony Iommi." I was still chasing Hendrix, but I was curious about all these other artists like John McLaughlin and Allan Holdsworth, and what they were doing. To me, it seemed like I needed time to stand still, so I could have another couple decades to work this all out. That's why I was staying in on Friday and Saturday nights practicing: because I was overwhelmed by the amount of talent out there. I would ask myself, "How do I get to the point where I sound as good as Jimmy Page and Jeff Beck? How do I play this Black Sabbath song and really sound like I'm where Tony Iommi is?" I was totally driven at that early age, from fourteen on through my later teens.

In high school, I had this brilliant music theory teacher, Bill Westcott, who really unlocked the power of the musical brain to me. His message was, "Your fingers may fail you, you may not turn out to be as physically talented as you think, but your mind can keep going, and the musician in your head is the one who's going to instruct your body how to best use your physical talent or lack thereof." This was a very important lesson to learn, and a very tough one when you're a punky teenager playing Black Sabbath and Led Zeppelin in a band and getting the adulation of your peers. To have some guy say, "Hey, you may suck when you turn twenty-two, and it may turn out everybody's better than you." So teaching me music theory, music history, ear training, learning how to sight-read better—all those things were invaluable. I really count that as the most important instruction of my whole life, those two years taking advanced music theory at Carle Place High School.

Me and high school music teacher Bill Westcott at Carle Place High School in '73

PHOTO BY SATRIANI FAMILY ARCHIVES

I remember very clearly back in New York—when I was already playing guitar at a point where I thought I was pretty good—sitting on my bed and turning on the radio, and on came a song by Yes. I remember sitting there listening to it, thinking, "I don't know what they're doing—what is that? How does a band create a piece of music so easy to listen to, and yet it's made up of parts I can't even recognize. How are they building that? How are they putting that together? How do they understand music rhythmically and harmonically and melodically, and make it all fit together?" And then of course the sound was fantastic as well. That's when I realized that I wasn't really that good after all, and that I could benefit from some music theory.

As a beginner, I would learn some chords, I would hit one chord I really liked, and then play another chord. I started playing them back and forth, and I would think to myself, "That sounds like a song," like I could hear somebody singing on top of that. So I would write the names of the chords down, and then I would say, "What does it sound like?" So I'd come up with a name for the song, and maybe write a description, like, "This song is about a bluebird." So every time that I would pick up the guitar to practice, that's what I would do, play my made-up little two- or three-chord song. This was before I took lessons, before I started playing with any other friends who played guitar. So I was left to my own compositional devices for material to play. As time went on, what I found was that it was more interesting, more compelling, and more artistically satisfying for me when I would play or work on music that came from an inner vision. Every time I went back to a song like that, I said, "This is where it's at; this is what makes the world go 'round for me. Not playing this other song that's popular in my school at the moment."

Early on, I experienced the emptiness of simply playing other people's music, even when it went over well. I realized that it wasn't like playing my own music, that I didn't have that insight into the composition process like I did with my own music. I learned in my music theory classes how conductors would really have to learn and understand a piece of music. They'd have to get into the heart and soul of the composer to properly direct the orchestra. And I thought, that's what it is—when I'm in a band playing a Black Sabbath song for a high school dance, I don't know why the guys in Black Sabbath wrote it. Well, no wonder I liked playing my own music, because this is a very long, accepted tradition in music, to be emotionally connected to what you're playing. That's the mark of a true artist.

What I started to understand was that the whole thing was a musical statement, that I couldn't just break it down and listen to the guitar part and say, "He's not doing much." That's when I started to understand that "technical perfection" had very little to do with it. So, for instance, when you hear John Lee Hooker singing "I'm in the Mood," you really can't find any way to dissect it, because what he's playing is such a beautiful, unique, and original statement that you have to figure out how to classify it in a way that doesn't break it down to its technical elements. It's selling the music short to say, "Well, he's playing the E chord, and then he's singing this note on top of it . . ." Because that's really not what's happening. If that's what was happening, then everybody who knew how to play a guitar could do it.

As I felt myself continuing to develop as a player, I applied my new listening lesson to Hendrix, and from there, I applied it to other players. Jeff Beck is so different from Hendrix; as players they're two different people. That's what we hear when we hear these guys: we hear *them*. Music gets filtered through their fingers and the technique they've picked up along the way, but their talent is really getting their unique personalities to come through their music. And that to me was the most important musical quest. I knew that's what I should be practicing at that age. I learned theory and fingering; I learned how to Travis pick, the details. But those are just little things in comparison to the real lesson: how to bring "yourself" out and represent it musically.

Jimi remained my greatest teacher throughout it all, directly influencing my use of feedback within melodies, solos, and even as harmonic beds. All that probably comes from him directly, from his recordings, both in the studio and live. He could use feedback to be musical—in other words, he would play with the notes melodically, just the way a horn player would. Before Jimi, people didn't really do that. They would use the noise simply to be a noise. I picked up on what Jimi did and it became part of my style. My blues style of playing is really based on his blues style; I know that his style is based on Buddy Guy and Albert King and a host of others, but I started with him. Then, as I got better at playing blues, I looked to Jimi's influences and educated myself all the way back. Today I know that every time I play blues, I'm pacing myself and looking for the same end result that I heard when I was listening to Hendrix's "Red House" back as a teenager.

By the time I was seventeen, I was so focused on mastering my craft and pursuing my dream that I actually graduated high school half a year early. I was a disruptive element and the school was happy to see me go. Hard to believe now, but back then, a rock 'n' roll playing, long-haired guy was just someone they didn't want in the school. It was a public high school in a small town on Long Island, and in retrospect, it's laughable, because that group of us who were musicians were actually the good guys, the harmless ones. The real troublemakers were the ones who didn't look like it, but society back then still did not like long-haired rock musicians, so we were vilified for wanting to do what we wanted to do. So they didn't want those of us who were good students but looked like rockers around. Maybe by getting a few of us who were musicians out of there, they were thinking, "They may not be playing at the high school dances anymore, but they won't be influencing the other kids to grow their hair," or whatever. They also probably thought we were doing drugs all the time, which we weren't. What I was doing all the time was practicing music.

When you're young, you don't realize you're being observed every day by your parents, and they're worrying about you. But that's what was happening with mine, and they must have thought that I was really crazy about music, but I just needed a little bit of help. My parents let us rehearse in our basement, which was crazy, and I don't know what possessed them to let us do that. I remember being very proud of them when they would talk down the police, who would come over to try to stop us for making too much noise. Once in a while, my mother would be concerned about the kind of songs we were singing, if she heard sexual connotations or demonic verses or something. We were just acting out, I suppose, trying to be like the bands that inspired us. But the neighbors hated us, and they would call the police, and I'd see my parents arguing our case and think they were really cool. They earned the respect of all my friends as well because they would stand up to the square neighborhood.

I still felt like I was going nowhere, mostly because the musical ambitions of the other guys in the band were different from mine. I still felt like I needed to understand the secrets of music, and I wasn't getting it from being in a rock 'n' roll band, and I didn't know what to do. I didn't know how I was going to understand what Mozart understood, or Miles Davis, or Jimi Hendrix, and no one was offering up any hints to me. The other big problem our band had was the lack of money. It was very difficult to make enough, and I didn't want to have to get a regular job. I was trying to figure out how musicians really made a living so they could take care of themselves.

Back on the academic front, I didn't get into Juilliard, which broke my heart. After that, I was accepted to the Berklee College of Music and went up to Boston to check it out, and I was horrified that it really was more like *Animal House*! I wanted the secrets of the musical universe unveiled to me, but it was so disappointing. My parents helped me look for a college, and we found this place on Long Island just starting up in their first year, Five Towns College. I attended that college for one semester, and that did not go well, because to me it was a joke being in classes with kids who knew one-sixteenth of what I knew. It was just a waste of time. So after a while, I told my dad I was ready to drop out and go pro. He said, "Go for it."

During this transition, I was fortunate to take two months of intense music lessons from bebop genius and father of cool jazz Lennie Tristano. He taught me what true musical discipline was. His ideas on improvisation as a way of life were eye-opening to me. However, his most important lesson was this: Don't live in the "subjunctive mood." Never worry about what you should have, would have, or could have played. Only play what you want to play. That's a lesson I still work on to this day.

I soon wound up in this disco band before it was called disco—they called it "progressive dance" back then, but it was really disco. For almost a year, I was in this band, and it was like being in hell, but I was working, playing music, and making money. The band was like this little corporation: The guys in the band were much older than I was, and they had it all worked out. Although I thought the music was horrible and didn't want to do it for the rest of my life, I really admired these guys who had figured out a way to be musicians and make a living. One guy was a music teacher but he played sax in the band. Another guy, all he did was this: He was the band leader, wrote the charts, and figured out how to get a loan to buy a van we could use to travel on these short tours around the East Coast. That was the first time I went on tour, the summer of 1975, and the whole thing was pretty interesting. Ultimately, that's also when I learned that I would never do that again, and that I should avoid it if at all possible, as if my survival depended upon it. It was a soul killer, something where you would slowly die as you stood on a bandstand playing popular music for people who didn't really care about you or what you had to say.

CHAPTER 4 ★★

Satch Goes West

In the winter of 1976, when I was nineteen, I made my way out west and moved into an apartment with one of my sisters in Berkeley. When I arrived in the Bay Area, I realized that everybody out here was an oddball, so I figured I'd fit in, too! It seemed like there was very little conformity going on. Even the number of famous artists who lived here did nothing to try to be like one another, and that was just something I liked.

To be honest, when I think back on what drew me out to the Bay Area, I have to say the weather was an obvious factor, because in Berkeley it was mild and gorgeous, compared to where I grew up in New York! No more suffering through freezing winters and humid 100-degree summers. It was also a lot cheaper to live out on the West Coast if you were at the bottom of the financial ladder. Since I was young and penniless, it seemed like a lot of fun.

I wound up renting a house in Berkeley right across from a music store called Second Hand Guitars, right next to Fat Albert's restaurant. I'd go across the street and play guitar all day long. One day the owner, Jim Larson, asked me, "Hey, you're not going to buy anything, are you?" I told him I wasn't, so he offered me a deal. I could come in and play as often as I wanted, so long as I also gave guitar lessons. I said straight out, "I don't want to get into that again," but he ended up convincing me.

"Let's just try it," he said. "I'll put an ad in the paper, and you can teach in the back room or during off-hours."

We worked out a deal where he got something like $2 off the top of what I was charging per lesson. It was very equitable, and it was fun to teach in a store that had fantastic vintage guitars on the wall and an overall cool environment.

Larry LaLonde, Primus lead guitarist: Within my age group around town, which was thirteen to fifteen, some of the other guitar players I knew had guitar teachers they were taking lessons from around the Bay Area, and it turned out in a short time we all learned that, ironically, OUR guitar teachers were all *taking lessons* from this guy Joe Satriani. And we were like, "Whoa, who's this guy?" And the buzz on Joe at that time, just locally, was that "this guy is better than Eddie Van Halen." As far as kids my age who played guitar were concerned, there was Eddie Van Halen and Randy Rhoads. So when we heard about this guy Joe, who at the time was also in this new band called the Squares, the question among my peers was, "How can we hear this guy?" because most of us were still too young to get in the clubs where his band played. So as fate would have it, I had around that time saved up enough money to go in and buy this Marshall cabinet at a place in Berkeley called Second Hand Guitars. And the day I went in to buy it, I saw this advertisement on the wall for "Guitar Lessons with Joe Satriani"! I couldn't believe it was him, so I immediately signed up for a lesson and he wound up becoming my teacher.

My teaching had to be flexible, because each student was so different. In one day, I might see Alex Skolnick, Larry LaLonde, David Bryson, and Charlie Hunter. Everyone who took lessons from me had to know the name of every note on the guitar and of every chord. I insisted on it, because otherwise we'd have no basis from which to move in whatever direction a particular student wanted to head.

Larry LaLonde: Joe was very good at assessing what your level as a player was right off, which for me at that time was still very low. The way it worked was: He would give you an assignment to learn over the next week, which was some form of exercise, a scale, for instance. When you came back in for the next lesson, he would also have you bring in a song you really wanted to learn, which he would figure out in two seconds. And the deal was, if you could pull off whatever technical lesson he'd given you to learn the week before, he would show you how to play whatever Van Halen or Randy Rhoads riff. So it was kind of a motivation to practice and learn the things he wanted you to, and it really made me want to practice, practice, practice whatever the technical lesson was that week. It would often be something repetitive and not that exciting from a playing point of view, but it was really fundamental exercise as far as getting your fingers together. It was the kind of routine where you would go up and down the neck of the guitar and if you'd miss even one note, he'd make you start over. So I would sit there and do these things that were hard exercises week after week, so even when I was practicing on my own, he had ingrained a discipline into me in which if I missed even one note, I would have to go back and start over. That turned out to be a really good method of practicing, and it helped when he started teaching me theory and how notes, scales, and chords went together, which at the time made no sense to me. So, for the first couple of months, he would explain these things to me, and I'd nod my head, secretly confused. Then I remember one day it all clicked and I was like, "Oh my God." It was a pretty amazing moment for me as a player.

Along with Larry, I was also teaching guys like Kirk Hammett and Alex Skolnick, who had gigs already where people were depending on them not only to write music, but also to shred. So part of the lesson always had to be about lead guitar, which would always involve more hard-core practicing. They had a real desire to get some work done fast. So if a guitar player like Alex came in and wanted to know how Allan Holdsworth, Hendrix, and Michael Schenker did what they did, then I'd tell them, and that's what we'd work on. That was our deal, and they happily took abuse from me because they said they wanted to be the greatest, and I'd always be very up front with them: "You want to be the greatest, and you want to be the greatest *by next week*? Then this is what it takes . . ."

Kirk Hammett, Metallica lead guitarist: Even back then he sounded like he does now. I mean, all the components of his guitar style were in place back then. I was just so totally blown away by his technique and his style. The first thing he said to me is, "Okay, if you're going to take lessons from me I expect you to learn your lessons. If you come in next week without learning the lessons, you're just going to be wasting our time and there's no real reason for you to be taking lessons." So he basically told me to have my act together when I came in the next week. So I had the lesson, learned everything over the week, and came back the next week. It just totally grew from there . . . I learned a lot of things from Joe, a lot of things about *technique* especially. I also learned that *feel* is better than anything and everything. So I've always strived be a player with a lot of *feeling* rather than a player with a lot of technique. I was always aware of the fact that you can say just as much with *five* notes as you can with five thousand notes. Learning that was very, very important to me.[1]

As I got more popular, I wound up with sixty students, and I could teach seven days a week, eight hours a day. I had a long waiting list, so that's how I made my living while I was playing with my band.

The Squares, my West Coast band, got together in late '79. When I first moved out to California, I had hung out with my sister's soon-to-be ex-husband, Neil Sheehan, a guy I'd written music with back when I was fourteen years old. He was a very smart guy and an engineer, but he'd also had a short stint playing with a pop band called the Critters that had some marginal success before my time on the East Coast. He was also a creative songwriter. He and I decided to try to put a band together where he could be a manager and a songwriter, and we both could find really cool guys to play with. He knew a little bit more about the local scene than I did; I was still quite young and not old enough to go to a lot of the clubs. So the Squares were born one night after my brother-in-law and I went down to the Old Waldorf club to see a local performer, Jane Dornacker, play. Her backup band was these two guys, Jeff Campitelli on drums and Andy Milton on bass. After the show, we went up to them and said, "You know, we're thinking of putting a band together from scratch, and want it to be this kind of a band. Would you be interested in doing it?"

The Squares playing in Sproul Plaza at UC Berkeley circa '80

PHOTO BY RUBINA SATRIANI

Jeff Campitelli, drummer: I remember Joe had come down to one of our shows to check out the band I happened to be playing in with one of his students, and we just hit it off backstage. We started talking and quickly found we had very similar interests in music, and he said he was putting together something, and he really liked my drumming and our bass player. So we got together at Joe's apartment the very next night and he started playing some demo ideas he had, and, of course, just listening to his playing, I

> immediately thought, "Wow, this guy's really good. He can *actually play*!" And at that time, I was coming from more of a school of playing with a lot of punk-type bands, just real fast three-chord stuff, and I remember being impressed by the fact that Joe could rock, but that he also had this incredible technical ability. So it struck me right away that it was pretty amazing. We all decided that night to get together and play. Within a couple days after that, we got together in my parents' garage—I was still living at home at the time—and played some Beatles tunes and a couple of Joe's tunes he'd been writing with his brother-in-law, and we just hit it off musically. It was one of those things you don't question; it just felt right. So we just started the band right there—we all said, "Hey, this is pretty cool," and started rehearsing. Andy had star quality without a doubt, and was one of those very strong yet extremely vulnerable, beautifully gifted singers. He was a fun bass player; he wasn't a guy who would ever consider trying toward any kind of virtuosity. He just wanted to rock 'n' roll; that was his thing. He had a beautiful voice, and the combination of being big, tall, and handsome and really sensitive was just this thing that made you want to watch him.

I could sense that Jeff liked the same drummers that I did, and although he was a lot younger than I was, he had elements of Ringo Starr, Charlie Watts, Mitch Mitchell, John Bonham, and Keith Moon. These were drummers who were all part of my foundation—they played in the bands that I thought wrote and played the greatest music, yet they were all different from each other. So it turned out that Jeff and I had this mutual appreciation for how different these drummers were and how they were at the core of the bands' ways of expressing themselves. If you had tried to switch their drummers out, they would kind of fall flat, so we knew it was more than just the technical ability: It was their feel, and that's what attracted me to Jeff's playing. I just thought he had a great feel on his own, and then when you presented him with music, he would seek out what he thought was the best feel for that piece of music, as compared to other drummers, who might simply take whatever you had and filter it through their "thing."

Jeff Campitelli: I remember Joe had a really great Marshall-amp rock tone, and at that time, he came into the group playing what was—and I don't want to pigeonhole him—a style that was a little more Van Halen-esque, because at the time they were huge. Back then, Joe was also playing through this Roland JC-120, which gave him a nice clean, chorus-y sound, and he could blend them together. I was coming from a more John Bonham, heavy-rock background. Back then, the Police were breaking, too, and New Wave was becoming more commonplace and breaking on a larger scale, and we were all three drawn to that. Once I heard Stewart Copeland, I thought, "Ooh, I can do a little fancy hi-hat thing," and Andy was definitely into Sting and trying to sing a little more like that. So we had a few ska-influenced beats and vocal parts coming in there, and collectively, along with my style of playing, I thought we stood out because we had this great pop vocalist and this heavy, great guitar player who really rocked. When we started rockin', it just felt right—an interesting combination of heavy but good melodies and some great background vocals, with some pop in there, too. So we thought, "All right, it's different," because nobody else was really doing anything like it at the time.

What made the Squares stand out from our Bay Area peers began with our very unique approach. For some reason, we decided right away that the band wasn't going to be about shredding at all—that was the part of the Squares that reflected New Wave music. It was guitar, bass, and drums, and a lot of the lead vocals were sung harmonized all the time, sort of like the Everly Brothers.

Jeff Campitelli: It was a really great music scene, with lots of clubs, lots of gigs, and lots of bands, and we immediately jumped right in. We had local management that came through Joe's brother-in-law—he did all the schmoozing with club managers so we didn't have to, because Joe and I didn't hang out a lot at these places. Andy was more social than me and Joe, but we were able to open up for some of the larger bands in the area. So for instance, our very first gig was opening for Greg Kihn at Keystone in Palo Alto, which was probably a 500- or 600-seat club. Then we found ourselves opening for Huey Lewis, and the Go-Go's would come through town and we'd open for them, and Squeeze, just all these great, larger touring bands!

We worked because we were different enough but still could fit in with some of the more punky, New Wave bands, so we played a ton of shows with bands like that. Then, when the metal stuff started to happen, some of those bands would open for us. So in a short time we built up a nice following, which allowed us to start headlining on the weekdays because we got to know all the club managers. We could just kind of keep up with everybody. We were all pretty good players, and I still get compliments to this day, like, "Man, you guys were the best band 'cause you guys could all play. We were all trying to write 'My Sharona,' and you guys would just come out and just jam for ten minutes on a song." Joe would stretch out on a solo, but we would hold the audience's attention throughout our shows. So quickly we also found ourselves headlining on weekends, and before long, we were selling 300, 400, or 500 tickets a show on Friday and Saturday nights.

John Cuniberti, producer/sound engineer: The first time I met Joe was when the Squares were playing their very first gig. I was actively involved in mixing live sound and hadn't really done a lot of studio work up to that point (although I was building a studio with a friend of mine at the time). I was mixing at the time for the Greg Kihn Band. They were local and had a hit record called *Jeopardy*, and they were packing them in, so I was mixing front-of-house for them. I remember one night, this band from Berkeley called the Squares was opening for Greg, and their manager came up to me and said, "Hey, it's our first gig, we're really nervous, the house sound guy here isn't very good, we like what you're doing with Greg, these guys are all from Berkeley, you may even know some of them—would you be willing to mix for them?' And I said, "I'd be happy to." And when they walked out onstage and started playing, I was instantly blown away! I said, "Who are these guys?" and specifically that guitar player—"Who is that?!"

I remember there was the general feeling that the band was unstoppable, and it was really going to be a big thing. There were bands at the time like the Knack who had clever, hooky little tunes, but they couldn't play like these guys. It was like the Squares were on another plane. I think their audiences would be divided between the musicians who saw them and would go, "Holy cow, these guys are on another level, and that guitar player is definitely someone to reckon with," and then there was the female side of the audience who just loved the lead singer because he looked a little like Elvis and sang like a bird. They were a very good-looking band, so people knew the Squares were doing something different and were going to go places.

Me onstage with the Squares in '81
PHOTO BY CATHERINE ANDERSON

We first met John while I was playing in the Squares and we were in desperate need of a sound guy. We were learning what you needed to be a good band, and that was the first realization: "Oh, the guy behind the mixing board, he's the Wizard of Oz! We need to find our own Wizard of Oz." We had heard John mix other bands, and we just thought, "If we could get that guy, that would be amazing." Whenever John mixed live, you heard the power of the punch in everybody's part, but you could still hear everybody's part. That's the key, because there's nothing worse than when you're watching a band and you see somebody do something, but you can't hear what they're doing. With John it sounded to us like how our instruments sounded when we played standing next to each other, so this guy must get it. After meeting him, we realized he was a musician himself—he was a drummer and had a history of making records—so he had been through several stages of his music life and brought with him that experience.

John Cuniberti: I think the sound and the presentation of the guitar in the band was definitely going to be an element, not unlike Andy Summers in the Police. The sound of his guitar in those early records was definitely instrumental in the sound of the band. The Squares also had a sound, and Joe's playing and sound and technique were definitely in effect; I think he even borrowed a little bit from Andy Summers. Because it was a three-piece, there was always this dilemma of, "How do you fill it out?" When you go to a solo, what kind of solo do you play when there's only a bass player playing? So Joe would rely on chorus and delay and reverbs to try to help fill out the sound. He was experimenting even then.

I just felt that Joe was serious. Up until then, I'd worked with a lot of people who weren't so serious, and I just knew Joe was going to be famous, from day one. I thought he'd be famous in the Squares—of course, it didn't work out that way, but I always knew Joe Satriani was going to be a famous musician.

I knew that first night hearing him play that I wanted to work with him. Two things really grabbed me about Joe. First, his command of the instrument, his authority. I'd worked with a lot of bands, all of which had lead guitar players, but those players were always looking at the necks of their guitars and struggling, trying to work to make their thing happen. By contrast, when Joe walked out, he just played things that were interesting and made it look effortless. His fingers would just flow across the fretboard. He would do things in one song that most of the guitar players I'd worked with up until then could barely make happen on a whole album. So his prowess and command of the instrument was the first thing. The other was that his solos weren't just typical blues-based phrasing and stuff. They were very melodic and singer-songwriter-like—in other words, thought-out. You could tell that he probably played the same solo every night the same way; everything was very structured and sculpted. But the whole band had a lot of energy and looked great, and I was immediately attracted to their music. So after they got done that night, I went backstage, found Joe, went up to him, and said, "Hey, man, I'm building a recording studio, and I want you guys to come in and record."

These guys were exceptionally well rehearsed. In comparison to bands I had been in and had worked with, which might rehearse two or three times a week if we were lucky, the Squares got together practically five nights a week. They were hell-bent on being the next big thing, and they knew that took a tremendous amount of practice. You could just tell by Joe's playing that he really practiced; he really made this a full-time job. I think he raised the bar for the other two guys in the band to also see it that seriously, because they had an attitude like, "This isn't for kids. If you really want to be successful, this is what you have to do: practice four to five hours a day," and Joe was a music teacher and came from that ethic of, "If you really want to learn how to do something, you're going to actually have to sit down and practice it—otherwise, don't waste my time."

He had no tolerance whatsoever for slackers. It's always been that way. You could hear it in his playing; every night those guitar solos were basically the same. There'd sometimes be some changes—sometimes he would change them completely, but only because they were still in development—but he played everything pretty much note for note, night after night after night after night. There was no jamming, the arrangements were super-tight, and the other two guys in the band had to get with the program. They had to learn their parts, and they had to play it exactly the same way, and Joe absolutely had no tolerance for "F-ing around." The lead singer/bassist, Andy, was a little looser, more old-school rock 'n' roll, you do it a little different every night, you drink a little too much, you have fun with it. Joe just couldn't tolerate that at all.

It was definitely insane, because we would practice five days a week, even if we didn't have any gigs during that period, for at least four hours a night, and we would just work it to death.

Jeff Campitelli: Four shows a month, easy, and we'd rehearse five nights a week, because we just loved to play, that was our thing. Joe would teach till eight o'clock, and then we'd start rehearsals at about nine and go until two in the morning. We did that Monday through the end of the week till our next gig. We'd take maybe one day off, and then do it all over again. We never really burned out because we really loved playing that much, and had a good time—it was our entire scene.

Compositionally, I was the group's leader. Andy was not as prolific, and that was a bit of a sore point because we couldn't get him to really take over in the role that we assumed he would. It's a funny thing: What he brought to the band, his voice, was so unique, none of us could even compare to it. It was a band where everybody had strengths and weaknesses. If I had one strength, it's that I was prolific, and if Andy said, "Oh, I'd love to write a song about this," I could write six songs about that for him, and that would be our starting point. Andy also was just a player by ear; he had no formal musical training and didn't understand chords or anything, so even with his own songs, he had to sit down with you and say, "You've got to help me figure this out. What am I trying to do here?" So a lot of musical work wound up on my lap, and I had to dictate how things were going to go, which turned me into musical leader.

Jeff Campitelli: We all played our part and shared in the writing credits because we all felt we brought something to the table that the other guys might not have come up with. Joe took the lead because he was definitely the most prolific. Joe knew music inside and out. He was a master of theory and of which notes went together and which didn't. How that worked was, Joe might come in with a riff or some cool chord changes, start playing them, and I would come up with a beat, and then either Andy would start working on a bass line and humming a melody or Joe would have an idea for a melody. Then we would give the melody to Neil, the manager, and he would write all the lyrics. So it was four of us who were contributing and sharing in the songwriting credits, but again I would say Joe was definitely the most prolific because he was bringing in the most stuff, and he knew the most about music theory.

John Cuniberti: Jeff, the drummer, was laid back, and was the youngest, and was just going along with the proceedings, and Andy was a bit of a loose cannon. He was a little unpredictable as far as his behavior, and he wasn't the musician Joe was. He tried, but he certainly wasn't going to be able to play the bass as well as Joe played the guitar. So I don't think there was any question that Joe was the musical leader of the band.

John understood us, and he allowed us to be ourselves during the recording process. It was great to be back in the studio with my own band. We had a sound; we had our own songs; and we had a lot of energy and momentum going because we'd already played in front of club audiences that really liked us.

John Cuniberti: At the time, my friend and I had just built our studio and had a 16-track, and because my background was in live sound, it was a fairly straightforward process to bring a band in, set them up, throw some mics up, and get the stuff recorded. Those first recordings we made were a good documentation of what the Squares were doing live, because in those days, in the very late 1970s, people made demos—you didn't make a record. Back then, only artists who had record contracts got to make records, so there was a real clear division between a demo tape, which meant cassettes, and a record contract where you had a real producer, worked in a real studio, and ended up with a final record that sounded like a vinyl album. There weren't a whole lot of overdubs done. There was one song where we put some acoustic guitars on it, and then there were some background vocals and double-tracking of vocals—stuff like that. But it was pretty straight ahead, and I liked the songs the Squares played, and the sound we made in the studio. I was doing other records with other musicians, but a lot of them—as much as I enjoyed the process of recording—weren't bands I went home and listened to at night. But with Joe and the Squares, they were actually making music I wanted to listen to, so that made it a whole lot easier.

Between Joe and me, I believe Joe saw that I was as passionate about recording music as he was about playing guitar. We both saw each other as allies in becoming famous recording artists. At the time, and still I guess to some degree now, recording engineers needed a band as a vehicle to become famous. You couldn't just be the house engineer and build a reputation by doing little bits of this and that. You really needed to be the guy responsible for a band becoming famous, and then you would be tied to that, and other bands would seek you out based on that reputation. So I was hell-bent and seriously focused on having a career as a recording engineer, and I think Joe saw that, saw my seriousness, when he showed up at the studio and noticed I'd been there an hour before and had everything set up. I'm a bit anal when it comes to everything—the gear, making sure everything's working all the time—and I think he was, too, and appreciated it.

That first demo John recorded and mixed for us is the way we like to remember ourselves. He captured the moment perfectly.

Ultimately, the later demos led to the band falling apart for me because it didn't seem like we had the right ingredients to compare with the fantastic singers and writers who were ultimately going to be our competition. We got more prolific, we got more detailed, but we never quite captured that "moment" again, and we never really got any better.

John Cuniberti: The first set of recordings I did with the Squares were the most spirited. They were very "ruckus," very straightforward, and just filled with life. Even back then, it was absolutely an ambition of Joe's from day one to get signed, so the next time we were back in the studio, that was when we started making more "serious" recordings. By then, I had moved to another studio in San Francisco, and we were recording on a 24-track in nicer rooms and stuff, so the management and people who were representing the band and trying to get them a recording contract had a lot of say in the direction of the band and the material. People were saying, "You don't have a hit song," et cetera, and I think their influence on the proceedings really kind of made it awkward for Joe. I think after the first set of demos, the band got steered in a direction that was uncomfortable for Joe, and he didn't like it. From my observations, there was way too much emphasis on trying to get a hit single and be really pop, and he didn't really have as much of a voice as he had before. He could only control it so much, but he wanted to be successful and was willing to make compromises. I just think those compromises that required him to be a pop star were really beginning to rub him the wrong way, and I think it showed in the material and the performances and ultimately led to the demise of the Squares.

As things with the Squares came to a close, it was complicated because I definitely felt musically like it was not satisfying anymore, that the band could not really grow how I wanted it to grow. That meant that as a team, we weren't writing songs that I liked anymore. The Squares was a power-pop band— how would I be able to express the elements that I put into *Surfing with the Alien* with that band? In a band that did not like long guitar solos, that was a thing we just didn't do.

Jeff Campitelli: Near the end, it got to be a little more trying for Joe because Andy didn't want to become a bass player with lots of chops; he wanted to be the singer. In fact, there was actually a time toward the end of the band when we were auditioning bass players, and Andy was fine with that.

Because Andy was not an improviser, you couldn't just wink at him and say, "We're going to do this for five minutes." He just couldn't do it, and didn't want to. It just naturally was not something he was into. It was one of several real problems with that band. One of our big challenges was we were not making enough money to survive, even as well as we were doing live. We had been turned down every time we tried to get a record deal, and our demos were getting technically better, but musically worse. The energy was not there anymore, and even though we all may have hoped we'd grow together in the same direction, we were actually splitting up over what we really wanted to do.

Jeff Campitelli: Our decision as a group to split up was mutual. What was happening at the time, in truth, is we were maxed out. We were headlining every club, to where I remember walking out onstage on any given Friday night to do our hour-and-a-half set, and the show would be sold out, and we were each making around $500 cash, but after a while it became a ceiling to us. We'd reached one level of success that was satisfying locally, but we all had bigger ambitions, and the groupthink near the end of the band was, "Man, we gotta get signed!" We were making a living just playing original music in clubs throughout the Bay Area, and it was a wonderful period.

As this was all happening and the buzz was going on around our band, we were starting to get offers from other, more established acts to join. For instance, I got an offer around that time to leave and join Eddie Money's band. Also, during all of that going on around the band, internally Joe and Andy weren't getting along all that well, and I felt after a while like I was just the nice guy in between trying to hold it all together. That in time would prove distracting to our focus compositionally, because near the end, if you listen to our demos, the music was just all over the place. One song would be more this direction, and another would be in the opposite direction, which translated to us scaring away ALL the big recording companies who were checking us out at the time. From all that it was just obvious that things were coming to a close. I remember talking to Joe one night and telling him about the offer from Eddie Money to play much bigger venues—2,000- to 3,000-seaters—and I just told him, "This is a good opportunity and I think I'm going to take it," and he was cool with it, because I think he was heading at that point in his own direction musically.

John Cuniberti: For a while after the Squares broke up, I got the sense Joe was really discouraged by the whole process, and I would venture as far as to say he was maybe even second-guessing whether the whole thing was going to be possible or not. I think that led him to take more direct control of his music from that point on and focus on becoming a solo artist.

I felt the artistic drive to strike out on my own, and I thought, I've got to do it in a way where maybe I'm not using it to make money or to be a career; it has to be a purely artistic venture. That's why I got so into playing, and to accomplish this, I was going to need to control it. I couldn't ruin it by trying to bring it into my reality as a working musician. I had to keep it as a new thing where I could control every element, where trying to make it go commercial never entered into it. I knew instinctively if I got the people I knew involved in it, that it would be compromised. Therefore, if I wasn't expecting to make money off of it, I didn't have to include anybody. It could be like sitting at home and painting weird pictures for yourself without worrying about the outside world and how people will review them or if they'll buy them or not. So once I'd crossed that threshold, I realized, "Wow, I can do whatever I want." So that was a great leap for me, intellectually and emotionally.

1. Courtesy of: www.GibsonGuitar.in, The Gibson Interview, May 6, 2011.

CHAPTER 5 ★★

Twists of Fate—*The Joe Satriani EP,* 1983–1984

"Though it's packed in a plain white cover with the artist's name in black block letters, this is anything but generic rock and roll. The much-needed clarification that 'every sound on this record was made on an electric guitar' is still hard to believe, especially with the sound effects that begin 'Talk to Me' and the popping 'bass' in 'Dreaming Number Eleven.' Satriani comes highly recommended by guitar wizard Steve Vai. Spacey but melodic and soulful."

—*Guitar Player* magazine

There was a place where we used to rehearse, next to this small publishing operation that did how-to books on just about everything—starting a business, getting a divorce, all kinds of things. We'd stand outside our barn door and have a smoke and drink and check out their Dumpster, which was overflowing with misprinted books. So we'd be standing there laughing at the books with titles like *How to Get a Divorce* and *How to Run a Juice Stand* and so forth. One day I spotted a book about starting your own business, so I took it home, read it, and realized I could start my own record company if I wanted to. I thought, "Why am I not doing this?"

At the time, I remember, I was trading phone calls, letters, and cassettes with Steve Vai, who had been living out in L.A. and working with Frank Zappa. He was obviously having the time of his life working with a genius who understood everything about how to use recording as a medium unto itself. Steve started experimenting with multitrack recording, and those early recordings were so wonderfully bizarre, I just loved them. There were tracks made of vocals sped up and slowed down, unbelievable guitar harmonies, unusual time changes—and of course he was recording with musicians who were absolutely incredible.

> **Steve Vai:** Back then, I was completely enamored with the idea of sound-on-sound recording, and the moment I had enough money to purchase a 4-track sound-on-sound recorder, I would record stuff all day long. Hanging out with Frank Zappa and watching the way he made his music was paramount. He taught me how to edit analog tape. The entire recording and editing process held infinite possibilities and I would experiment constantly. Recording things backward, sped up, slowed down, overdubs on top of overdubs, using EQs and any effects I could find, building guitar and vocal harmonies that were previously impossible, recording conversations, events, TV commercials, cats screaming—you name it and I'd figure out a way to use it! Then taking that stuff and cutting it up and recording over it, streams of consciousness, bizarre guitar riffs with beautiful and disturbing harmonies, et cetera, et cetera. I could have been the sixth Beatle! It was like every day was Christmas.

Toward the end of high school, I had inherited another Sony 2-track reel-to-reel tape recorder, and not only would I be making 2-track guitar recordings, demos, and things like that for the band, but my friends and I would also make these goofy comedy recordings that were like the Fireside Theatre. So I remember playing that stuff for Steve when he was a young kid taking lessons, and he of course was fascinated with it. I think Steve has a recording from that machine of the two of us improvising at a guitar lesson.

When I left New York and moved to California, I no longer had this tape recorder, but I did take with me all those hours of experience playing with tape recorders, and I kept thinking, "I've got to get back to that one of these days." So fast-forward five years, and I'm in the studio with Jeff Holt (an engineer I'll introduce you to in a moment), thinking, "I remember doing this, and I know you can create fantasies with a tape recorder." Even though we'd made all these demos for the Squares in professional studios, they left me feeling flat. They still just sounded like really great recordings of the band, and I already wasn't really happy with the band, so obviously these recordings didn't mean much to me. But the recordings that I had from my previous life in New York meant much more to me, even though they were really weird sounding. So I had these tapes, and I'd listen to them and think, "That's just so much more satisfying because it's so odd," and that brought me to the realization that I needed to make what became the *Joe Satriani* EP.

It all started to crystallize: knowing Jeff, taking in Steve's recordings, listening to stuff by Robert Fripp, Adrian Belew, and the like . . . Plus living in Berkeley, where there certainly were a lot of oddballs that I identified with, exposed me to artists who were producing their own music and going against the commercial trends of the time. All these elements came together and made me realize, "Wow, this is something that's been part of me since I left New York, and maybe I want to go back to how I started out."

So I took three or four weeks off from practicing incessantly with the band, and during that break I decided that I would start my own company and record an album. My experience with the Squares was winding down because the conflict in the band was winding up, so it was almost like a knee-jerk reaction: "I'm going to make a record, and I don't want to deal with band politics, so how do I make a record by myself?"

Musically thinking, I knew there were many artists like Brian Eno, Fripp, and Belew who were all making music that engaged me.

I realized I had all this odd music that I suspected would get spoiled by a band, because the drummer would want to rock, the bass player would want to create his or her own riffs, and the "unusualness" of my music would be compromised by being made accessible. I didn't want to be accessible. I knew I had to do something to catch this odd approach to music, but I wasn't sure exactly what that something should be. That's when I started making phone calls and hooked up with Jeff Holt.

I'd first met Jeff because he was volunteering to record the Squares. I got to know him and I thought, "I like this guy. I think he's very talented as an engineer, and he seems to be at the right place at the right time with the right kind of ideas." I felt Jeff fell into this rare category of someone who understood that different bands need to be recorded in different ways. He had his own studio, Likewise Productions, which meant he could do whatever he wanted because he wasn't answering to a studio owner. So I got to know him better when I called him back years later with the idea of doing this solo EP, and he was not only receptive but he also had the inclination to try to pursue it with me. Neither of us knew exactly what we were doing, or how it was going to turn out. But he had a very positive attitude and the engineering chops to improvise with me.

Jeff Holt: When I was working with a local San Francisco FM rock radio station, "Rockin' the Bay KMEL," I was also writing and recording seven-second sound clips at my studio, Likewise Productions in Oakland, California. The radio station was celebrating its fifth birthday and asked me if I knew any local band that wanted to record a version of "Happy Birthday" to be played at a concert at the Greek Theatre in Berkeley. I figured it'd be a great chance to record my favorite local band. So I had Joe, Jeff, and Andy come in on Thursday, December 8, 1983. We came out of the session with a slick, quick version of "Happy Birthday." Kind of like the Squares meet Van Halen. I remember Joe playing through a Marshall half stack with great tone. Jeff had that fresh pop on the snare and

> bright cymbals, with Andy through a Countryman direct box. Once we had the sound dialed in we did about seven takes. It was a blast! So when Joe called me up, I was excited about the chance to work with him individually, which stemmed from an admiration standpoint, too, because by that point I was very familiar with his live performance and just really dug his sound. There weren't many guys doing what he was doing, and I definitely knew he was going to be "the guy," so to speak. Joe definitely had that aura about him, so it was all exciting, especially with his concept for the EP because he wanted to create these songs using just the guitar, which meant tapping on his pickups for the kick drum and above the neck for the snare.

I remember arranging the songs for the EP while sitting on the front stoop of my Ward Street apartment, notebook in hand, asking myself, "Okay, I'm going to produce this album, so what do I want to happen? How does a producer do this? How do they write a script or a storyboard, a musical timeline that is more than a musical manuscript?" I would write out these particular chord progressions with a note for scraping technique, and then I would write, "Kick drum will be Allen wrench on neck pickup for the whole piece," with a note to myself: "When do I record this?"—that would be a note I would write to ask Jeff. Next thing would be, "What do I do for cymbal-type activity?" because I knew I was going to need quarter, eighth, or sixteenth notes to replace the typical hi-hat/ride cymbal pattern. So I'd write a note saying, "Scraping strings over the peghead," or "Cymbal hi-hat simulation." And I would write these little things where they would go for a certain amount of time and stop, and then it would come to a point where I might say, "Guitars coming from reverb abyss to the forefront totally dry and in your face. How do I do that?" You can see how personal this music was. It wasn't like the Squares' stuff where we were aiming toward an idea of a band—this was really strange music that came from inside of me, that I wasn't compromising at all for any reason. So I was ready to lose myself in bringing this sound to life.

Jeff Holt: On the first day of recording, Joe came in with a notebook full of ideas, and I could see he was just ready for it. It was all new territory for him, being his first one-on-one experience recording in the studio. Still, with Joe, you're dealing with a very adept solo artist. I could see that in the eighties, there was an unwritten law that the engineers and producers should keep the musicians on the other side of the glass, if you will, so that they held the mystique and control of getting musicians to get their sound. Being a musician myself, my theory was that if I can teach these guys about faders and panning knobs, stuff like that, really try to get them involved in their own sound, they would come back to work with me again. And especially with a guy like Joe, he definitely was a sponge, soaking it all in, and he was really interested in knowing what made the transmission of his sound to tape. I felt that was one of the reasons he chose to work with me on this first thing: I gave him total access. I don't know if I was really breaking any unwritten rule, but I felt that by going about it how I did, we had a good working relationship. Even though we were working in a really small studio, there weren't other people around, because this place was in the basement of my house, so it was definitely a private situation where Joe could focus without distraction on his vision for the record.

It proved a very conducive atmosphere to getting him behind the controls and showing him as much as I knew. It's amazing how in instances where you work with people of Joe's talent they wind up teaching you, because they're asking all these questions. Some musicians don't want to know about recording—they get really uncomfortable—but Joe fit right into that role. I know in my case it helped me out a lot because, as an engineer, you're able to perform what an artist wants right there while they're sitting next to you. So I was getting the immediate response of the effect I was putting on because Joe was sitting right there with me in the control room, which was important. He definitely wanted to know as much as he could, and he was the guy listening in the middle of the speakers to the stereo pan, to make sure that imaging was there.

As we started recording, I remember being really fascinated from day one with the recording process itself, and there were so many times when Jeff would show me something, and I would look at him like a little kid and say, "You mean I can do that?"

All of this was important because I was learning a lot about how to make some of my crazy ideas a reality based on his experience, and Jeff was open enough to teach me how to do it as if he were teaching another engineer. I think it was necessary for him to understand what it was that I was trying to achieve, and for me to be happy artistically. Likewise, I needed to feel that I could gain control of those engineering elements. So he was there to enlighten me on how to use the studio to complete what I started on the guitar. How could we get the vision from my brain to the guitar to the tape? So as I would come into the studio with these notes, Jeff and I would talk about the song.

Jeff Holt: From the first day of recording, those conversations were wild. I remember Joe instructing me that the first thing we were going to do was go into the reel of tape, advance it, and flip the reels over. We recorded the backward intro that can be heard on "I Am Become Death." "Wow," I thought, "this is going to be a crazy set of studio sessions!" The record had no live drums or drum machines—the whole idea was Joe would tap with an Allen wrench on his pickup to get the kick drum.

A word on how an Allen wrench became my drummer: When I worked on music in my apartment, I'd have to play with headphones, so I was sitting there using that 4-track tape recorder. The Kramer Pacer I was playing would go out of tune if you just looked at it, so I was endlessly tuning it with an Allen wrench. Ultimately I'd be sitting there with the headphones on, changing strings or something, and the magnetic pull of the pickup would pull the Allen wrench against it, and I would hear a thump. And I guess that just registered in my head as a cool sound. So I started to play around with that, and it crossed my mind, well, if I've got a thump, how would I make a snare sound? So I'd go looking for some other part of the pickup or something else on the guitar to hit with the wrench. It really started from that.

When I brought it to Jeff, I said, "Listen to this! I'd like to use it for the kick drum." He said, "Well, okay, how do I control this sound that's got this huge transient? How do we get it to fit in?" So he looked at it as if it were a guy on the other side of the glass stepping on a kick drum. That's when I was introduced to how we could use limiting, adjust attack time and threshold, and manipulate equalization so we could carve the sound that we wanted. By muting the high end so the listener would hear the thump of it, and with the right limiting, it would always come in at the right volume. That was the genesis. Accidents sometimes create innovation. Maybe Johnny Cash's famous dollar bill flew between his guitar strings one day, and he said, "Wow, that sounds cool . . ."

Like all good engineers, Jeff knew the relationship between the pitch of a note and what frequencies were its most fundamental, and so we were able to get that two-note *bom-bom* on "Banana Mango" to sound like it was some kind of a Taiko drum or something, but it was actually just me playing a detuned guitar string. That same guitar is on that track playing these beautiful harmonics, a '54 Fender Stratocaster. And as I mentioned earlier, a lot of it came about when Jeff would ask, "What do you want to do next?" I would tell him, but I would also end with a question, like "This is what I wanna do. How do you think we should do it? Should we play it loud? Should we do it quietly?" And he would have to make that decision, because I didn't know anything about microphones, which mics to use, and I'm sure he was thinking, "Well, Joe wants this to eventually be a very low-sounding piece, where there's a lot of low-end being accentuated from it," so he might suggest to me a different volume level so that he could use a different mic that was better at picking up low frequencies. If it was a really biting, typical lead guitar thing, he might suggest the traditional setup with an SM57 and just go out there and turn it all the way up. Those were the things he had to interpret for me.

By that point, I also had two guitars for which I had gathered all the pieces from scratch. They were mostly made from Boogie Bodies; one of the guitar necks was an ESP, and the other may have been a Boogie Body neck. As far as the parts I bought, I think I had Seymour Duncan pickups. Bill Knapf did all the wiring, and a local guy did the finishing. Those guitars looked beautiful. Also, toward the last year of the Squares, I bought the Kramer Pacer, which had the very first version of a Floyd Rose vibrato bar. This was a big deal, because in trying to extricate myself from the late sixties and early seventies and really embrace the eighties, I'd gotten rid of playing with a vibrato bar, just as I'd sworn off ever using a wah-wah pedal again. But at this point, I noticed that everyone around me was using this Floyd Rose bar, and I started thinking that maybe there was a way I could use the bar and not just sound like someone who wanted to play like Eddie Van Halen. So Jeff Campitelli and I hit the Guitar Center in S.F. for one of their "midnight madness" sales, and I picked up the Kramer for about $400. It had all the wrong hardware on it, but I loved the guitar. It really did have a beautiful tone, and I just totally got into the vibrato bar it had. After I'd avoided using the bar for years, it revolutionized my playing style, so obviously that's all over that first EP.

Another thing I loved about that guitar was it allowed me to indulge in being the Hendrix freak that I was. I worked on depressing the bar, getting the strings to be slack, bringing notes up, and then connecting them to a fretted note. This was something I'd picked up from Hendrix, who had used it a lot on *Electric Ladyland*, and specifically on "Machine Gun," so there are little things like that where I'd be paying homage to Hendrix. I noticed that I started trying to make some unusual noises, like taking the bar and pressing it against the strings itself, which would give me all sorts of strange clanking and metallic noises—that was something that I didn't hear anyone else doing at the time and I worked that into different songs.

Jeff Holt: On the EP, it was very impressive because Joe came in with everything together gear-wise on his end. He came in with a notebook full of ideas and some crazy stomp boxes. We experimented with mic placement on the speaker cabinets to get different tones. I remember he was definitely using a Marshall, and Randy Stapman, the local guitar tech, worked on Joe's amps and was able to change the bias on the tubes, and it was all about getting the combination of the tubes. So early on, Joe was into maintaining his gear, and he would usually use a couple of half stacks—he never went for the double stack. He had a lot of little stomp boxes—the DS-1, the MXR, stuff like that. He didn't have a tech that set any of that stuff up; it was all me and Joe. He had a van he'd pull into the driveway, and we'd set all his gear up together.

At that time, I believe I only owned two Marshall half stacks, because that's what I had been using in the Squares, and I didn't have any extra equipment. So I had the two Marshall slant-bottoms and the two Marshall heads. One was a late-sixties 100-watt, slightly modified, and the other was the MKII Lead, but I didn't own any small amps. I believe I had an MXR Flanger. In different moments on that record, I definitely needed distortion, and I think I had my original Big Muff Pi by Electro-Harmonix, which was still working at the time, and DS-1 and OD-1 Boss pedals. I used my two Echoplex tape delays as well. Every time Jeff and I would start recording, it was a brand-new experience for me.

Jeff would always come in with a good word of caution. For instance, on "I Am Become Death," after the backward stuff, the song is a bunch of single lines and harmony, and I was using the pick to scrape the strings down by the bridge to create a violin-bow effect. And I'm describing to him how I want it to sound, and he, of course, being the voice of reason, is saying, "Let's record these things flat and dry, and then we can add the stuff later."

I realized he was right, that I didn't want to commit too early to certain things, just in case they didn't work with the other things

I wanted to try out. Jeff never knew exactly where I was going to take everything, because I wasn't clear in my own head—there was always 10 or 20 percent where I was going to wait to see how it developed. But we had to start somewhere.

I'd first come across the Maxon Digital Delay rack mount when they'd just started putting out consumer-level, rack-mounted digital delays, in '83 or '84. Jim Larson, the owner of Second Hand Guitars, where I was teaching, was importing some of these things, and I realized they had this hold-and-repeat function. You could set it at 1,000 milliseconds, you'd play a figure, push the button, and it would just simply repeat that figure. It was trial and error, but Jeff and I were able to create the end of "Banana Mango" with a set of hold-and-repeat figures that would go left channel/right channel, left channel/right channel. When we were recording that ending, to me it sounded like something no one had ever done before. It was just so unique, and I remember being so excited at how much it sounded like I had imagined it. Sampling is one of those things that maybe goes past people today, but back then it was just being born because of this technology. We were fascinated that a unit could capture a short burst of something, manipulate its time, and use it as a rhythmic figure, as if it were a recording of somebody doing something over and over again perfectly. Plus it had a little bit of distortion, just a certain tone, slightly degrading as it repeated. It was something that we found beautiful, and it finished that song so wonderfully.

Jeff Holt: Joe had been using digital delay live at the time as an outboard effect, because a lot of the live clubs back then just had basic reverb and delay. It was a real high-end piece of gear, and it was rare for a player to walk into a club with his own outboard gear. So both onstage and when he brought it into the studio, I thought that was a really cool example of his natural desire to push the boundaries of what other people were doing in context of his own sound. We came up with this thing on one song where the old machines had this VSO feature where you could slow the tape down, so we played around with that, and also with panning, and I had this really cool Lexicon Prime Time, which had different outputs, so we were able to throw the sound around in different delay lines.

Control room at Jeff Holt's Likewise Productions, '84
PHOTO BY JEFF HOLT

As we finished the part of the record-making process that I greatly enjoyed—creating and playing—we arrived at a part I *wasn't* so crazy about, where we might be almost finished with a song, everything's perfect, and then something would suddenly go wrong. A piece of equipment might make a noise, or a knob was acting funny, or when you made that one little fader move, maybe you went a little bit too far. For instance, when you pushed a fader up it might react a little differently each time, and you've got two people leaning over each other with their arms on the board making moves. Jeff would say, "I'm going to do tracks one to seven, and when we get to here, do me a favor, reach over and turn this knob like that, and then I'll move over to that part of the board." It was like a four-handed organ performance, and one of us would always do something a little different.

When we were dealing with nonautomated mixes, the good side of it was you had to make a decision, and then you moved on. Those were things I learned again later on, from Andy Johns, who said that in the old days of multitrack recording, they had to commit on the spot to effects and submixing of vocals and guitars. He would tell me, "The idea was: If you had a guitar part that was in reverb, you just recorded the guitar part with the reverb—done." You never went back and said, "Oh, is it too much reverb; is it too little reverb?" You'd just say, "I made that decision, and now we're living with it," and that's how you made records. That's why, when we go back and listen to the records made in the sixties, what we're hearing is bold decisions made by people who knew how to make decisions with the attitude of "Damn the torpedoes, full speed ahead!" They got good at cutting tape, too, which John Cuniberti would introduce to me later during the making of *Not of This Earth*. His idea was that if we couldn't get through the mix in one pass, we would mix only those sections we could get through. Then we would mix the next section, and so forth, and then we would splice all the sections together and have a final mix. I thought he was nuts, but when I heard the result I just couldn't believe it, because it sounded like one beautiful mix.

From that experience I gained a new respect for working with another person. Every time Jeff would say, "I think we have it," or "I think we should do it again," or that it should be brighter or less bright, I trusted him, and when we went back to it, I realized he was always right. When you're the one actually playing the music, you can't truly evaluate the performance. Certainly the way that I play, I lose perspective. I go headfirst all-the-way emotionally into a performance, but that's the only way I can get the whole "Joe" into the music. But the lesson was that I needed somebody to tap me on the shoulder and say, "Do it again," or "I'm not going to let you do that again because it's so unusual." That's another way Jeff helped me—by telling me when I got it right—because he would say from time to time about a particular performance, "I really think you have it. That's so unique, please don't make me erase that," and he was correct each time. So you've not only got to find that person you can work with, but you have to learn to trust them. You have to be open to when they give you very interesting comments, be they technical or emotional. They might say, "We've got to change the mic," or "You've got to go outside and walk around the block"—you never know what it might be. That was the most important thing I learned while working with Jeff, and I remind myself of those lessons every time I make a record with anybody.

Jeff Holt: I think making that first record was something Joe needed to get out of his system—doing an instrumental, all-guitar record. This was a very different approach, which is why it falls in the category of experimental, because when the EP was done, it wasn't a traditional record, more of a sound-effects type of situation. That record was a big break-out moment for Joe from the band construct, and he proved to me he was a very deep musician and composer, because he was coming up with stuff that wasn't consistent with the power pop of the time. From a production standpoint, Joe has a great ear for tone and I could tell he was taking it all in. I'm sure these early experiences behind the board helped him with ideas for future projects.

At that point in the mid-eighties, we were doing things on that EP that other people hadn't done before. For instance, on "Banana Mango," I tuned the guitar to a D7 with an added 4th, and I put the guitar in my lap, and with both index fingers I tapped the guitar on the twelfth fret—almost like I was tapping a dulcimer. After you hear the initial rhythm guitar come in, which is just a single-performance figure, when you hear these other dulcimer-sounding harmonics come in, that's me tapping the guitar as it's sitting on my lap in the open tuning. And to this day, whenever I listen to those three guitars, I think, "I have never heard anything with that sound, *ever*." It's a dream. It sounds so un-guitarlike, and yet Jeff and I just did it on a Stratocaster with some interesting tuning.

After the record was finished, I showed up with the recording at the next series of Squares rehearsals and said, “Look what I did, guys! We should be doing this, we should be going our own route.” And it was a very interesting moment, because the manager hated it, the bass player hated it, but Jeff Campitelli said, “This is cool.” That was unusual because the record had no drums on it, so you'd think a drummer would say, “I hate this,” but he said, “This is really cool. You did this on your own?” Those reactions were a big part of what started to make me think, “This band is going nowhere,” because, besides Jeff, I didn't think they understood what was happening in the world. I knew in my heart that was the real end of my days with the Squares.

CHAPTER 6 ★★

Not of This Earth—1985-1986

When the EP was done, I was excited because I was so pleased with how Jeff Holt and I were able to capture all these unusual moments. The record was a funky little EP that most people played at the wrong speed (I'd manufactured it as a 12-inch EP at 45 RPM, and most people played it at 33 RPM) and thought I was on heroin or something. But artistically, I thought it was fantastic. I couldn't believe that I'd made all those sounds. I was so happy because I thought I had been captured completely without compromise, being as weird as I could be, combining R&B phrasing with all the odd recording techniques and scraping and all the other odd things I had done. But as pleased as I was with it, I realized that for people to really get into my style, I needed to record an album with bass and drums.

Leading up to that time in the mid-eighties, I was always thinking that I would be lucky to be like a Jimmy Page–type figure in a four-piece rock 'n' roll band, with the singer being one of the quartet. That classic rock-band model had always made sense to me, and as I got older and more honest with myself about my abilities, I began thinking that that's where I could thrive the best. I knew I could write—I was prolific—and I liked working with vocals-oriented rock music. The music I listened to over and over again, year after year, was made by bands pretty much like that: these three-, four-, and five-piece bands, guitar/bass/drums/singer, maybe a keyboard. So that's what I kept working on. It really wasn't until after I did the record with Jeff Holt that I started thinking there was any hope of playing instrumental music professionally.

John Cuniberti: With Joe, we've always seen that he has a rhythm section, then a melody guitar—and it can have harmonies or not, usually a harmony to the melody would happen at some point. And that could be a two-part, three-part, or even five-part in some cases. Then there's what we'd call the solo sections, and we always saw those three things separately. It's not unlike a pop song where you have your rhythm section, you have your lead singer, and then your soloist. So the records have always been constructed in a very similar manner. In other words, when Joe says to me, "I'm going to do a rhythm guitar part," I know what that means—it doesn't mean a solo or melody part. And when he says he's going to do his melody, I know it doesn't mean a solo; it's what someone would sing if there were a singer. It's what's played during the verse and what is played during the chorus, and what might be played during the bridge—it's the melody line. So he could take his guitar and make a full band out of it.

I arrived at that evolution in my sound after I recorded the EP, which I felt was more of an experimental calling card. In other words, I had to make that record just to show people how artistically odd I was, that I wasn't just the professional pop-rock guitar player that had been gigging around town with the Squares. And because there was no outlet where I could do that music, the only way I could do it was to record it, send it out, and see if there was someone out there who would respond to it. Even then, I wasn't thinking about replacing vocals with my guitar playing—I was writing serious, original guitar music. It really wasn't until I saw a review of the EP in *Guitar Player* magazine that I caught a glimpse of my musical future.

This was when I was selling the EP out of the trunk of my car, and there were maybe fifty copies floating around, so I had no real idea who it was reaching. That changed one day when I was at a rehearsal with a band I'd been playing with following my exit from the Squares, and I remember our bass player, Bobby Vega, came in with a copy of *Guitar Player*, handed it to me, and said, "Hey, you're in this magazine," which was a little surreal. I remember as I read the review, they were talking about this guy, Joe Satriani, who they thought was one of the strangest, most avant-garde guitar players they'd ever heard. Once I read it, I realized they didn't know who I really was. They thought I was some obscure musician, somebody new on the scene. They had no idea I was Joe, formerly of the Squares and now struggling to find another band to play with.

Promo shot for NOTE
PHOTO BY PAT JOHNSON

That's when I knew I wanted to be that guy they were talking about. I wanted to be that odd, new guitar player. I saw a glimpse of my future, and said to myself, "You've got to figure out a way to be 'that guy.'" So I quickly left that group I was playing with and decided I had to figure out a way to make a record with real bass and drums, because my EP could only get me so far. That really was the next step in putting together what would become *Not of This Earth*. The challenge was how to maintain my odd sense of tone, harmony, and melody, while bringing in the elements that people relate to—drums, bass, guitars, and keyboards, playing together like a band.

Before I recorded the EP, Steve Vai and I had been communicating with each other regularly. He was still sending me these odd tapes, just some of the most bizarre recordings of the stuff he was making in L.A., where he was becoming a composer, learning all about recording on his own, and actually becoming the Steve Vai that we all know. He'd been up to see the Squares, and thought it was fascinating and yet strange that I would be in a band like that, because he knew my other self.

Steve Vai: I would send much of this stuff to Joe. Stuff that I would not dream of letting anyone else hear. Tons of stuff that, to this day, he may be the only one who has. It was all obviously very crudely recorded with little real production value or time spent on things to make it actually sound good.

I had all this unusual music in me, and now there's this magazine review, and they have no idea that I'm this struggling guitar player here in San Francisco. They think I'm a successful nut job who's at home in his studio creating this odd music, and the outside world actually thinks that's who I am, because it's written down in this magazine. And the review was actually quite favorable, too!

John Cuniberti: Honestly, at first, I'd been terribly disappointed when the band broke up. It was like, "God, after all that work . . ." Because we had recorded nearly two albums' worth of material, and there were a couple of trips to L.A. for showcases, but they could never get themselves a record contract, so after a while everything just dissolved. So when Joe's band broke up, he went about his way and I went about mine. I was making records with other people, and I didn't see Joe again for at least a year and a half to two years, and he was teaching and did his first solo EP with Jeff Holt, which was an all-guitar-based recording.

Once I had John in place as engineer/coproducer, I realized I needed to bump up the budget. After I'd formulated this idea for the record, I assumed that I could get what they used to call a "spec deal," where you go into a studio, they front you the time to record, and then—and this is right out of the film *Boogie Nights*—when you get a recording deal, you pay everybody back. That was a very naïve way of looking at things, but I had so much confidence in it, even though John was of course the first guy to tell me, "Are you out of your mind? Nobody is going to front you money for instrumental rock, it's not even a genre anymore!" And he was right.

I remember returning home from that discussion feeling quite deflated, worrying that I'd never get this project off the ground. By some stroke of fate, the next day I got a credit card in the mail, preapproved with a $5,000 credit limit. This was the eighties, when banks all over the country were sending out preapproved credit cards to total strangers. I probably qualified because I'd been successfully paying off the van we'd purchased so I could drive the Squares around. They didn't know that in reality I was a broke musician. The letter said something like, "Joseph Satriani, because of your good standing in the community, we're giving you this credit card and it comes with $5,000 worth of checks." So I took that checkbook to John and said, "What if I paid you up front, what kind of a deal would you make for me?" So

John worked out this deal where I would pay him and the studio up front, and I wrote $4,700 worth of checks to the studio that day so I could get *Not of This Earth* recorded.

John Cuniberti: I was managing the studio at the time, so I had a little bit of leeway with what Joe's rates were. We'd worked a thing out where he'd come in some days after a session had ended at seven or eight at night, and we'd work till three, four, or five in the morning at some ridiculously low rate, and we did that a lot for that record.

As a player by this point, stylistically, I was a weird combination of a guy who would listen to Prince and Van Halen and would tune in to dance music stations, but also would still be into Weather Report, John McLaughlin, and Alan Holdsworth. I've always been the kind of person who listens to a wide variety of music and really identifies with all of it. Along with that, there was a lot of music at that time, in the early eighties, that was drum machine driven—a lot of new rock from the UK and Europe. I was also a fan of bands like Kraftwerk, and there were very few bands like Kraftwerk. But you either responded to that music or you didn't. Part of me really loved that strange, drum machine style of music, with humans overdubbing on top of repeating drum machine patterns. When I started to hear the way the new bands were getting a drum machine to sound like a drummer in a big club, I started to get more excited about it. I realized that the music I was writing didn't really have that sort of verse-verse-chorus-bridge thing where we really needed typical drum fills. What I was really writing was stuff that had more of a "stream of consciousness" approach to it. That was the phrase we used a lot.

John Cuniberti: He'd done demos at home with a drum machine, and he'd basically write and build his parts and create his sound in a song with these relentless, perfect-time drum machines. But when we first got into a studio and attempted to use a real drummer, the whole thing would fall apart. Joe would say, "Those parts that I'm playing—that picking during my rhythm guitar parts—they don't make sense now when you've got a drummer out there thrashing around. They don't work anymore." So when we started *Not of This Earth*, I just assumed we were going to use Jeff or some other drummer to play the stuff, but we learned early on that absolutely wasn't going to work. So Joe had basically developed his whole sound style around the fact that everything was more or less locked.

The decision to go with drum machines was also a sonic decision. John and I had worked together in the studio for five years previous to this with the Squares, and we both had a bad taste in our mouths from trying to get these modern drum sounds. So we thought, to hell with it. Let's listen to all these bands that are using drum machines. If you remember the New Romantic era, music was coming over from the UK around this time made by bands playing New Wave pop using drum machines, but they had drummers playing along with them as well, playing cymbals and overdubbed percussion. John was well aware of that, and he had produced other bands this way, so he said, "We can do this. We can have Jeff come in and only do the snare drum and the hi-hat for *Not of This Earth*, and we'll use the kick drum from the machine because it's very dependable and we can use that as the element that's always perfect." So we were going into it thinking we wanted part of this to sound like modern rock, as we called it, which was the sound of machines and synths together with guitars. So it was an artistic decision, and it worked with the budget, too!

John Cuniberti: We soon discovered that these drum machines actually weren't perfectly in time. They would drift, and that became quite problematic. We started to realize it during *Surfing*, when we started actually using MIDI and computers. We started to realize, "Man, these things just don't feel right. There's something funny about the feel of this thing." So we really, really, really struggled with it. For *Not of This Earth* it was a little more straight ahead.

The drum machine we used for the broader album was an Oberheim DX, and this particular one had chips in it that you could pull out and replace with different kick and snare chips. We had a couple of different snare and kick drums we could use, so we would mostly do kick and snare with the DX. Joe and I (and sometimes Jeff) would write the drum parts, we would record it, and that was it. Then we'd unplug it and put the thing away, and then Joe would play everything against that machine. There was no time code, no MIDI, nothing.

I remember very clearly one very embarrassing moment when a friend of ours, who went on to be a successful songwriter, came into Studio D at Hyde Street, after we had just done all the bed work for the song "Rubina," and he's listening to it, and he said, "Wow, that's really beautiful. How did you do this . . ." I explained how John had engineered some really great stereo recording of Jeff, with John and myself playing random percussion instruments on top of the harmonics guitars, the synth bass, and the drum machine pattern. "That's really great!" he says. Then he asks, "So you put down time code so you can replace and reprogram the drums later?" And I realized I didn't know what he was saying, and I was kind of embarrassed and just answered, "Oh yeah, yeah yeah . . ." When he left, I asked John, "What's time code?" And he looked at me like, "I can't believe you don't know what time code is!"

I realized how naïve I was about recording with these machines, because I literally did not know that these machines spit out a code that you could record, and that later you could reprogram the machine, and the time code would instruct the machine to play it in synch with everything else. So when John explained it to me, I asked, "Why didn't we do that?"

And he said, "Well, there's two reasons. One, you didn't tell me you wanted to do it because I thought Jeff was going to come in and replace everything, and two, there are some problems with time code." So he advised, "If we're doing these quiet guitar things, we can't have time code sitting on an adjacent track, because you'll hear it."

John Cuniberti: Another challenge within this process came with the fact that, in those days, drum machines had really terrible cymbals, because a lot of them were just 8-bit. Joe and I recognized very quickly that the cymbals sucked, so Jeff played cymbals on everything. Every song that had a hi-hat or a cymbal crash on it, Jeff played it. We would set up the cymbals, and he would sit there like he was sitting at a drum kit and just whack those cymbals.

Jeff Campitelli: When we were doing *NOTE*, Joe had a budget, a tight, tight budget, and of course this was Joe's baby, and he had for any given number of songs, four, five, or even six guitar overdubs with every little part worked out. So he would work for hours and hours and hours and hours to get the guitar parts just right for each song. Well, when it came time to head in to record, originally the plan was: "Okay, on Thursday night from midnight to 8 A.M., we're going to record the drums for the entire album." And I was thinking, "Oh yeah, Joe and I have been playing together forever. I'll just sit down and start playing drums and we'll play ten songs in a row and the thing will be done."

That was NOT AT ALL how it wound up working out. I remember one of my drum students had just invested $5,000 in this brand-new Simmons kit, and didn't even know how to use the damn thing, so we borrowed it, brought it in, and originally I didn't even bring a regular drum kit. Joe and I were both thinking we could just use the electric drum sound for something new and exciting. Well, as it worked out, it was like playing on a Formica tabletop: hard, plastic, and no one had any idea how to run the thing, so we couldn't get the sounds right, and the outputs were all plugged in wrong. After a while tensions were running pretty high in the studio.

I remember by 2 or 3 A.M., we didn't have anything recorded, and Joe was freaking out because we only had the budget at that point to go on for another day recording drums. So we raided a closet, found a little twenty-inch kick drum without a front head, I threw my jacket inside the drum, and we found a bass pedal, and luckily I'd brought a really good snare drum. So we cranked that up and found a couple of cymbals, and we just basically put together this makeshift kit on the spot! We didn't have any toms, so we tracked the song "Memories." It was just whatever we could do to finish a song that night.

That full set of Simmons electronic drums was another thing that went wrong with the percussion on *Not of This Earth*. We brought them in because we had some songs that would use drum machines; we wanted the whole album to have this sort of semisynthetic drum sound, and we couldn't afford to spend all this time miking drums. We needed to be able to plug something in and go with it. But it was such a disaster. I remember the evening Jeff came in to work on the song "Memories," and after hours of trying to get these things to work, we had to abandon it. But I had to record Jeff that day—we had to get it done. So we literally put a drum kit together with drums that were in the building from various different studios, and Jeff somehow—by two or three in the morning—was able to perform on this totally held-together-with-rubber-bands drum kit made up of all different drums and cymbals, and we recorded this beautiful performance for that song. We were so wiped out after that, that we were all like, "Oh, the hell with that, no more live drums!"

I had the Oberheim drum machine at home, so I wrote as much as I could from the drum machine patterns. Jeff would then "play" the drum machine in the studio. It had dynamically sensitive pads, so a really good drummer like Jeff could become comfortable with it and create cool performances.

Jeff Campitelli: That experience basically made up the blueprint that Joe decided to follow from there for the rest of the album's rhythm tracks. It was a real shocker because I didn't want to record that way, but we didn't know how to do it any other way. It wasn't like, "Oh man, we're heading in this amazing direction: We're gonna have the kick drum from the DX, and then Jeff, you're gonna play live snare and overdub some hi-hat. Then you'll do the tom fills and crashes." So we were just really winging it, and while I was thinking, "Well, of course, I'd rather be playing live drums all at the same time and really giving a good performance," as we went along, the songs were taking on this kind of eerie quality and a life of their own that—being a musician first, and a drummer second—I thought was kind of nice, and inspiring, too. That process defined the sound of the album.

Once we turned to recording guitar tracks, I think John was fascinated with the fact that he could elicit performances out of me by creating the proper environment in the control room. He was very good at that, from a producer and engineer's point of view. He was very sensitive to my moods and would try to get me as comfortable as possible to create the proper performance. That's why I liked being in the control room.

John Cuniberti: In setting up at Hyde Street Studios to record the album, it made sense, because I'd recorded there a lot with the Squares. So it's not like it was new to me; I'd been there a lot. I was comfortable working there because I thought it sounded great. Every room sounded like a real recording studio. It had been the original Wally Heider Studios, and great, great records had been recorded there. So when I walked in there I realized, "It's totally my fault if I can't make this place sound good, because there's been so many classic albums made here." And I think at the time, coming into the city had sort of bumped up my energy level as well. I was still living in Berkeley then, which was a lot more laid back, so when I'd come into San Francisco—and Hyde Street is in the middle of the Tenderloin, a horrible neighborhood in the city—I enjoyed it. That whole grittiness of interfacing with the city and coming into this building

> that had four studios running in it. There were a lot of people coming in and out of there, and the next client would always be standing by the door looking at you, wanting you to get out. The attitude there was exciting, and everything that Joe played always sounded amazing and wasn't like anything I'd ever heard before. That was always very exciting to me, too. So when Joe started playing that stuff, I thought, "Oh my God, I've really got my work cut out for me."

The first solo we were going to do was "Memories," and I remember John was thinking, "I've recorded Joe before: We do a solo, it takes twenty minutes, we're done." So we go to the section, and the song has a long guitar solo, and three and a half hours later, John asks, "Oh my God, Joe, is every solo going to take this long? 'Cause we're going to have a problem with the budget." So this was John's brain really working very well, while mine was not because I was just completely emotionally involved in the music. All I kept thinking was, "The guitar solo is like the ultimate expression of the song, and that's what I'm going to put into this record." And of course, John was thinking, "If Joe's going to take three and a half hours for every one of these guitar solos, then that's thirty hours or more!"—and I'd given him my checks, so he knew how many hours I had paid for. So once he informed me of this potential problem, I said, "Look, I don't know, sometimes the solos will go quickly, but the guitar solo for each song is going to be the most important statement of the song. So if we have a problem, then we'll deal with it, but I'm not going to skimp on this."

That was a very important day, because a lot of things happened during the recording of the "Memories" solo where I learned about how John could punch me in to fix certain sections. Then, when I started to hear the artifacts that were created from punch-ins, I liked them, and started to ask John to punch me in to places where I hadn't made mistakes but where I just wanted the sound of the artifact to be part of the solo. He thought I was nuts, but I really loved the effect, so I had him punch me in in all these different places for the effect. I drove him crazy, the poor guy, because I had him punching me in and out in 32nd notes, 64th notes, so he had to sit there and we'd have to go over it dozens of times before I could explain to him exactly where I wanted him to punch. It was pretty nerve-racking for him to have to punch somebody in so precisely. We became quite a team after that record because of his ability to adapt to what I was learning about the studio, how you could punch in and out to create very compelling musical statements.

John Cuniberti: There were things that would evolve in the studio that would bring something to the song that we didn't expect, and it was a pleasant surprise. Joe always came into the studio very organized and prepared for the day's events. During the recording process, every night when we finished, he would bring a cassette home with him of what we'd done that day. Joe would then come back the following day with an idea about a new part, or possibly a change to something he had done the day before, or wanting to completely redo something—you would never know. It was always a surprise.

John, Jeff, and I often reminisce about how we would leave that studio at 3:30 in the morning with the worst indigestion from drinking the studio coffee, which had been burning in the pot for five hours. We were always there between midnight and 8 A.M., because that was when the time was cheap, but it was very stressful working on that schedule. It was also exciting, and even felt musically dangerous at times, because anyone who might have stuck their head in the studio and listened to what we were doing would have said, "Why are you guys wasting your time with this?" None of our music sounded like anything that was popular at the time, so anybody listening from the outside would give us that sort of dismissive look. I think that emboldened us even more and made us feel we were doing something quite unique, and that in the end, we would show everybody because we were doing something quite artistic. That played into how we used all the effects that we had, and made sure we got them recorded, because the guy who ran the studio liked to move equipment around and sell it, so you never knew if the cool gear was going to be there next week.

John Cuniberti: When Joe first played me what he had in mind, I remember thinking, "I've got to do something now with the sound of everything else to make that work." How do you play something like that, which is truly not of this earth, and just have it go along with a silly little drum machine? How's that going to work? So I spent a day looking for that drum sound, and we found it on a reverb by EMT, the 251, which looks like R2-D2, it's a little rolling thing that was fairly rare and stupidly expensive. Dan Alexander, who co-owned the studio and was an audio dealer, just happened to have one in the studio. So this EMT 251 reverb had a switch on it called "Non Linear," and that's what those drums are on *Not of This Earth*—it's the kick and snare run through the EMT 251 switched to "Non Linear." Well, Joe and I loved the sound so much, and wanted to feature it, but I was so afraid Dan was going to sell that unit before we were done with the record. Sure enough, when Joe and I came back a week later, the thing was gone! And he said, "Oh man, the reverb's gone," and I told him, to his relief, "Don't worry, I printed it on two tracks, we still have it." Because that really made the difference. That track would never be as cool if it didn't have that on there.

The EMT 251 was definitely one of my favorite pieces of outboard gear, first of all because it looked really cool; it had these funny robotic arms with little rubber things around them. It was just the funkiest-looking thing ever. We did a lot of crazy things with that machine. For instance, on "The Enigmatic," where the snare drum comes out of a deep reverb and then is suddenly in front of your face, John manipulated the 251 live while tracking! He was so comfortable with the EMT that he would play it like an instrument. The studio was truly his realm.

John Cuniberti: "The Enigmatic" was my personal favorite of all the Satriani recordings I have made. We were using the DX drum machine, and Jeff was playing crash cymbals and a huge artillery shell. The song starts with me starting the MTR-90 tape recorder at the same time Jeff hits the brass artillery shell. Because the machine takes time to get up to speed you hear it slide down to pitch. It took me and Jeff a long time to make it work, with Joe wondering what the hell we were doing.

The progression of guitars I had used through that point began with the Hagstrom guitar. Then I bought a Telecaster that John Riccio found for me in the local classifieds. I believe it was a 1968 maple-neck model that somebody had refinished black, and it had a Bigsby vibrato bar on it. I later went into Manhattan and had Charles LoBue and Larry DiMarzio put in a humbucker in the neck position. That became my main guitar through all of those high school bands. Then right at the tail end, I traded it for a Les Paul Deluxe in a private trade, and that became my main guitar until I had more money from all the work I was doing with the disco band. At that point I bought a refinished '54 Fender Stratocaster, and that became my go-to guitar for quite a while. So during that period, from the start of that twelve-year run, I had this Les Paul Deluxe and this Strat. Eventually I got rid of the Les Paul and started building my own Stratocasters with humbuckers in them, because Boogie Bodies had come into existence, so for the first time you could buy separate body parts. I was teaching at Second Hand Guitars then, and through being in that store, I realized I could buy every component and screw together my own guitars.

So many guitar players of my generation—the easiest one to point to is Eddie Van Halen—grew up loving Hendrix and Jimmy Page, Jeff Beck and Eric Clapton, all of whom had their Fender period and their Gibson period. And so what did we all do? We wound up creating guitars that were Fenders with Gibson electronics. When *Van Halen* came out, I felt vindicated, like, "Yeah, here's someone doing what I've been trying to do, and he's going to legitimize it for all of us," and that's what Eddie did. I think that first Van Halen record shocked people because they didn't realize there were thousands upon thousands of guitar players around the world who felt the same way that Eddie did. We wanted a Strat guitar but we also wanted the Gibson sound; we wanted a bar but we also wanted it to be in tune. We had these desires because we'd grown up on the classic rock records, which were a combination of the Fender and Gibson scenes. We were products of all those third-generation electric blues players and we wanted to propel their sound into a new era, but we needed a new piece of gear. And that's what it was: it was the 25½-inch-scale guitar with the Gibson sound. For me, it just let the melody speak. It gave me the fatter sound I needed because I was playing in the Squares, which was a trio. So I built these two guitars that were sort of retro-looking, because part of our scene was New Wave. I was playing stereo into two Marshalls, a Wall of Sound kind of approach, so I needed that humbucker fatness but I wanted the snappiness of the Fender scale.

For the '85 studio sessions, I started plugging my guitars into a Tom Scholz Rockman, which I really liked as a direct amplifier, primarily because my record didn't sound like traditional rock music at the time. I had played through 100-watt Marshalls for a good five years already, and I was getting kind of tired of the straight-ahead guitar-into-a-Marshall approach. My competitors were all doing that—they were in studios with their Marshalls turned all the way up, trying to continue the dream of the late sixties and early seventies. And I thought what would really sound more modern to me, especially if I had some drum tracks that were drum machines, would be to get the guitar into that space as well. So if I've got a drum machine and a synthesizer, how could I get the guitar to sound like it's coming from the same space as them?

That's where the Rockman came in. It sounded like it was coming from the same aural space as the Prophet-5 synthesizer and the Oberheim DX we were using. It made them more mixable, to my ear, and they presented a more unified sonic sound. We rarely used big amps—we were using very small one- and two-speaker Fender amps for this stuff. The sound seemed to be more easy to place; I liked the fact that it was somewhat compressed, and the drums were very much like that as well, because they were coming from a drum machine and already had a sort of recorded sound.

> **John Cuniberti:** Throughout the album's recording, there would be occasions where Joe would need to get close to his amplifier for a particular sound, but it was very rare. Even then, he was using foot pedals for distortion and setting his amp up clean. He never really took to the loud amplifier-standing-in-the-room kind of approach.

John wasn't always a fan of me using small amps, and I remember there were moments when we would definitely argue back and forth about it, because John had a long history of getting great guitar sounds out of amps, so he was pushing for using mics. I remember I showed up for that record without an amp, and John asked, "What do you mean?" And I said, "I want to use whatever the smallest little amp is you've got," because I was really Mr. Antithesis, and I just didn't want to waste time getting a big rock sound because I thought it would never fit. As we got deeper into recording for the record, I think he understood that sometimes the part would sound better technically if it was played through the Rockman. But other times he would provide me a more upscale path and say, "I know what you want. Let me show you how to do it better," and we'd go direct. He introduced me to going into a vintage mic pre, directly to tape, and then using very expensive signal processors to recreate stereo chorus and delay. So we wound up using that instead of the Rockman. It was a balance, back and forth.

Along with the Rockman, my go-to traditional amplifier was the

Roland JC-120. We used it quite a bit, and I still have that amp; it's fantastic. It wasn't really great at distorted guitar sounds, because it had this high end that revealed itself as being a transistor amp. But for clean sounds it was excellent, because it had a quick, snappy, transient response in the high end, and it had that unusual, wide stereo chorus effect. It's a unique acoustic phenomenon, and recording it is tricky, but we got good at it. I found some small silver-faced Fender amps in the closets at Hyde Street that I would borrow sometimes, and if I needed a Marshall, I still had my half stacks.

John Cuniberti: As far as effects pedals, Joe was primarily playing through his orange Boss DS-1 Distortion pedal and CE-2 Chorus and that was pretty much it. All the echo-delay types of effects—reverbs, chorusing—we did with outboard gear. Typically, I would use a Universal Audio 1176 limiter for rhythm guitars and bass, and a Universal Audio LA-2A limiter for melodies and occasionally solos. Because again, those were limiters you would use for a singer, and since Joe's phrasing and playing and arranging were that way, I tended to use the same processors as I would if there were people singing. An LA-2A's not unusual for lead vocals, so of course that's what I'd use on Joe's melodies.

Along with all the guitars, I decided to play all the bass guitars and keyboards on the record. I've played bass for as long as I've played guitar, so composing bass lines has always come naturally. I've written quite a few songs on bass, too. While we were tracking, I remember that recording DI, direct-input, was a new thing for me. Because I'd never been a bass player in the studio, I really didn't know how bass recording was done, so John was saying, "We gotta do DI. We'll get more control over everything, and it's more mixable." And then for some songs where we needed some sort of distorted element on the bass, we would send another signal out to a bass amp we would borrow and use that Boss OD-1, and then blend the upper frequencies of the distorted bass with the solid, low frequencies of the DI bass.

John Cuniberti: One really interesting thing I remember about this stage of recording was that there was a lot of experimenting going on with miking. I was a big fan of the AKG C-12A, a really great-sounding microphone. I used that exclusively on *Surfing* and quite a bit on *Not of This Earth*. The mic had a very smooth but extended top end; it didn't have the high-frequency bump that an SM57 would, but it also had a really remarkable low frequency. In other words, it had an extended range both on the highs and lows, and was a very wide microphone, but it could also handle the dynamic range of a guitar. It could handle the sound pressure level like a 57 does, but it has a wider dynamic range than that mic, and didn't have that ugly presence peak. That mic could handle anything Joe would be throwing at it from the playing side. The C-12A and the Shure SM57 were the two microphones I used 80 percent of the time.

Among the many techniques I employed on *Not of This Earth* was pitch axis theory, which I learned in high school from my music teacher Bill Westcott. It is a compositional technique that was actually developed at the turn of the last century, so this is something that had been around for a long time. I remember Bill saying, "I'm going to teach you this very cool compositional technique," and he sat me down at the piano, and he went, "Watch this: I'll hold this C bass note, and then I play these chords, and each chord will put me in a different key, but it will sound like C 'something' to you . . ." I was fascinated by it, because I thought, "That is the sound I'm hearing in my head." To me it sounded very "rock," because rock songs don't travel around in too many keys, and it was the antithesis of the modern pop music that had been around for fifty years. It was the total opposite of most commercial jazz, but not all jazz, as I learned when I started really listening closely to modern jazz. I realized, "Wow, John Coltrane is using pitch axis theory. Not only is he doing that, but he's going beyond it with his 'sheets of sound' approach," where in addition to building modes in different keys off of one bass note, he was building modes off of notes outside the key structure as well. He had taken it a step further.

But that's not what I was looking for, except for in a song like "The Enigmatic," which has that sort of complete atonal-meets-psycho melodic approach. I was more interested in using the pitch axis where you really could identify with one key bass note, in a rock and R&B sort of fashion. Then all the chords that you put on top would basically put you in different keys. So on *Not of This Earth*, you have these pounding E eighth notes on the bass, and your audience says, "Okay, we're in the key of E." But the chords on top are saying, "E Lydian, E Minor, E Lydian, E Mixolydian in cyclical form." And I thought, "Well, this gives me great melodic opportunities, I'm not stuck with just the seven notes of one key. I've got seven notes for every different key that I apply on top of this bass note." And I just love that sound, so I applied it to quite a lot of my music.

With the title track's sequence of angular, dreamlike chords bouncing back and forth, I knew I wanted sort of a stream-of-consciousness rhythm section behind it. I wanted the rhythm section to sound and feel like it was on its own unstoppable trajectory, with the melodies and solos trading off and embellishing the track at different times. The song, after all, was about someone who was "not of this earth," so everything about the song and the recording had to reflect that.

As I readied my experimental concepts and techniques for the studio, I knew that I would need help getting them on tape. During the sessions I would present them to John and he would help me brainstorm a recording plan. He might suggest, "Well, maybe we should change the guitar sound dramatically when we get to this point, go from a faraway to a close-up, or a close-up to a faraway, change the microphones . . ." He would come up with all sorts of ways to answer my desires that were more on the artistic side of things.

The recording of *Not of This Earth* had kind of a dramatic ending, too. John's car had been broken into behind the studio, and while we were mixing the last song, he went out to take a look at it. As he was trying to get the thing in shape so he could drive it, he wound up cutting his hand. So he came back into the studio, his hand was bleeding, he had a Band-Aid on it, and he said, "We need tape." This literally sent us into the garbage pail! We had to pull tape out of the garbage, because we had no more mix tape and needed a long fade-out, and John had to splice it all together with his hand all bloody. It was crazy watching the mix go by, made up of tape of all varying lengths, covered in blood. I was just trying to get the record done, but at the same time I was fascinated that you could make a record with bloody pieces of tape from a garbage pail and still have it sound great! And that's to John's credit. I don't know how he pulled it off technically. It was funny because he would always work hard to answer my musical questions, like "How do I get a train noise to go into a double hammer-on whammy thing?" He would just work out how to record and mix it. So when I informed him, "I don't have any more money for another reel of mix tape," he figured out a way to pull tape out of the trash and splice it together.

The drama continued through the very last song we recorded. I remember we had almost finished the album, and there was a song called "The Last Jam" that was part of that disaster night when the Simmons drums didn't work out. We had a performance from Jeff, but the drums were all distorted, and John refused to put it on the record. I agreed with him—the whole thing just didn't work out. So I said, "We'll do another song," and I went home and wrote this other song. When I brought it in, John said, "Well, we need another reel of tape, or we have to erase that other song." Well, I didn't have any money to buy another reel of tape, which was $150, so I said, "Erase the song, the hell with it." It was a big deal to do that, but these were the decisions you made in the old days with tape. So we simply rolled over that piece of music, recorded this new piece of music that went down pretty easily, and Jeff came in and helped program the drum machine for me, the Oberheim DX.

We had to do that really fast, because I was late in ending the session, and people were standing at the door with their arms folded, fuming. It was like four o'clock in the afternoon, and I was still trying to do these arpeggios, because I'd told John after we did the main guitar that I wanted to double it, and he was like, "Are you kidding me? How are you going to double that?" And I said, "I know I can do it." Meanwhile the clients are standing there looking at their watches, saying, "Will you guys get out of here?" because they were booked to start at four. So I finished that track, "Driving at Night," with people breathing down my neck.

Mixing was equally as pressured because, first, from the technical side, we only had so many tracks within a given mix to work with. In those days, it wasn't like Pro Tools, where you have unlimited space for tracking and mixing. When you were dealing with analog tape like we were, you had to have plans. It wasn't like you could just keep going, because you'd run out of tracks very quickly, so everything had to be thought out. Every step of the way, if you got an idea, you had to deal with the problem of space. "Where does it go? How's it going to be mixed? Is there another way to achieve this idea?" So you always had to be planning.

We were constantly aware throughout recording that we would be battling the clock right up until the end, so from very early on, if we started going creatively to a place John knew would be unmixable later on, he would say, "We have to pause and make a decision." So if he asked me, "Is there anything else?" and I'd say, "I want to add two more guitar parts," then he would tell me, "Well, then we're going to have to take some of what's recorded and mix it now into a submix," which meant we had to make a mixing decision because once the tracks were submixed, they couldn't be unmixed and broken out again. That was a dangerous decision, so we didn't do that very often.

Looking back, I was grateful for John's ability to get me to economize, and I was very impressed with that from the start of recording all the way through the end of tracking. Instead of saying, "Oh, it would be great to have six guitars," he'd ask, "Why? Let's figure out a way to get two guitars to do it. Is it the way that you're playing it, or is it the sound, because if we can do it in two that will leave us so much more room." It got me to focus more on how to make each performance on each track really count. I learned from John that if you just fill things up, every new thing you put on may cover the tracks of the previous thing. Again, being the guitar player and the writer, I'm really focused on that main instrument sometimes, but I had to learn how to pull back and pay as much attention to the drum kit as a unit, and the keyboard as a section, and the bass as what it needs—just the way an engineer would look at everything and try to get the whole band to sound good. Since we had no band, the danger was that we'd just start piling one thing on top of another. So, for instance, if we wanted the drums to sound like we were in a big room, that meant we had to hear the room, so we couldn't cover it up. And if I came with a guitar part that on my demo had lots of echo on it, John might say, "You know, if there's all that echo and delay and stuff on it, it's going to cover the performances by these other instruments, so let's start flat and see where we go." So as the track would get built up, I'd begin to see his wisdom about leaving room for the other instruments so the audience could hear their performance, too.

I have to admit that in those early days, beginning with *NOTE* and for the first couple of records, it was just so emotionally traumatic to listen to a record when it was done, because I had to really let go. I realized I couldn't mix it anymore, so I had to come to grips with my disappointment in, say, my performance or my writing, or the way I thought the album was going to come out. And I didn't have sophisticated listening gear at home, just average consumer-grade stereo systems, so it was hard for me to know if what we were doing was right. John would call and say, "It sounds great in the studio. I've got this gear at home, and it sounds great." And I'd go, "I can't hear the guitar," or "The guitar's too loud," and he'd ask what I was listening on, and I'd describe it to him, and he'd say, "You can't evaluate your record if you're listening to it on that crap."

John Cuniberti: Amazingly, for as much work as it feels like, looking back on it, I would say we probably didn't spend more than two weeks of studio time making *Not of This Earth*. That was spread out over maybe two or three months because of Joe's teaching and studio availability, and my schedule, but it went very, very quickly. We only had so much money. Joe had gotten this credit card in the mail with a $5,000 limit on it, and he went, "We're going to keep recording till this thing is full." And I was working for $20 an hour, and getting him studio time for $25 an hour, so we got a lot of studio time for his $5,000, but once the money was gone, the record was done.

CHAPTER 7 ★★

Relativity

At the end of recording *Not of This Earth,* I was $5,000 in debt, the maxed-out limit on my credit card. I couldn't make the payment on it, and I had the credit card company telling me they were handing me over to a collection agency by Friday—and this was a Monday. I remember being at Second Hand Guitars, giving lessons, thinking, "This is really bad, how did I get myself into this?"

Unbelievably, a lightning bolt of luck struck about a half hour later in the form of a phone call from Steve Wright from the Greg Kihn Band. He sounded panicked. "Joe, it's Steve. We're recording at Fantasy Studios and our guitar player's strung out. Would you please help us out? We'll pay you to finish the record, and if you agree to be with the band for the next year, this is how much *more* we'll pay you just so we can get this record and tour off the ground." That call was my saving grace.

After hanging up, I canceled the rest of my lessons for the day, went right over, and by the end of the afternoon, we had recorded three songs. The manager gave me a couple thousand dollars cash, and then laid out terms for a salary if I decided to join the Greg Kihn Band. I couldn't believe it! The very first thing I did the next morning was call the credit card company and tell them, "I'm sending a check and paying my balance off." Once I paid them, I suddenly found I had a completed album, recorded on my own label, published by my own publishing company, and I was in a band, making a salary, *and*

I didn't have any more credit card debt. In a matter of weeks, my life had totally changed!

Me and Greg Kihn live at a UC Berkeley outdoors show in '86

PHOTO BY ZAK WILSON

When I got into the band, it was clearly falling apart. Back when I was in the Squares, we'd done a lot of shows opening for Greg Kihn, and I just knew them as a really great local live band. But as I drifted away from pop music, I had paid less attention to them. Still, from having played with Greg, there were several things that I immediately found very impressive about the band. For one, Greg himself was a fantastic front person. He had the gift. I think he was the first lead vocalist I ever worked with who had it and was comfortable with his position. He could walk out onstage with very little planned, talk to people, and get them to have fun. He was a great talker, he had a good voice, and the other guys in the band were very much what you would expect for their positions in the band. Especially Steve Wright, with his personality as a bass player and his great bass technique: how he played, how he tuned his amp, how he used compression live—I'd never known a bass player at the time to use a dbx compressor in his rig. I was so surprised that someone would do that, but he got this big fat sound and it was fantastic.

Once I started playing with the band, I remember standing behind Greg Kihn every night, saying to myself, "This is what a lead singer is supposed to be doing." I thought Greg and Steve were just so unique. Everybody else in the band was new; we had a new drummer and keyboard player, and me, the newest of the three guys, so it was more like a gig to us. But Greg and Steve were the original guys, and I just thought they were exhibiting the sort of great rock 'n' roll musician traits that I should be paying attention to. It came to a tragic ending—I was with those guys from the end of '85 to the end of '86, and it was like being on a 747 that was on fire, slowly crashing into the ocean. It was kind of sad in a way, but at the same time, during the better gigs and moments when they were very good at what they did, I was able to learn from that professional side of them. The other benefit of the tour was that I had started writing "Surfing with the Alien," "Ice 9," and other songs for what would become the *Surfing* album, and recording demos in various hotel rooms between shows. I wrote many of the album's songs that year.

While I was out on the road, Steve Vai and I had been talking on the phone, and I told him that I'd decided to release *Not of This Earth* as the second record on my own label, which at the time was called Rubina Records, after my wife. Steve told me about this label in New York that had agreed to manufacture and distribute *Flex-Able*, Steve's first solo record. That piqued my interest a little because Steve's record was much stranger than mine, and so he said, "You know what, if this guy is going to put out *Flex-Able*, I bet he'd put out your record. Can I give him a copy of the cassette?" I agreed, but I wasn't expecting anything to come of it.

Steve Vai: Once I moved out of Carle Place, Joe and I always stayed in touch, exchanging tapes and stories and marathon phone calls. That's when I was able to shed much of that high-school-kid bewilderment and teacher–student dynamic and allow our bond as true friends to grow. We obviously had a great bond, though, and shared some personal moments in those early days. There was this huge field between the schools, and now and then Joe and I would drive there in his Volkswagen and sit and stare out into the field and just talk for hours about everything. We called that area the "Sea of Emotion." Those were treasured moments. But the greatest moments were when my lessons evolved into these long jams in his backyard, up to six hours at a pop. We would just sit back to back and play. There's a very intimate place you can go with someone you are sharing music with, if they have the ears to listen and respond creatively and without prejudice. And to this day, those backyard moments of pure sharing and expressing musical ideas with Joe are my favorite musical memories. There is nobody I have ever played with who can listen and respond like Joe.

There has been, and still is, amazing synergy in our careers together. After I recorded my first solo record, *Flex-Able*, I tried to find a record deal. It was difficult, and the one label that offered me a deal presented something that was a music-business eye-opener. Conventional record deals at the time seemed completely lopsided (and still do today). From working with Frank Zappa, I learned to never get emotional about a deal or sell myself short. If it doesn't feel right, just don't do it. Do something else. So I set off to get my music out on my own and studied the infrastructure of the music business. I discovered that I could start my own little label and go directly to a distributor instead of a label, thus cutting out the middleman that would usually take ownership and control of your music and pay you a mere pittance for it. What I didn't realize was that finding a distributor was more difficult than finding a label that would sign you. I sent my stuff to everyone, and the only person who responded was Cliff Cultreri at a distribution company called Important Records. Cliff actually knew some of my work with Frank and saw that I had some kind of a built-in audience because of that. He gave me a distribution deal that was much more lucrative than a record deal. Because Joe and I were trading tapes all the time, I sent some of his stuff to Cliff and hooked them up. It was a good pairing.

Cliff Cultreri: I had known Steve Vai for a while, and one day in early 1986, he stopped by my office and was hanging out for a bit, and I remember he kind of nervously pulled this ragged-looking cassette out of his pocket and said, "I usually don't like doing this, but you really have to hear this guy, I've taken some lessons from him and he's really something special." So I put it in the cassette player and a minute or two in I stopped the tape and looked at Steve to ask, "WHY did you wait so long to give me this. What the hell is wrong with you?" I listened to that tape over and over. Well, Steve had Joe's phone number on the tape, and so the very next day I cold-called him, introduced myself, and he started firing away questions at me.

During that first conversation, Cliff let me know that he really liked my compositions. It was a real boost of confidence, and a recognition that my approach to strike out on a different path from everybody else was perhaps worthwhile artistically. When you do something different from the popular crowd, you really feel you're out on your own. You realize, "I don't fit anywhere. Nobody's doing this like me." When people hear your music for the first time, you're afraid they won't know how to categorize it, or how or when to listen to it. And all it takes is one person to say, "I get it, I know what you're doing, DON'T COMPROMISE. Keep being yourself." For me, Cliff was that guy.

Cliff Cultreri: As we began talking back and forth about a P&D [pressing and distribution] deal for *Not of This Earth*,

Joe was really sensible about it all—that's the best word I could use. Among his concerns were the guitar lessons he was giving at the time, which was how he made his living, and his questions were things like: What does he do to replace that? How does he support his wife? How does he support himself? What becomes of his students? How soon does all this happen if it does happen? He was very smart about it, and certainly expressed interest in wanting to do it, and he explained what his situation was and what his needs along the latter lines were going to be to make it happen, so I tried to put a deal together that worked for him and protected him. That was no problem for me because I already knew I wanted to sign him before I called him.

One thing I knew was that for instrumental guitar rock to be successful in that era, it had to take the place of the lead vocalist, and it needed to be lyrical. Those guitar riffs and lines had to put the listener in a place where they're sort of making up their own words to the music, and Joe was completely about that. Every song, all the way through each song, was just so incredibly lyrical and memorable, so you could just let your mind wander with the music. I thought if anybody was going to break through as an instrumental artist, he was the one.

If you sort of look at history, there was a big instrumental hit with the *Miami Vice* theme a year or so before I started talking to Joe, and ten years prior to that, there was a huge hit over in Europe with Jeff Beck's *Blow by Blow*. So it seemed like every so often, the cycle repeated where instrumental music sort of got its foot back in the door and got some of the attention it deserved. So to me, hearing Joe's album was perfect timing in that context, because the guitar was back dominating again, and you had the new wave of British metal bands, you had a new wave of American hard rock and metal bands, and even the alternative rock that was popular at the time was shifting from synthpop to more guitar-driven pop music. So the guitar was certainly in the limelight.

After my first phone call with Cliff, Rubina and I drove down to L.A. one weekend to meet him. It took almost the whole year to get the deal done, but Cliff really wanted to get it released. So I thought, "Okay, I'll hold off on putting it out myself." In the interim, I had the gig with the Greg Kihn Band, so that sort of tided me over until Cliff was able to work out my deal with Relativity Records to get the album released, which finally came in November of 1986.

John Cuniberti: I thought the album was pretty amazing when it was done, but honestly, I didn't ever think anything was going to come of it really, for the simple fact that *Not of This Earth* began as essentially a vanity record. It wasn't for a label, but rather I think something Joe had to do musically for himself. He had all this music in him, and all these frustrations from the Squares, and he really needed to prove to himself that he really could do something remarkable and special. I never remembered a time when we were together making that record where we thought to ourselves, "Man, this is gonna be a fucking hit." Remember, this was an instrumental record, and was way before there was any progressive music movement, so there were no record labels dedicated to this type of thing. Everything happened for a reason—it's quirky, it's weird, you can shoot holes through it, or take exception to it, but as far as I'm concerned, it's a perfect little piece of art and I couldn't have done it better. I just felt it was something Joe had to do to show the rest of the world that he was a guitar player who was going somewhere.

Along with the support I received from John and Steve along this journey toward getting signed, Cliff Cultreri was now providing me all kinds of energy—catalytic, creative, and supportive—which is what makes a great A&R guy. He really made things happen for people. Very often, artists just need that one person to help them with the creative connections that make an album happen, which was absolutely the case with my next record, *Surfing with the Alien*. Cliff was the one who really pushed Relativity Records president

Barry Kobrin to bring me to New York for a showcase so everyone at the label could see me do it in the flesh. He knew what kind of record we were making, and no one had really made a record like that before for Relativity, so they were in virgin territory as well.

Cliff really believed in me, partly because he and I thought alike. I liked him, I liked his taste in music, he understood where I wanted to go with my album, and he was very encouraging all the time. After I got off the road from touring with Greg Kihn, Cliff hooked me up with this Swedish bass player named Jonas Hellborg, and I was off on this crazy tour of Scandinavia for about a month. It was a very interesting time, where a lot happened in a period of two months, as I continued to lay the foundation for my future as a solo artist, finishing with a make-or-break showcase that Cliff had set up for me at the China Club in New York.

I remember this clearly: The first time I met Barry Kobrin, he shook my hand and in front of everybody from the label, said, "You don't look like a rock star." He was sort of laughing when he said it, but I think he was nervous, because I think he was looking for someone that looked more like Steve Vai: somebody tall, handsome, with long hair, wearing leather and chains, doing what rock stars did during the mid-eighties. I was not that guy at all.

I remember the afternoon before the show, I'd brought bassist Mark Egan and drummer Danny Gottlieb down and showed them the songs literally about an hour before we were going to play. They were really cramming. The executives at Relativity were basically checking me out to see if they wanted to go beyond the P&D deal that we had for *Not of This Earth*. So when everyone from the label got there, we played some of the new pieces, and I think it was "Satch Boogie" that convinced them of my direction and style. I'd told them I wanted to make a guitar record that celebrated all the aspects of rock guitar, from Chuck Berry to Hendrix and everything else. Relativity was primarily a thrash metal label at the time; that's what they were really putting out, so this was a test, a showcase of sorts. When Barry heard "Satch Boogie" and saw me play it, he was completely knocked out and finally "got it." He shook my hand and said, "This idea you have"—which was going to become *Surfing with the Alien*, although it didn't have a title at the time—"I get it. I understand you now, and I want you to go do it. Let's make a deal."

CHAPTER 8 ★★

Surfing with the Alien—1987

> *"In 1987, with the release of his multi-Platinum album* Surfing with the Alien, *Joe Satriani rose from obscurity to worldwide prominence."*
>
> —*Guitar World* magazine

***Surfing* was an** important album for me, partly because every single song on it contained elements of what collectively crystallized into my signature style. The writing process was different for each song as well. Sometimes I would start composing a melody and immediately have a full grasp of its primary inspiration and how I wanted its message to unfold. From there, I might ask myself, "What kind of band could play behind this?" Other times, it would just be a groove, along with a mental image, and I would write a musical story to go with that image. The inspiration for the compositions always came first, straight from the heart.

When we started *Surfing with the Alien*, we were all excited because we felt we were going to make a record that hadn't yet been made by other guitarists in my field—we felt we were on our own cutting edge. At the same time, I also wanted the album to be a celebration of all the styles that made up my musical roots. There were things I really loved about the records that made up my foundation as a young musician: the guitar playing of the mid-sixties through the early seventies, that was my foundation and how I learned to play. The late-sixties guitar sound is really what woke me up to wanting to be a player, and I wanted to put a modernized celebration of that into the record. I didn't want to make a self-promotional shred record where it was just me playing fast and furious all over the place. The songs had to be "classic" high-quality compositions, not simply vehicles for improvisation. I wanted each song to be very different from the next, with variety not only in the way I played and composed them, but also in the way we recorded them. Equally, I didn't want to come in with such a preconceived idea of a song that I would shut myself off from the spirit of the moment.

As a guitar player, I was excited to make the kind of record that showcased some of the new ideas I was working on, both compositionally and technically. For example, *Surfing with the Alien*'s first solo is announced by an unexpected high-register trill. What's different there is the way that I used it and how I did it. I used the edge of the pick instead of my fingers to execute the trill, which gave it a pronounced, almost glassy tone. Compositionally, I'm using it to announce the first solo section in its new key, using the root and flat 9th of the Phrygian dominant scale. It's a very dramatic shift of key signatures and the pick-trill is a signature moment. It's brought to life with a wah-wah, a Chandler Tube Driver, and a Marshall 100-watt half stack.

Quite a few guitar players over the years have mentioned to me the opening phrase of the solo in "Echo" as another signature moment. It announces itself boldly and then has a way of just "tumbling down" and ending on a low tone, then taking a breath. Players would say, "I never thought that you could do that, build a guitar solo by making an opening statement, then waiting, using silence, then continuing on, and building the solo with a variety of phrases." I didn't even notice what I'd done while recording it. I was just following my muse, channeling the great saxophonist Lester Young, I think. But it opened other players' eyes up to the possibility of what you could do with an electric guitar solo. We used a DS-1 into a Roland JC-120 for the melodies and solos, miked with an AKG C-12A, I think.

"Echo" turned out so cinematic-sounding partly because it had a traditional-style melody utilizing big intervals over lush chords, and it was in an odd time signature, too. The chorus's chord sequence is very unusual, moving through a few different keys, but the way it resolves is quite traditional. I was really trying to subvert that sort of chord journey that you hear in almost every commercial song when they go into their B-section, or when they're leading into their chorus. My style of playing over multiple key changes and in odd time signatures focuses more on smoothing things out, making the listener feel more comfortable, and delivering the song's resolution gracefully after a long melodic journey.

On the whole record you hear me using feedback, using the whammy bar, picking a lot, or using legato. I'm throwing in about everything that you would consider the history of guitar techniques for the last 100 years, by players like Jimi Hendrix, Jeff Beck, Jimmy Page, Billy Gibbons, Eric Clapton, Brian May, Tony Iommi, Alan Holdsworth, and John McLaughlin—to name a few!

From Left: Jeff, John, me, and Bongo Bob Smith at Bill Graham's house in Mill Valley

When I wrote *Surfing with the Alien*'s title track, I was inspired by the thought of being visited by an alien, but with a twist: The alien would want to do something fun while visiting Earth, and so we all go surfing. That was really it, just a little daydream that popped into my head.

"Always with Me, Always with You" began as a love song for my wife, Rubina. I remember composing most of it in my Berkeley apartment one afternoon. The chord sequence uses suspended triads arpeggiated over a major-key bass line. On top of that, a lyrical melody in counterpoint with the arpeggios, and a little pitch axis B-section. There's even some two-handed tapping in there as well! John, Jeff, and Bongo Bob Smith helped me keep the end result sweet and as light as a feather by adding the perfect accompaniment and a unique final mix. All the guitars were recorded using a Rockman, and then straight into mic pres on that song—no amps!

With a song like "Circles," I'm using dyads to create a harmonized melody against an exotic rhythm section that shifts gears suddenly with Jeff Campitelli's amazing footwork on the kick drum. It's a crazy arrangement that was a lot of fun to work out in the studio. DI guitars for the main melody, amped-up rhythm guitars combined with the Rockman for the solo. For me, it was a new way of combining melody, rhythm, and harmony to create a memorable hook. The trippy ending with all the swirling percussion and sound effects completes the song's fantasy.

I was sixteen or seventeen years old when I came up with the two opening chords for "Lords of Karma." I had returned home from partying on a Saturday night and couldn't sleep. It was an hour before dawn, and I was sitting on my bed playing the guitar when I wrote those two chords, repeating back to back. Two things happened: I was writing down everything I was feeling at that moment about what those chords represented to me, and night was fading—you could tell the sun was going to rise in about an hour or so. So my young musical brain at the time was saying, "I think no one's ever put these two chords together before." I sorted through my musical mind but couldn't recall borrowing those chords from anybody or find them in my memory of any rock, jazz, or classical compositions.

"Wow," I thought, "you've just created something nobody's done before, those two chords as a cyclical chord progression." It represented my take on the pitch-axis style, where each chord changes the key, but I was still using A as my bass note, my main key note. The chords: A (no 3rd) add +4 to A 13 sus4 (no 9th). The keys I built off of the chords were A Lydian and A Mixolydian, respectively. That fascination stayed with me for over a decade, but I couldn't write a song around these chords to save my life, so when I was getting ready to record *Surfing with the Alien*, I said, "You're finally going to finish this song!" It just flowed out. That song is very special to me. Every time I play that chord sequence it brings me back to that place—being home, the sun coming up, guitar in hand, having a profoundly creative moment.

Back then, critics would really focus their energy on the lead player, who had all the chops. What I wanted on *Surfing with the Alien* was a record that had the instruments sounding as if they were played by an actual band with a unified vision, so you didn't have everyone trying to show off their fusion chops, or whatever school of playing they were coming from. When I look at the techniques on the record, I feel like I made a conscious effort to pull back, to tell you the truth. On the title track, for example, the rhythm guitars are very straight-ahead rock 'n' roll rhythm guitars, and I'm doing Chuck Berry licks and Hendrix-y things. They wanted you to do that "over the top" rock guitar thing at that time, but I wanted to be different. I wanted to use more space, stronger phrasing. That's what I heard in the music I grew up with. Jimi Hendrix and Keith Richards are masters of that. They came up with these great riffs and solos that you remember forever. It's not a matter of filling every space; it's picking your moments. That was an important lesson I put into making *Surfing*.

I also worked hard trying to innovate song structure. Take "Satch Boogie" with its pitch-axis-meets-two-hand-tapping chord sequence. From a compositional point of view, the song starts off as a swing piece, turns into a rock boogie jam, then breaks down to a half-time beat with a pitch axis composition stuck in the middle of it. It's got the weirdest bridge ever, too! I started with what was very popular at the time, a very Van Halen–like two-hand tapping technique, but I did something very different with it by playing a chord sequence that veers way outside the rock idiom.

The visionary Cliff Cultreri and me at a platinum award presentation dinner

There were things on *Surfing* that we thought were really groundbreaking for its time. John's use of nonlinear reverb and the FS-1 Cyclosonic Panner for 3-D imaging of sound I thought was quite unique. The way we used sampled instruments to enhance sections of songs like "Hill of the Skull," "Circles," "Lords of Karma," "Midnight," and "Surfing." These were things you wouldn't normally find on a rock 'n' roll guitar album. We were trying to make this something extremely fresh and artistic, and I suppose that's the best way to explain it in the fewest words.

John Cuniberti: Every time Joe picked up the guitar and started playing it, I heard something new. I don't think I ever took it for granted, but it was absolutely stunning how he could just continually pick up a guitar, play it, and produce music that you'd never heard played like that before. The chord changes he would pick and the way he would construct music was unlike anything I'd ever heard. So I was always excited to hear what he had to play; everything was always a surprise, especially with the material he brought in for this new LP. I've never known where he gets that stuff from—what are those chord changes he's playing, what key is that in? I was always mystified by him musically.

There was a lot of planning when it came to how each song on the album was supposed to sound. John Cuniberti wanted to make sure that everything sounded unique and specific for each song. He was great at finding the sweet spot out of any amp's speaker, too. "Crushing Day" and its triple-tracked rhythm guitar sound is a good example of that. A song like "Hill of the Skull" has at least six electric guitars on it, using one Marshall head daisy-chained into another, really loud, very distorted. There was literally nothing else on the album that was recorded like that. Similarly, if you take the first three songs, "Surfing," "Ice 9," and "Crushing Day," each of those was recorded quite differently in terms of what amps and stomp boxes were used. Back in those days, "the team" was me, John Cuniberti, Jeff Campitelli, and Bongo Bob Smith. John and I were the principals, but Jeff and Bongo had a big influence on *Surfing* as well.

John Cuniberti: Joe was comfortable with the strict time of the drum machine, because up till then he always worked in a band with a drummer and wrote and played music that worked in a band-type scenario. Once he found a drum machine and started playing to that, he completely changed the way he wrote music. It opened up the door for him to do all sorts of very interesting things rhythmically, where if the guy was throwing a big fill in or changing the pattern on the hi-hat, it kind of made Joe compositionally change what he would have to play.

Bongo Bob's musicianship had accelerated and gone into this new era of programming where he could play an SP-12 drum machine with his fingers and make it sound like it had more feel than a real drummer! His body was very musical, and yet his head could also get into the programming aspect of music, which was great. He had a university degree in ethnic percussion, but he also knew his way around the latest technology, either synthesizers or drum machines or the latest cutting-edge samplers. He could come in and program the drum machine with great feel, and then add some African percussion on top of that.

Bongo Bob Smith: At the time, I was working as a drum programmer for the biggest producer in the world, Narada Michael Walden, and we were doing what I call the crap of the eighties, but doing it very well, from Whitney Houston to Lionel Richie. I wouldn't say it was crap so much as it was not a musician's kind of music. I was doing that by day, so when Joe came to me saying, "I have this idea for this record . . ." to me, it was like, "Oh my God, I would just LOVE to be a part of that," because it just sounded really interesting. I'm a percussionist, so I had studied African, Cuban, Brazilian percussion, the migration of rhythms out of Africa into the Americas, and that was my life. So the idea of what sound could do and what rhythm could do to a particular song was very, very important to me. I think my biggest contribution was, "How far can I go to stay out of the way? To what depths can I go here to stay out of the way?" Because NOBODY has ever said, "Wow, those drums on *Surfing with the Alien*, those are amazing." [laughs]

They've never been spoken, those words, and I applaud that, because the idea with what Joe had set out to do with the drums was to have them *support what the guitar was doing*. The simplicity was very important because it really propels the guitar. It made his guitar bigger than life because everything else—the keyboards, the bass and drums—are just so simple around it. So as we recorded, we were thinking, "How are we going to make this stuff really speak and how can we contribute when there's no singer?" Because up until that point, I had always been taught, "You're here to support the singer," and in the world of production—from back then until now—any great producer's going to sit there and ask, "How am I going to get this piece of music to fit around the singer? How do I sculpt this?" And in our case, the singer *was the lead melody*, so we were trying to always inspire that.

I wasn't playing perfectly to the machines. I was dancing *around* them. Bob pointed that out to me one day. The curious effect it created was a "hook"—it drew you into the music. The drum machine "performances" actually had this very interesting quality that made the music more listenable in a modern, cinematic way, and when you removed them, there was some sort of charm that evaporated. I couldn't figure that out at first, because all of our instincts were to have a live guy playing drums, but the live kit would somehow make the music sound less special. At the same time, there were other songs where it was so obviously better, like with "Satch Boogie" or "Circles." For the songs on *Surfing* where Jeff did wind up playing live drums, it sounded amazing. So what we wound up with was a lot of songs where the drum parts were essentially a hybrid of live and programmed.

John Cuniberti: Initially, Joe and I would get together with Bob, play him the demo, and then talk about what a real drummer might play, and where the fill might be. And if there was going to be a fill, what kind of fill is it, and when does he come off the hi-hat, when does he hit a cymbal, all that stuff. Joe approved all the drum parts, but he wasn't a drummer, and so was happy to have the assistance of a real drummer who could come in and program the machine to play like a real drummer would play it, but with this real strict groove and time that was necessary for him to be able to play these songs the way he envisioned them being played. We'd made what was, in my opinion, the brave decision to dive headfirst into MIDI and computer-generated drum machines.

So what we did was Joe and I would huddle with Bob around his computer, and we'd lay out what we believed to be the drum performance, and that was based off Joe's demo, what he heard for the song, and how complicated he wanted to be. I would decide on the samples we were gonna use and what Jeff was ultimately going to have to play, because again, I never liked the cymbal sound and wanted Jeff to play hi-hat and smash cymbals to get a sense of fidelity. Once that was done, we would book the studio, and Bob and I would go in there, and I would take all these outputs from our tape drum machine samplers and plug them into mic pres and EQs and get them printed, and get the whole drum performance printed. It wouldn't include Jeff's performances, as those would come later, but we would have computer-generated brass for guide tracks for Jeff to hear later and know where to put them.

John Cuniberti and me at Hyde Street in '87 . . . shirts tucked in!

PHOTO BY JON SIEVERT

Bongo Bob: Alongside Joe and John Cuniberti, Jeff Campitelli and I worked together in the studio in kind of a backward way from what was traditional to the times in that it wasn't, let's say, him playing a drum set and then me playing, let's say, percussion or bringing in the drum loop. The way we worked, he actually came in and laid down his live drum parts as overdubs *on top* of the drum machine part, from drum fills to whatever he wanted to add to the groove, and then together we would both spice it up with cymbal hits to different other little percussion bits where we were trying to add to the collective.

John Cuniberti: Because the drums back then were being generated by computer, we were always given eight or ten tracks, then other tracks were set aside for rhythms, others for melodies and solos. So when we started a song, I would pull out a track sheet, and go, "Okay, give me an idea of what you hear in this song, how many tracks you're thinking about, et cetera, so I can start laying this thing out." Because I didn't want to run out of tracks and get to a point where I had to say, "We don't have any tracks for that because I did those last two guitars in stereo." I kind of needed to know ahead of time what he had in mind track-wise—how many guitar parts he heard, if he was going to add a keyboard, if the harmonies were going to be one- or three-part—and the track sheets would be laid out more or less the same. So as we'd work through the project, there would always be a couple of empty tracks until there weren't any, and there were times when we'd get to a point where we were filled up, and I had to start moving some things around. Then I would print all these drum parts. Once it was all printed, then Joe would start to build the project. He oftentimes would pull out a bass and play a bass track. More times than not he would lay a guitar track and just to be sure the thing was feeling right—if he got through the thing and it still felt good to him, and he liked the way it sounded—then we would move on to other tracks till we'd finally built the song up. That process could take a day or it could take a week; it just kind of depended on the song and how evolved it was by the time he arrived at the studio, and then what happened as we recorded the song.

I knew that I had to be flexible, because there were some great ideas that John would have after listening to me play for a bit. Also, we would work on the parts of these songs—the bass part, the drum part, the first rhythm, the second rhythm, the keyboard—for hours before we would get to any kind of solo part.

John Cuniberti: Joe was always in the control room when he recorded, and from then on throughout his career, he spent most of his time in the control room with just him and the engineer, one on one, just layering his guitar tracks. As he tracked, we'd lay a drum machine down first, and then he'd play either a rhythm guitar part of some kind or bass, and then we'd build the tracks up like you would any rhythm section. He'd do rhythms, then bass, then melody, and then there might be some clean guitars that come in during the bridges or choruses, and we'd build it all up until it got to the point where it was time for the lead singer, so to speak, which in Joe's case would be the melody guitar. I would say he's stayed loyal to that structure throughout his career. When Joe and I worked on guitar overdubs, generally the rhythms pretty much stayed what they were in the demo. If the arrangement called for a solo, he would have worked on something at least stylistically ahead of time, so that he knew where on the neck he wanted to play and what technique he wanted to showcase for a particular solo, and he basically would know more or less how he wanted it to end up.

We wanted every song to have its own vibe and unique juxtaposition of instruments. It wasn't going to be about Joe and his guitar technique. It was going to be about the songs, their melodies and their arrangements, the guitar tones, the use of outboard gear, and the technique of recording—bringing the art of engineering and mixing to a higher level, making a record that you could listen to top to bottom and walk away from with a feeling that you'd just been blown away.

John Cuniberti: When we would listen to his demos, or when we would start recording a track, a lot of times I would be inspired by what I heard. So for instance, with "Always with Me, Always with You," I thought, "The simplest we can make this, the better," so let's not have a drummer playing a drum part; let's just keep it super simple. Other songs might have a vibe to them, a sound that would inspire us to do more reverbs or delays. So a lot of times the music Joe would play would inspire me to do studio tricks, and then the studio tricks would in turn inspire him to play differently. So it was kind of a circular, organic process we would go through. So from *Not of This Earth* through *Surfing* and really all the way up through *Flying in a Blue Dream*, it was highly experimental. Joe didn't really know what these records were going to sound like till they were done, and neither did I. I had a lot of free rein to do a lot of screwy things to the sound, and Joe allowed me the freedom to try anything I wanted. He may not have always liked it, and if he didn't, I would dump it and try something else. But I had a lot of latitude.

Once we laid a rhythm track down, and maybe he had played a melody or a solo, he might say, "Something's missing. It would be nice maybe if there were these other guitars playing this other part. Give me a track, let me try something." A lot of times, he would come in and start playing, and I would make suggestions like, "It's too bright or too muddy, maybe we should make it more ambient. Let's put this delay on it . . ." Then he would start playing a solo a little differently because he was actually playing now to the sound that we then created in the studio, which of course was something he couldn't do at home.

My ideas would build a song over the course of a couple of weeks. If we were spending a week on the rhythm section, the next week we would do rhythm guitars, and then we'd rent a keyboard for a couple of days. The solos didn't get on the album until maybe a month or two later. By then, I'd had a lot of time to both think about what I wanted to play and to just *react*. So as I was listening to a rough mix of the guitar, bass, and drums, no melody or solo, I'd start to imagine, "Wouldn't it be great if the solo did something like this?" So I'd go into the session and maybe say, "John, this solo is going to be very in time, very structured," like "Crushing Day." For the solo on "Echo," I might have said, "I don't know what I'm going to do here, but it's going to have me starting and stopping, playing long phrases and using some open spaces."

With "Echo," I was looking for a very emotional sound out of the melody and solo guitars, and John thought he could record the guitar coming out of the JC-120 and limit it "before" it went to tape. I was getting really into the tone he was getting by limiting the guitar this way, but it was a dangerous thing to do because we had delays running through the amp as well. Once recorded, we'd be stuck with those repeats, so if we'd wanted to do a punch-in or something, it might get problematic. But that's a good example of me reacting to how the sound was evolving, and to what John was suggesting as he listened to me play.

Prior to working with John on these records, I just assumed you put a microphone in front of an amp and its cable went into the wall and then it made its way to the desk and the tape machine. John would flat-out say, "Let's NOT put your guitar through the desk. I want people to hear your guitar just like it sounds when I stand in front of your amp." I gave him carte blanche to figure out the most direct way to get my guitar onto the tape. He had these Neve mic pres, and other ones from old recording desks that were used on classic records, and we would use them religiously. Since we were doing single tracks, one at a time, we could use the same mic pres for all the guitars, all the bass guitars, and so forth. I really loved the sound I heard coming out of the speakers so much that it helped with my performance.

John Cuniberti: When we'd started *Surfing*, I had gotten a hold of a pair of Neve 1073 mic pres, which at the time was unheard of. I wanted to record a record on a Neve console, but we didn't have one—in fact, there wasn't one in the Bay Area, particularly not an old one. My friend who owned Hyde Street Studios had gotten a hold of an old Neve and had pulled out all the modules, and when I saw them, I asked him, "Can we put these in a box, so I can use all these mic pres and EQs?" I went to a woodworker right here in town, said, "See these modules? I want these in a box and upright, and an aluminum back panel, etc. . . ." and the guy built me a box, and I had those for years after that. Relative to Joe's sound, we primarily used that one on every track. Because we were recording one track at a time, I got to record the album on a Neve. So my plan was to record it on a Neve and mix it on an API. That was my game plan for *Surfing*.

I recorded the album on just a few guitars: my home-built black Boogie Bodies "Strat" thing, another similar guitar that my wife had painted for me, my two Kramer Pacers, a borrowed Coral Sitar, and a Fender P-Bass. I was very comfortable using the Kramer's Floyd Rose bar, which by now was a tunable Floyd Rose. I had one on my white Kramer Pacer, but the body's wood was so soft the bar would eventually fall right out of the guitar. Back then, luthier Gary Brawer had to put hard wood dowels into the guitar body so we could screw the Floyd Rose unit in again and again. My Boogie Bodies Strat from way back in the Squares days had two different pick guards: one with humbuckers, one with the three single-coil Stratocaster-type pickups. So sometimes, like with "Circles," I took the humbuckers out, put in the single coils, and recorded the song's main melody, and then did the same thing for all of "Midnight." When I wanted a crunchier sound, I'd put in the humbucking pick guard configuration.

John Cuniberti: Even as we were making all this amazing progress, it was definitely difficult for us to complete that record, both because of the timing and the money. I think the mix process produces high anxiety, because as long as you're recording, there's hope. There's always this sense of, "Well, the rough mixes don't sound right, or the song isn't really working yet, but when we mix it will be fine." When you start mixing is when you realize what you have or in some cases don't have. It can be devastating. You can spend a lot time of recording, thinking that you've really got something, but when it's done and you push up the faders you say, "What happened?" By then it's too late because the money's gone.

It was difficult for me to complete the record because of scheduling and budget issues. Sometimes I'd wind up with three hours at one studio and four hours in another studio but only between eight and midnight or midnight and four in the morning. I couldn't always get John when I needed him, so the recording schedule dragged a bit. We couldn't afford lockout time, so I had to just book hours here and there that were sometimes separated by days, weeks, things like that. We were also working on different equipment, so we literally would finish two hours of recording in Studio C at the Hyde Street building, pack everything up and move to Studio D, set up all over again, and record some other part of some other song. It was crazy.

Relativity originally set the recording fund at $13,000, which was ridiculously low. We reached that $13,000 limit pretty fast, so I kept having conversations with Cliff Cultreri, my A&R guy, asking for a doubling of the fund. Cliff was an inspirational guy who really believed in me and argued my case every time I called the label asking for more money. We eventually spent $29,000, which is still a tiny amount to make a record.

What was never reflected in the budget, however, was that I was trading studio work, hour for hour, for studio time to finish the album. John did everything he could to find a way for me to get free time or trade my services at any studio that was functioning at the Hyde Street building. I was working with Sandy Pearlman, the producer who was working on the Blue Öyster Cult album *Imaginos*, and instead of getting cash, I said, "Just give me studio time." So I'd do a session midnight to 4 A.M., then show up the next day at noon and use those "earned" hours myself! I did other sessions in the building for the Hyde Street studio co-owner, Michael Ward, and some other clients that John had arranged. With *Surfing* we really needed a lot of extra studio time because it was just a few guys making the record, one small step at a time. It wasn't a rehearsed band where you could go in and play your whole set in a couple of days. Every once in a while we'd have Jeff come in to do percussion, or Bongo Bob, and even John got in on the action sometimes, but I was doing 99 percent of the playing.

The biggest stress of that final schedule was going back to Hyde Street, working hard hours, day after day. Having a home studio in later years helped me tremendously because I could put a song to bed, then two days later, come back to exactly the same spot on my Pro Tools session, capture better performances, and get a better handle on what I was really recording.

But back then, my schedule had me teaching, playing, and performing ten hours a day, and it took a heavy toll. Good things can come of it if you've got a good team with you, but you can wear your hands out that way, too! I would be playing a lot of different instruments as well, going from guitar to bass to keyboards. On top of that, if the song wasn't working out, I'd have to rewrite that part right there in the moment, which was definitely stressful. Remember, we recorded the album on only three reels of 2-inch tape! The only performances saved were the final ones. No outtakes left behind.

By the time we were finally ready to mix *Surfing*, I remember not liking anything I'd done! I really felt I needed another ten years to work on the album. Mixing meant you were finished playing, so I came into the process with a lot of anxiety. Of course, John, having mixed so many records before, thankfully knew what mixing was really about. I was using it as an extension of making the record, but John had other, more practical things to get to first. Balancing in the days before automated recall, for instance, took a long time, and engineers need to be given the space and time to get that balance right, and that's *before* you'd start to get crazy with mixes and things like that. John was meticulous in making sure the album sounded gorgeous, and he somehow always found a way to make cool ideas we came up with work.

John Cuniberti: Some of the songs were easier to mix than others—as always. In those days, I would start a mix, and then Joe would come in and sit down and we would finish it together. That was pretty much how we did it. Sometimes Joe had working titles for his songs that stuck, but oftentimes the titles came much later, after the songs were finished. He would come up with an order during mixing and run it by me, and I might like it or make suggestions, but the track order and the song titles usually evolved after the mixes. For *Surfing*, I think we'd gotten $25,000 to do that record, and by the end of recording, we did wind up going a little over budget, because after the first round of mastering, we decided to remix at least one or two songs, and then had to go back and remaster again. But $30,000, even in those days, wasn't a lot of money for making a record. So oftentimes, by the point where we'd gotten to the mix stage, we were either almost out of money or damn near, so it wasn't a situation where if we didn't like a mix, we could come back the next day and do it again.

One morning, returning to the studio to finish mixing "Lords of Karma," we found that the cleaning staff had removed our "magical" mix of the song's bridge, which was hanging on the coat rack, and thrown it in the Dumpster! It couldn't be saved, so we had to mix it again, using more precious mix tape, which was getting harder to pay for. And the drama didn't end there.

When we first heard the final album mixes at Bernie Grundman's mastering studio, it was a shock. Side one had a noticeable left/right balance discrepancy. It turned out to be a recording-desk issue back at Studio C where it was mixed. After a few angry phone calls to the studio manager, we packed up and returned to S.F. to remix side one. The label thought I was nuts, but I insisted. We had to get this right. We returned a week later with properly balanced new mixes and mastered the record using the new Dolby SR system. It sounded beautiful, and Bernie did a wonderful job cutting the album to disc and preparing it for CD.

I should have been overjoyed. I wasn't. I was so emotionally distraught after the album was finished that I could only listen to it—I kid you not—slowed down and distorted. I'd put a cassette of the mastering on my 4-track and slow it down and turn it up. It was the only way I could get through it without having a heart attack. I thought it wasn't good enough. I'd put everything I had into it and thought it was the last record anyone would ever let me make. I loved *Not of this Earth*, but I knew it was a little weird, so I didn't think it had too much broad appeal. *Surfing* was the first record that was sanctioned by and paid for by Relativity Records, and they were expecting something great. *Surfing* really crystallized a moment for me. Why wasn't I satisfied with it? It summed up all the different styles that I related to musically and everything I'd been working on as a guitar player since I was a kid. Yet despite all the trials and tribulations in making it, *Surfing* turned out to be a real gem after all.

CHAPTER 9 ★★

Launching the Silver Surfer

"Joe Satriani's 1987 breakthrough can be seen as the gold standard for guitar playing of the mid-to-late '80s, an album that captures everything that was good about the glory days of shred."

—*Billboard* magazine

Steve Vai: I always knew Joe would be recognized as a musical guitar giant, and it's easy to say that now, but the truth is that I always saw him that way from when I was twelve years old. But I did not know how things worked in real life, if real talent could be recognized or if it was just luck when someone became successful. In looking back and knowing what I know now, it is unequivocally clear that there was no other way for Joe's career to have gone but up, up, and up. It's very comforting to know that true talent can be recognized.

Lords of Karma was the original title of the album before its release, but after a journalist expressed his displeasure about it I started to have second thoughts. I scanned the record's songs for a new title and thought how could anyone object to *Surfing with the Alien*? It's so obviously a title with a sense of humor. So I called the Relativity office in New York and told production manager Jim Kozlowski my new title. He responded with, "Let's put the Silver Surfer on the cover. It's my nickname!" I replied, "What's a Silver Surfer?" Jim sent me a few issues of the comic straightaway and I was blown away. The Silver Surfer was the perfect image for the cover. It was bold, iconic, and positive. I could identify with the Surfer, even though I had never been on a surfboard!

Cliff Cultreri: Now that the record was done, we needed a cover concept that was as exciting and original as the music and the record's new title. We approached Marvel Comics and got the license for using the Silver Surfer art for the cover.

Our next move made sense because I knew that the odds were definitely against us in terms of, "Can he become a crossover artist to any degree? Can we get MTV? Can these types of things happen for him?" I knew in my gut there was a possibility of it, because there was really nobody like him happening at the time, and again, I felt if anybody had the music to do it, Joe was the one. But in the end, his first big break didn't actually come from radio or TV or any of those traditional venues that record companies use to break new artists and get the momentum behind an artist.

What happened was the music committee for the Winter Olympics approached us wanting to license the rights to use some of Joe's songs during some of the winter sporting competitions, and so naturally we said, "Great, what's the deal?" They said, "We'll give you X amount of dollars and you supply us with a master," and I started sort of kicking and fussing, asking, "Well, is there any way we can turn this into something bigger?" So what we came up with was instead of taking the up-front money that was being offered, we asked if in exchange they would show Joe's name and the album's title somewhere at the bottom of the TV screen while the music was being played so viewers would actually know who he was. That was the problem when you had these sporting events that used an artist's music: Unless you're on a stage playing at halftime and being announced, most people don't know who the artist is performing the music. So they agreed to that, and now we had—just like when an MTV video is playing—in the bottom left corner of the screen, every time one of Joe's songs came on, something that read to the effect of "Joe Satriani, *Surfing with the Alien*," the name of the specific song, and "Available on Relativity Records," et cetera.

It wound up being a boon for us promotionally, because they ended up using a *gang* of songs from the record. I remember we were getting such great promotion during those Olympic Games that sales started picking up, and pretty soon radio started to come on board. So all the bits and pieces of promotion we were doing culminated in what proved to be a pretty big piece of the puzzle, and I remember feeling Joe's music was a perfect fit for it. With so many millions of people watching the Olympics, it was better than having a video in rotation on MTV!

Mick Brigden, Manager: The day Joe came down to S.I.R. Rehearsal Studios to audition for the Mick Jagger gig, we had background singers, all the moving parts of a big stadium show set up that day. When Joe walked in the door, I remember being instantly impressed by the fact that he was not intimidated at all. He still was exactly the way he is to this day, and didn't change from that moment to this moment as the guy I know. He had his guitar in his hands and was comfortable playing whatever anyone threw at him, and they were throwing a bunch of material at him—not just Stones songs, but everything they were going to play onstage. They were just grooving and jamming, so there was a bit of blues going on, and some riffs going on, and Joe was just feeding off people, and Jagger was staying out of sight deliberately, because he didn't want to make it about who was onstage.

I was watching this all, and Mick just waited, and then at one point came out from behind the amps, blowing a harp on a blues jam, and just fell in with the groove, and Joe didn't bat an eye! There was no change in his state of being, and Joe's obvious talent came to the fore, and Mick looked around and gave me a thumbs-up, like "We've found him, haven't we?" So that's all it took—Joe just had to show up and play, and Mick was blown away and everyone in the band thought, "This guy can do anything we want to do," and they didn't even know how much Joe could do at that moment. They'd just had a two-hour taste, but it felt like Joe was born for this moment.

I had managed to get on the covers of a couple of magazines, but the success of the record hadn't really kicked in yet. It was that first Jagger tour of Japan and the following spring and summer solo tours of '88 that made things start to happen. I did two Jagger tours that year, separated by about five months of my own touring. Touring with Mick and the guys was so much fun and very intense, playing the Stones catalog and Mick's solo music. I was influenced by this historical rock 'n' roll library that I was playing every night, the lifestyle, and Mick's professionalism in general. I started to understand that it was okay to have fun and do whatever you wanted to do musically—in other words, "Don't be afraid, don't hold back, just do what you want, put your heart into it. If things don't turn out, be a man about it. Take your lumps if people don't like it, but you definitely don't wanna hold back, and you definitely don't want to do it because you think it's going to make you popular. You've got to love it and live it."

Cliff Cultreri: Once *Surfing with the Alien* really started to click, I knew Joe was definitely writing a new chapter: he was that next great, great musician to take the guitar and bring it to the forefront and really just push the boundaries. There were a lot of great rock-metal players doing their thing, from Eddie Van Halen to Angus Young, and they created a sound, a rhythm, and a feel, but Joe took the instrument and pushed it in every direction. He really just pushed the boundaries like nobody before, and it was a remarkable thing to watch young players listen and start learning from it—that was a tremendously important thing. Not only was Joe entertaining people, but really anybody who was listening to him was getting an education in playing.

The thing is, it's easy to say—especially with *Surfing* because the record was a multiplatinum success—that "Everything that happened in the studio was good." But had the record not been a success, it would have been just as easy for us to say that everything that happened was bad. Ultimately, you can only rate the record on its artistic success and how fans embraced it. Playing live onstage and hearing people shout in excitement when you start to play a song, like "Always" or "Memories"—even the first few notes—that's pretty amazing. I remember when there was none of that, and now all of a sudden, there are millions of fans and they know my music. They put it on at all times during their life—that to me is the most important thing ever, because it's the thing I've used to connect myself with other artists, too. That's how we all use music: We put it on when we need it, and it's extremely important in our lives. You put on a jacket when you're cold, and you put on music when your soul is in need. And when millions of people choose you and your music, nothing gets more profound than that.

Cliff Cultreri: The album was such a hit. Did I expect it to be a hit record? No, I was hoping it would get recognition and acclaim, and I think it outperformed everybody's expectations, which I think turned out to be a tremendously pleasant surprise for everyone.

It was a big deal. I believe we wound up selling more instrumental guitar records than anybody else has in history. That was cool, but personally, the audience knowing the material was the main thing for me—and they loved the material. That was the most striking thing, because before the album really took hold, I'd heard about people playing *Surfing* on the radio, but it didn't register with me until I was playing it before them live. I just couldn't believe that people knew every song on the album, and quite a few from the previous album, too! To me that was the greatest part. I knew you could win awards, you could get on the cover of magazines, you could be on TV—it didn't matter. Being famous was *not the same* as being embraced by your fans; it was very different. To actually connect with fans, and have them sing along, clap, and acknowledge full songs or even parts of songs . . . I was overwhelmed that this connection had been made. It was the same one that I had with artists I liked, and I thought, "Wow, that means it's really happening. People really love the music on the album." This was the most important thing to me, the connection with the audience.

Jonathan Mover, me, and Stuart Hamm after a San Francisco show in '88

PHOTO BY PAT JOHNSON

Postscript: Late in 1987, just before everything was about to "pop," *Guitar Player* magazine asked me to record an original piece of music for a Soundpage to be included in the February 1988 issue where I was to grace the cover—my first! I jumped into the studio with John and Jeff and recorded two pieces of music: "The Power

Cosmic," a solo guitar piece, and what would become a hit for me, "The Crush of Love," a soul song with a lilting wah-wah melody over a funky bass and fat backbeat. With my new Ibanez 540 Radius guitar in hand, Rockman amp, and Casio CZ-101 keyboard, we recorded and mixed the new music in a few hours at Hyde Street Studios. It eventually was added to a live EP called *Dreaming #11* that was released about a year later. The live performances, recorded at the California Theatre in San Diego, featured Stuart Hamm on bass and Jonathan Mover on drums, my touring band that year.

CHAPTER 10 ★★

Flying in a Blue Dream—1989

"One of Satriani's most brilliant early strategies: to subvert, re-energize, and recast common blues-rock licks as catchy and memorable instrumental 'verse' melodies played over irresistible rhythmic grooves."

—*Guitar Player* magazine

By the end of 1988, *Surfing* was still on the charts, and I was on the covers of magazines around the world, and I had just finished two tours with Mick and a few of my own as a new solo artist. With the release of the live EP *Dreaming #11* coming up, change was in the air. I had lived, celebrated, and survived that whole year, and come off the road thinking, "I've got to do something new and challenging, something to push me into a new artistic space."

I never intended to go into this genre as though it were going to be my career. I was still a rock guitar player, and I sang in bands my whole life, so I kept thinking, "Don't fall into the trap that many artists do of thinking they have to cater to their past success, because it will kill you in the end." So I said, "Look, I'm going to take a big risk: I'm going to sing and I'm going to play a larger variety of music. Artistically, I'm going to take it more out and more in. This record is going to be big and sprawling." I wanted to take that risk.

Because ultimately, the people who heard me on the radio only heard three songs at best: "Always with Me, Always with You," "Surfing with the Alien," and "Satch Boogie." They didn't hear "Midnight," they didn't hear "Hill of the Skull" or "Echo"—those things never got played on the radio, so they were thinking, "Joe Satriani is this boogie guy, who also has a fascination with aliens," but that was only a little part of me. So I had to bump it up and say, "No, it's going to be 'Big Bad Moon,' 'The Mystical Potato Head Groove Thing,' and 'I Believe,' and it's going to be 'The Forgotten (Parts 1 and 2)'—it's going to be *Flying in a Blue Dream*!"

I knew that John felt the same way—that we should just make a more adventurous, better-sounding album, and try to do things we'd never done before. We wanted to expand on what we'd accomplished with *Surfing*, and the good news was, in contrast to that record, when we started working on *Flying in a Blue Dream* my budget was something like $125,000! What that meant was lockout time! This was a gift for any recording artist, because now I could rent a studio for two weeks and no one was going to go in there, from the time I started renting it till the end of that two-week period. So all the amps and microphones, console settings, everything was left set up, which was a great time saver.

John Cuniberti: When we got together for preproduction sessions on *Flying*, there was a pressure I could see mounting on Joe being newly successful. There was now an infrastructure relying on prosperity based on his record making.

Initially, we moved to a new studio, Windham Hill's Different Fur Studios, and ran into technical difficulties almost immediately, beginning when we went to lay down some chunky rhythm guitar for *Flying in a Blue Dream*. As we were trying to get this guitar sound in the control room, I noticed that every time I started to turn my volume control up, this radio or TV broadcast would come through. Well, we quickly discovered the studio had a problem with RF interference. We wound up recording and using the RF we were picking up as part of the intro to the title track!

John Cuniberti: As a solution, we first tried a Faraday shield, which was basically chicken wire, which this expert said we needed to run around the entire building. This was a two-story building in the middle of San Francisco, so we couldn't do that. Then I tried to build a shield—basically a smaller chicken wire fence—around Joe, and that didn't work either, so we left after a couple days. Following our departure from Different Fur, my plan had been for us to set up shop at Fantasy Studios in Berkeley, but it wasn't available right at that moment. So we wound up back at Hyde Street working out of Studio C, where we'd done *Surfing*, basically with our tail between our legs because they had been pissed that we weren't going to do the new record there. In those days, when a band decided not to do a record at a studio, that produced a lot of bad blood and a lot of hurt feelings.

To try to alleviate getting bogged down, we picked a schedule that gave me breaks. So we didn't go in for two months straight and finish the record in one shot, with all those songs. We wound up going in for three weeks, and then we would stop and I would have a chance to do rewrites. So it wasn't unusual for me to be continually writing like that. But having the breaks really helped, because physically it was rough. I couldn't maintain a schedule of every day for two full months; I just wouldn't have been able to handle that kind of thing.

John Cuniberti: Our work schedule was erratic. We'd work for four or five days, and then I wouldn't see him for two weeks. Then we'd get together, and he'd listen to everything and want to redo it all. He'd come up with new ideas, throw some old songs away, and get some new songs, and then we'd get together for a couple of days and record some more stuff. It went on like that for months, which made it difficult to book studios and try to get a momentum and feel for the album. There was a lot of things going on for Joe, and his life got very complicated very quickly.

At the end of '88 two things happened to me that would drag me down physically for another year. To start, I contracted the intestinal parasite *Giardia*, which went undiagnosed for twelve months! I must have picked it up in Jakarta while playing a show there with Jagger. I'd have these incredibly painful attacks and have to go to the emergency room, where they would always fail to figure out what was wrong with me. Second, I decided to get a full compliment of dental braces to correct a TMJ problem. I told my orthodontist he had a little less than one year to get the job done. He could put me in as much pain as he needed to, but in eleven months he had to take all the braces off because I was going to be photographed and filmed. I was miserable continually for a year. I lost weight and felt uncomfortable in my own skin while trying to make this big artistic leap forward. And that wasn't all.

As we started recording *Flying*, my father suffered a massive stroke. He had suffered a smaller stroke years before, but this one sent him into a coma from which he never recovered. I realized then that he was gone. In my heart I knew that if I stopped working on the record and traveled back to New York to be with him, I'd probably just stay until he passed. I knew that wasn't what he would have wanted, so I stayed in California to finish the record, hoping he would hold on until I was finished. It didn't turn out that way. "Into the Light" was about the situation my dad was in. The song is more a prayer, a spiritual message. That's the best way to put it. He passed away as we were mixing "I Believe" in July that year.

I wrote "I Believe" about that whole period. I poured a lot of emotion into the performance, which made it even more difficult for me to sing, because the song was about dealing with hardships in your life. I first had the idea for the song when walking past this painting in the hallway of the Berkeley apartment where Rubina and I were living. It was a large multimedia painting that a friend of my wife's, Nunu Skrimstead, had made, and Rubina was the subject of this painting. Rubina was my emotional rock and the inspiration for the song, so concentrating on her portrait helped me focus on writing a song about hardships in general and how I believe you can turn things around no matter how hard they get.

Me at the mic in Studio C at Hyde Street, getting ready to sing "Strange" in '89
PHOTO BY KEN FRIEDMAN

"The Bells of Lal (Parts 1 and 2)" also came out of this period. My wife came home with these bells that were called Bells of Lal, and she told me they were put around camels' necks when they have a long journey through the desert. The sound distracts them from the hardships of the journey and keeps them moving forward. The bells were on this thin metal harness, almost like a necklace, and because they were very old and rusted, they had a very unique tone. I hadn't heard bells chime like this before. I realized I needed my own Bells of Lal to put around my neck to keep me going so I wouldn't stop and dwell on the harshness of the reality of what was happening in my life. I imagined I was in a vast desert. And I wondered, "If you could fly very close to the surface of the sand, over thousands of miles of desert, what would that sound like?" I thought the idea of a long journey should be represented not by a song that's got short little parts—versus, bridges, and choruses—but rather one long part.

John Cuniberti: We moved over to Fantasy Studios from Hyde Street around this period as well. Our feeling was that it was a better-run studio. It had very professional maintenance staff, it had a better microphone selection, the rooms were bigger, the quality of the assistant engineer was higher. I lived in Oakland, so it was very convenient for me. Most of all, it served our end of being a different venue—we just really needed a different atmosphere, a fresh start all around, and Fantasy definitely gave us that because it was a big step up. First off, when you walked into their huge, multistory building, there were pictures of Creedence Clearwater Revival and just about everybody else that's famous on the walls there. It was just a full-time studio that made you feel like you were moving up. That album was recorded in three different rooms, I think; we were definitely in D, where we mixed and did some drum recording; we were in B; and I remember doing something in Studio A. So I think we used almost every room except for the MIDI room.

When Joe was at the studio recording, he didn't accept anything less than your very, very best from anybody. Throughout my career working with him, if you're not at your best, he can't tolerate it. He hates people fucking around in the studio, and in those days, he really saw himself as the star in the room, and that was true. Everybody else in the room really was working for him. And he was really starting to build an infrastructure of management, family, engineers, assistants, and a guitar tech. They were all relying on Joe and his talents to pay their bills. This was kind of a new thing for him. The pressures on him to make bigger and more successful records were really nearing a pinnacle at that point, so this time Joe basically couldn't suffer fools.

When I'm playing and recording music like that, I'm not really hearing it the way other people do. I'm hearing the music coming a few bars ahead and I'm still listening to the music that I've played a few bars back. It's just an emotional way that I experience the music, so when I'm sitting in a studio, listening back to something falling flat, it annoys me because it sounds nothing like what I've played. Of course, John will say, "That's exactly what you played," but I can't get the exact feeling of the experience of how I'm playing onto the tape, so I'll look for effects like backward delays that represent that transcending of time I experience when I play music. I don't feel that I've ever fully been able to represent that properly, but things like backward reverbs and backward delays are my best attempts to convey how the music sounds to me as I'm playing it in my head and my heart.

The album's title track actually came to me while I was working on "Big Bad Moon" and was taking a break from trying to write lyrics. I played these two chords and thought, "This is about me having flying dreams as a kid. Wouldn't it be great if there was a melody that was so smooth it would 'fly' over these chords? What's my guideline for the opposite of what I've been doing for 'Big Bad Moon'?" For some reason, I thought of Frank Sinatra singing these songs where he starts off mellow at a lower register before ramping it up. The lyrics would reveal more of the "story" while his vocal line rose in pitch, and the chorus was the last few lines of his story. I'd always thought that was a beautiful way of playing a melody, because it wasn't an obvious verse-bridge-chorus kind of thing. It was a very elegant, simple way of telling a story and putting it to a beautiful melody, then having it peak. From that flash of inspiration, recalling my flying dreams, I wrote the rest of the song right there in about two to three minutes, all while taking a break from writing another song!

"The Mystical Potato Head Groove Thing" was another favorite from the *Flying* record that took a lot of work. I remember telling John I'd written this song and wanted it to be on the record, but it was going to take me two or three weeks to prepare for the recording. I'd come up with this idea to use arpeggios as the song's chorus, but they were so hard for me to pull off. Up until that point, I don't think I'd ever really experienced any kind of arm pain before, but after three weeks of practicing those arpeggios almost eight hours a day, I had a pain in my left forearm and hand that was unbelievable! When I brought the song to John, I said, "When the chorus comes, it's actually just this flurry of notes, but we have to create this beautiful tone, and it's got to be perfect." I played them on my Ibanez "Black Dog" guitar using a DS-1 into a Roland JC-120. I tied a scarf around the neck of the guitar at the 5th fret to keep the string noise down, while muting the strings a bit with my right hand at the bridge. It's all left-hand hammer-ons performing the arpeggios.

John Cuniberti: The success of *Surfing* allowed Joe to broaden the palette and maybe have a little bit more fun. I think he wanted to branch out and do other types of music and presentations, and there's a danger in that, of course—there always is. I wasn't surprised that he wanted to sing. I remember he was quite nervous about it, and I think Rubina and I were the only two people who thought he could pull it off! I thought it was great, and in fact, my favorite song is "I Believe," one of the numbers he sang on; it's one of the highlights of the record for me. The way he sings it is just beautiful, the lyrics were heartfelt, and he really believed in what he was singing. And he really suffered in the studio singing that, and when he nailed it, I just thought it was great.

I really had to follow John's lead when I sang in the studio. John knew I was a background singer and that I had no knowledge of how to record a voice, nor what microphone was best suited for what kind of song. John had years of experience at this working with singers, so he would just say, "Oh, we're going to use this kind of mic today," and I wouldn't even know what it was. My world was in the headphones, and if it sounded comfortable to me there as I sang, then John could get a good performance out of me. I'm not a real singer, but I feel really good singers have this ability to communicate that supersedes their range or vocal quality. Bob Dylan and Neil Young have unusual voices but are great at being lead vocalists because they have that gift of communication.

Each of my vocals on *Flying* is sung "in character," which made the album more interesting for me. The vocals for "Big Bad Moon" weren't working at first, but we figured out a way to make my voice sound more menacing by changing the song's speed, singing to it at a faster speed, and then returning it to its normal speed—that did the trick. We'd heard a lot of other artists did this, including Prince. Once I heard it back, I thought, "Okay, that's my character."

Cliff Cultreri: Joe would always be sending cassettes and DATs—"What do you think of this?" and "Check that out"—and I remember hearing bits and pieces and knowing it already had become a very different writing process for him by his third LP. So on *Flying in a Blue Dream*, you can really start to hear tremendous stylistic variation in the makeup of the music and the songs. He always had that going on, but I think not to the degree of *Flying*, and he did it in a way where he took you along for the ride. It wasn't different for the sake of being different; it was more like a natural evolution where he really took you on a ride on a lot of those songs. In a way, it almost was more of a progressive style of writing on many of the songs on that album, but it still was very listener-friendly—I don't think it put off any of the *Surfing* audience. I think what it did was take them further out much in the way Hendrix did. Here Joe was doing it his own way.

Just as I was finishing the recording of *Flying*, Cameron Crowe called me out of the blue and asked me to write a song specifically for his directorial debut, *Say Anything* . . . He filled me in on what the movie was about, then sent me a very rough cut of the film on VHS. Cameron wanted something rocking that would represent John Cusack's angst during a kickboxing scene. "Just do what you do," he said. "I don't care what you do, just be Joe Satriani." So I wrote "One Big Rush" and he loved the way it turned out.

Looking back, for me as a multi-instrumentalist and solo artist, *Flying* was a lot of work. Making records with Chickenfoot, by comparison, is really easy because you go in as one of four guys, play a song half a dozen times, and that's it. On *Flying*, I played all the guitars, basses, and keyboards, and I sang on six of the eighteen songs. Sometimes, after a hard day of recording, I would return home to get some rest and wake up the next morning having dreamed that I was in the studio and would feel like I hadn't slept! I think the biggest stress of having a recording schedule like that was having to go back in day after day. It was fun, it was exhilarating, I loved it, but at the same time the process of making that record was definitely stressful!

John Cuniberti: The record was a huge advancement from the first two albums. It was incredibly ambitious. I thought it was going to blow people's minds and really be well received. The song "Flying in a Blue Dream" was the most beautiful thing he'd ever done. I was really, really proud of the record.

Mick Brigden: We were lucky in the fact that the success of *Surfing* opened all these doors, so Joe was a headliner overnight. He didn't go through the phase of being an opening act. He went straight to headliner. Joe's set obviously had some landmark material, but he didn't have an awful lot of it. That changed very quickly when he promoted *Flying in a Blue Dream*, because he gave us a broader scope instantly and he brought in vocals. We wanted "Big Bad Moon" as a single. Joe felt the title track was the most important song on the record. Relativity and management knew that if we could get "Big Bad Moon" on the radio and the video on MTV, it would be a hit. We also knew we had "I Believe" in the back pocket. We shot great videos for both of those with a then unknown David Hogan. We put a lot of effort and time into broadening Joe's audience, as did he, because ultimately it all comes from Joe. He handed in a record with such a wide variety of sound and composition that he opened the door for us to have so many different ways to market this guitar hero beyond just six strings.

My personal take on *Flying* once we'd completed work on it was that I'd moved to this higher level that was new for me. I'd elevated my technique and was playing new things that you'd never heard on the first two albums. There were stream-of-consciousness clusters of notes, like in "Flying in a Blue Dream"; very worked out, purposeful-sounding arpeggios like on "The Mystical Potato Head Groove Thing"; and crazy out-and-out soloing on "The Bells of Lal (Part 2)." Then there was the personalization of the legato technique, which was a continuation of what I'd just started with "Echo" on *Surfing*, and I wasn't afraid to use this legato technique as the forefront of my musical statement on *Flying*, too. It wasn't something I just dashed off with for eight bars for effect, because I knew it was going to be a cornerstone of my technique.

Me and my six-string Deering banjo at Fantasy in '89
STILL FROM JOHN CUNIBERTI'S VIDEO

Looking back on some of the other techniques I had fun with on *Flying*, I had taken my two-hand tapping style to another sort of extreme compositional level. "Day at the Beach" is a good example in that it was more developed and complex as a song than similar stuff on the first two records. I felt that if I was going to put my own stamp on tapping, I had to move it to some higher level of compositional expression and drop the "wow, look at me" factor.

Oddly enough, when "Flying in a Blue Dream" was released, the star of the album actually wound up being the *title track*, so the one that nobody thought anyone would ever play turned out to be the one that got the most airplay. It was the same thing with *Surfing with the Alien*: The label never picked "Always with Me, Always with You" as the single; instead they picked "Surfing," "Ice 9," "Satch Boogie," but "Always" was the one that everybody wanted. For this album, the record label actually really wanted to use "Can't Slow Down" as the first single, but one of the A&R people at the label just had a real problem with the solo section (I never figured out what it was that she didn't like about it), so eventually they went with "Big Bad Moon" and "I Believe."

We started out the live shows feeling everybody was going to like the whole album. We always knew "Flying in a Blue Dream" was going to be a great song live—it was just a perfect opener. The lights would dim and then the recording of the RF intro started and those beautiful chords and the feedback would unfold. It just had so much drama to it and was so unique at the time. There really wasn't a song like it. "Big Bad Moon" turned out to be a great live song that has stayed in the set to this day. To our surprise, songs like "The Mystical Potato Head Groove Thing," "I Believe," and "One Big Rush" became fan favorites, too, and stayed in the set for a very long time.

CHAPTER 11 ★★

The Bearsville Experiment

When I decided to begin working on my next album after the *Flying in a Blue Dream* tour, I wanted a change of studio scenery, and the legendary Bearsville Studios in Woodstock, New York, fit the bill for me because it had a big live room and it wasn't in an urban setting. As far as John was concerned, he felt the studio had the necessary facilities to handle what we were looking to accomplish, and I think I was just attracted to going back to New York because I grew up there. When you say "Woodstock," it just has an allure because of its history, but I had never been there before, so I arrived like a tourist to some extent. I was looking for a musical adventure.

I think the experience of being a live act for the last three years was the biggest factor in my decision to shift from computers to a live rhythm section in the studio. After touring not only for the first two records, but also with Mick Jagger, I was thinking, "Wow, I've gotta work more of this live energy that I've experienced into the next record." I figured, "I'm just going to trust my instincts, go to Woodstock with John and with the guys from the Jagger band," so I hired Simon Phillips on drums, Phil Ashley on keyboards, and Doug Wimbish on bass. I wanted to introduce more musicianship into the mix, and that sort of creativity you get from having different kinds of players in the band, but I also wanted to make sure I could control it. That concept really blossomed on some songs—"New Blues" and "Rubina's Blue Sky Happiness," for example—because each of the players felt (I think) he had room to move creatively.

Unfortunately, everything broke down when I discovered I couldn't get them to follow this disciplined approach to instrumental rock that John and I had pioneered on the first couple of records. So, for instance, trying to get them to play and create the same effect we got on "Flying in a Blue Dream" or "Ice 9" was very difficult because they didn't think or feel that way as players. It was entirely my fault, because I picked these guys and they're amazing at what they do, but, in retrospect, they were the wrong musicians for the project.

John Cuniberti: This was ironic to me, because those guys are so creative, and they love music so much, that as soon as they walked in the room and picked up their instruments, they would just play and play and play—and Joe enjoyed that. Where I could tell things weren't working for Joe was, traditionally on his prior records, when he would come in for a playback and listen, you could tell when he felt a drum part wasn't working if it was a live player, and he would turn to the drummer and would basically be directing the drummer on what he was looking for. Well, at Bearsville, when he attempted to do that, Simon would either argue with him about it, or say, "Yeah, sure," then go back out in the studio and play whatever the fuck he wanted. Simon played Simon Phillips music, which is like this progressive, showy style. It seemed like Simon felt, "Joe's been making these weird records with funny drum machines. Now he wants to make a real record with real players in a real room, and that's why he's hired us." So that's exactly what Joe got, and it's exactly what Joe *didn't* want.

I remember at one point Phil Ashley taking me aside and saying, "Perhaps you need to be more descriptive, more detailed in what it is you're trying to get out of Simon and Doug." I thought the songs were getting softer and having less of an impact when drums, bass, and keyboards were allowed to wander through the arrangements, and this was a problem because these guys were very expensive! The whole trip out there was very expensive, and suddenly we're running into a problem where I started thinking, "I won't be able to overdub on these performances and get them to really hit hard." So I started to realize after a few weeks—and I think John was pretty shocked when I told him this—"I'm not happy with this. I don't like what my songs are becoming."

As it had started to build up, I had a few key realizations, the first being that they didn't respect me enough to take my direction seriously. I could understand that because I was the "new guy." The second was that they didn't understand my directions because I couldn't figure out how to be more descriptive. So each morning, I'd go to the studio telling myself, "I'm going to turn it around today. I can try to see where their influences will make the song better, change my approach, and see if I can explore their approach. Maybe they're right." But each day, the opposite would happen, and I'd wind up getting a little bit more discouraged, and I would walk back to my cabin at night, thinking, "That didn't get better, that got worse."

When we started "Summer Song," that's when I really knew it wasn't working. There was a small dining room off the kitchen where we used to eat communally, and each morning, John would prepare the previous day's roughs for us, and we would sit there in the morning and listen to everything. I remember everyone listening to "Summer Song" and feeling really good and excited about it, while I was thinking to myself, "That is weak," because I was used to the hard-edged rhythm sections on the *Surfing* and *Flying* records. I felt that was a signature of my sound by then, and I noticed once it was removed that there was something NOT better with what was replacing it. I think my creative faith at the time was that once I removed the rigidity, the music was going to blossom, but I didn't hear that at all. I remember it blindsiding John when I announced, "I'm not happy with the way this is going," because he had originally figured—as I had—that these were the greatest musicians we'd ever worked with, but now it was, "How could it not be working?" He probably was trying to figure out, "What is it that Joe's not hearing, and what can I do to help him out?" Because he was my partner in this, and to a certain degree, I was not being totally open about what I was disappointed with, because I didn't want to totally spoil the vibe of the sessions. I didn't want to stand up and say, "This sucks!" even though that's precisely how I was feeling.

Eventually I had to pull the plug on the Bearsville experiment. That was an even scarier decision because of the money I had spent, and maybe wasted.

Phil Ashley, Doug Wimbish, Simon Phillips, and me at Bearsville in late '90

PHOTO BY JOHN CUNIBERTI

John Cuniberti: There were times when Joe would walk into the control room for a playback and just stand there like he was pissed off, and I'm sure Joe went back to his cabin every night shaking his head, asking, "What have they done to my song? I came with this idea to have this song that looks like ABC, and instead I have XYZ, and I'm supposed to go into the studio tomorrow at $2,000 a day and record that?" So as the session started to unwind, Joe opted for what I thought at the time was a soft landing of sorts, because he was pretty unhappy and he decided it was time to take a break. We came home the day before Thanksgiving, and after the holidays we talked, and he said, "I want to get back in the studio. We got a lot of good stuff here. Let's book some studio time in the Bay Area here, and sort of address all the issues."

Following that, when we went home for the holiday, John and I started to plan around the idea that maybe we'd be able to reconvene and do what we did before. John offered, "Let's go back to San Francisco and you record your guitars just the way you always do it. Then we'll bring in a drummer, or we'll do the drum machine thing."

John Cuniberti: Joe had played and we had recorded a lot of great guitar takes, and he was trying to preserve a lot of those performances: rhythm guitars, solos, melodies. So he started replacing Simon Phillips's drum tracks with drum programming, and trying to manipulate the music the way he wanted, and I remember it was very, very, very difficult. We started to run into tuning issues, and tempo issues, and those guys were much more free-flowing, so Simon was playing all over the click—in front of it, behind it, around it—and everyone's playing to him, so when you take his drums off and try to lock a drum machine to it, nothing made sense anymore. We struggled and struggled trying to put Band-Aids on it, and got a few nuggets that were pretty nice that ultimately ended up on the record.

CHAPTER 12 ★★

The Extremist—1992

> *"The chugging 'Summer Song,' the warm 'Friends,' the slamming 'Motorcycle Driver,' and the crunching 'The Extremist' show Satriani's talents as a guitarist are undiminished, while the more traditional neo-folk approach to 'Rubina's Blue Sky Happiness' and the bluesy 'New Blues' are different from anything he has done before!"*
>
> —*Billboard* magazine

With *The Extremist*, I felt like my playing style had really grown and I had sort of reconnected with a lot of guitar playing that I grew up listening to, like Jimi Hendrix and Jimmy Page. My other records were a little more modern for their times, but with this record, I was not holding back from bringing out my roots of the late sixties and early seventies. So that meant I was showing more of what I could play, which was an important part of my growth as a musician. I also think that the range of composition was HUGE on this record. At the time I was wondering, how was I going to get "Tears in the Rain," "New Blues," "Why," "Cryin'," and "The Extremist" to stylistically fit together on one record? How was I going to justify that there was a song like "War" on the same record as "Rubina's Blue Sky Happiness"? Were people going to like the sort of Celtic country style of "Friends," because it was very much not like "Ice 9"? I also felt that I'd really matured compositionally, and that was something John had felt at the beginning, too. He just thought that the material

I'd brought in was really exceptional, and I think his reaction to it also gave me a little bit of courage to see it all the way through.

Even though I was conceptually excited about this album, starting over after the Bearsville debacle was so difficult for me because there was this incredible sense of guilt that I had spent too much money and had failed to pull the project together. It really affected me in a creative way, and I distinctly remember calling Bill Graham Management from Studio D at Hyde Street one day and telling Kevin Burns that I didn't feel like playing my guitar anymore. I had lost all the necessary drive to continue.

When I called the office that day, it was to ask Bill and the management team, "Can I stop, again?" Their answer was, "Of course you can, just pack up and stop." My management company was great; they told me to take some time off and not to rush back into it, which was the right advice, so I just shut everything down and took a year off from recording. My wife and I had recently bought a house up in the Sierras at Lake Tahoe, and we finally got to spend some time with each other, because it seemed like we had been working like crazy for years and years. I'd spent a lot of time on the road, and she was working as well, so I think we just needed time to hang out together. I also performed at the Guitar Legends Festival in Spain that year, so by then, early '91, it was the first time Rubina and I had a chance to travel together.

With the time away, I was starting to reevaluate everything I was doing in the music business. I started to think that it was just a matter of stepping out of it for a while so I could come back with a fresh attitude. That led me to think, "I've got to be more like other musicians. I've got to play around." Bill and the guys at the office were saying the same thing: "Every artist we know eventually works with new musicians, engineers, and producers."

Months later, on October 25, 1991, we lost Bill in a tragic helicopter accident. It was a staggering loss for his family and all of us who knew and worked with him, and a huge loss for the music world.

We had to continue on. I had to pick myself up and complete my vision for *The Extremist*. It was time to find some new collaborators. I'll admit, I found that thought to be frightening at first, because John and I had shared some of the greatest moments, creatively recording and mixing together. We would spend hours in the studio stretching ourselves into areas where we felt we were just walking on the edge, and then we were ultimately rewarded by platinum success, but I wanted to keep pushing myself. By the end of the year I realized this was where we were, so my manager, Mick Brigden, started to field ideas about working with some different producers.

I traveled down to L.A. and met with a few producers, including Mike Clink (Guns N' Roses) and Dave Jerden (Jane's Addiction, Alice in Chains), and then I met with Andy Johns at Eddie Van Halen's studio. I found myself feeling a little starstruck. I couldn't believe that I had a chance to work with somebody like Andy because I'd been listening to his recordings ever since I was a kid. When we first met, Andy was like a total wildcard. He was a very colorful character and very animated in a rock 'n' roll way. An important part of Andy's talent was that he was extremely musical. He was a musician himself; he may not have been able to play drums, but he could zero in on the delicacies and intricacies of drum patterns and go out there and instruct a drummer. He could help you arrange keyboard parts and harmonize guitar lines—he was that musical. The conversation we had in just the few hours we spent listening to my demos at Eddie's studio that day reignited my passion for the project.

Andy Johns: I invited him to meet me at Eddie Van Halen's house because I was producing a Van Halen record at the time, and so just for a joke, I said, "Why don't we meet there?" which was a little mean, because Joe was still a little bit starstruck. So he was very happy to meet Ed, and he played me some stuff. Up to that point, Joe was still into using drum machines and playing through boxes, not using proper amplification, and the way I work is very organic—I

> like to have people play off of each other and use real amps and all that. So that was sort of a condition, that we try doing work that way, and he was more than cool with it.

As excited as I was to be working with Andy, it wasn't the same as starting fresh with a new producer. I had no intention of starting fresh because I'd put so much work into quite a few of the tracks, and thought "New Blues," "Rubina's Blue Sky Happiness," and "Why" were beautiful tracks that, if anything, just needed some touches on them. With "Summer Song," all we needed were new drum and bass performances, since John and I had finished all the guitars and keyboards earlier in San Francisco. Andy realized that we had a lot of it done, and he loved what John had recorded, so he thought, "How hard can it be?"

Once I was ready to start working on the album again, I started asking different people for opinions on players. Steve Vai suggested the Bissonette brothers, two guys he'd been playing with, and sure enough when I was down in L.A. actually auditioning a bunch of people, Matt and Gregg turned out to be the best team I played with out of four or five sets of players. No matter what I threw at them, they seemed to rise to the occasion. Since they had worked with Steve before, I knew that they would understand any odd directions they might get from me. They would understand how sometimes you've got to play it really straight. I think maybe some musicians, when they get famous for being themselves, they're rewarded for idiosyncratic behavior, and then that's all they can play. Other players who naturally take direction well and are versatile develop an attitude and technique that furthers their abilities—and that makes sense. When I would ask Gregg, "Could you reverse that beat, and play it super loose?" he would do it. Then if I said, "Sorry, I changed my mind. Could you play that straight and forward?" he would do it, and he seemed to really relish taking direction and providing me with what I wanted. He never had a negative attitude about trying it again in a completely different manner, and I had never played with anybody like that.

Matt Bissonette was the same way. They both had this fantastic attitude in the studio of wanting to make the session work. And they were very creative and intuitive, so when I would say things like, "This part really needs to soar. I want it to fly," Gregg and Matt both understood what I wanted them to do, instead of needing concrete examples. I think that's how we wound up getting keeper takes for "Summer Song," "War," "Motorcycle Driver," "The Extremist," and "Friends." What they did with "Friends" was just so amazing, and it was because they could take direction, not only from me but from Andy as well.

Matt Bissonette: We were at Mount Rushmore playing softball, looking at the presidents' heads, and just goofing off, and I'd heard Joe's name because Steve was always talking about him. I remember all the roadies were listening to *Surfing with the Alien* on their headphones, and they were all way into it and kept telling me I had to hear it. So I finally heard the album, and of course figured out right away that he was an amazing guitar player. After that, I started listening to him more and more, and then when he called Gregg and me a few days later to come and audition for *The Extremist*, we showed up and just started jamming really well.

With my new producer and band now complete, we settled on legendary Ocean Way Studios in Los Angeles. Everyone from Ray Charles to the Rolling Stones had recorded there. The first day we got to the studio, I remember we were playing in the big scoring room, and it sounded so beautiful! It's just one of the most beautiful-sounding rooms I've ever been in. It's just a magical, magical room where music sounds wonderful, no matter where you put stuff, and just listening to the sound of the drums and bass coming from the room is amazing. Allan Sides had designed the control room's speakers, and the control room itself was tuned beautifully. And here is this legendary, towering figure in Andy Johns—drinking, smoking, laughing, screaming at the top of his lungs—at the helm of it all. Andy was very rock-star, rock 'n' roll royalty: high energy, lots of emotion, lots of drama. When he was happy, it was infectious, and he got everybody up and the performances were great. It was a lot of fun, because when you did something right and he got it on tape, the experience in the control room with him playing it back at 120 decibels, hugging everybody, smiling and joking, leaning into the speakers, just thoroughly rocking out to the recording, was very inspiring! It was just one of many things that were exciting about that time.

Me and my favorite JS6 in '92
PHOTO BY NEIL ZLOZOWER

On top of that, when I arrived in L.A. to start the rehearsals for the record, I remember being pulled into the room with Matt and Gregg and getting a phone call from Rubina telling me the wonderful news that she was pregnant with our son. That was a huge motivator for me, because suddenly the album stuff was not nearly as important as it was before getting the news. All at once, everything was put in perspective, and I think I lightened up a little bit because the most important thing in the world now was that we were starting a family.

Andy Johns: My foremost focus heading into work on *The Extremist* was on getting drum sounds with Gregg to replace those blasted drum machine boxes, which have as much soul as a stamp, perhaps less than a stamp because I collect stamps. I did come up with a theory of using room mics, which in actual fact I had started with Blind Faith on the "Can't Find My Way Home" album [*Blind Faith*]—it's all done on just two mics. Then when I did "When the Levee Breaks" with Led Zeppelin, I got Bonzo out in the fucking lobby and used two mics, so I was trying to get the drums to sound like they actually sound in the room. Gregg Bissonette, being an experienced cat, had some very good stuff, and I fiddled around with his kit a little bit, and I remember thinking that we got a pretty good drum sound on that one. We had this big live room with that old, sort of '50s linoleum tile, which is just great for drums. I put a couple of room mics in *behind* the drums—for some reason that seems to work in that room. And I had a 1308 mic pre to run the toms through, so that they showed up in the room mics a little bit more. Then I just found the right drums and tuned them right, and that was the secret, you know—the source of the sound has to be recordable.

On Gregg's kit, everything was miked up. When I'm getting a drum sound, what I do is, I listen to the room mics to see how the balance of the kit is in the room, because if one cymbal is really loud, or the toms are dead, you're fucked. So when I started, I added in the bass drum, then added in the snare, and built it up like that. Take "Summer Song," for example. What I did with the kick drum to get that sound is, I liked to have the front head off without a bloody hole in it, cut a piece of foam to size—so it's just like a quarter of an inch—over the lip of the shell, and then where the air hole was, I got one of the techs to cut a cable and run it

> through the hole, then solder it back together, and had like a 421 on a mic box or something, so it was not resting on the foam inside. Then I put a FET 47 on the outside, and I tried to get the drummer to use a wooden beater (they always complain, "Man, this thing keeps bouncing back," because they're not used to playing with a proper front head). So I used coated Ambassador heads for the bass drum—none of that rubbish stuff with all the fucking foam going 'round the edge. Then I deadened that down myself so I could adjust it, and of course, you have to have the right drum. That's the most important thing—because I knew where the mics go, fuck if I didn't know that by then. I had a snare drum that I've used on a couple of number ones, I think, and a bunch of other hits, that I'd tote around with me for insurance; I called it my "Black Beauty," and we used that on *The Extremist*.

Andy understood when I told him that the problem I had was "swinging versus straight," and that I wanted the album's sound to be big and heavy and to rock, that I did not want a fusion or jazz album. I didn't want an easy-listening record, and that was my struggle even before recording *Surfing with the Alien*, explaining that to people. We were not doing "easy-listening background music" or fusion. The songs were rock songs; they had verses and bridges and choruses and solo sections, and everyone had to play specific parts. I think Andy liked that and took the project on because he understood what I was trying to accomplish.

In a way, working with Andy was a return to the earlier way John had recorded me with the Squares, having me plug straight into my Marshalls and play live in the room with the band—the main difference being Andy was doing his "Andy Johns" thing, which was creating this huge foundation of drums and bass guitar with all this powerful ambience, which was entirely new to me. There was a bass going into an SVT and DI, and there's drums miked up in a huge room, with the kick drum being put into its own PA and then being pushed out into the room and re-miked.

And then with my guitars, I was plugging into a vintage Marshall 100-watt full stack turned up to 10!

Andy Johns: Joe had a bunch of Marshalls which sounded really good. He had a nice 100-watt combo that we used, too. Now, when we're doing the record, we had five different amp setups, and about fifteen guitars, so therefore you could find any fucking sound you wanted appropriate for the room. My miking would probably have been a couple of 57s and a 414, my standard setup of a 57 on the speaker, another 57 about 45 degrees so the phase is all cool, and the one that's angled gives you the bottom end, and the one that's straight up gives you the top end. The 414 you mount on another speaker on a 4×12 and you get a bit more woof. And now, in the end, it sounds like one of the best rehearsals any band ever did; I was quadruple-tracking rhythms, and doubling them through 4-tracks, but it meant he had to play in time, and he went for it.

A lot of the guitar work on that record was done using my original Black Dog JS and my new JS6 prototype Ibanez guitar. As far as the amps: I had a nice collection of old Marshall heads and cabinets, a Soldano 100-watt head, and a Boogie 4×12 bottom that had two different sets of speakers in it. Part of our aim once the record was in Andy's hands was to make the guitars a little bit tighter, and to prepare for more overdubs that would complement each other. So, for instance, when you hear the rhythm guitars on "Friends," you're hearing one live electric guitar on the left side, my JS6 going into the Marshalls turned all the way up. On the right side, you're hearing a stack of six-stringed instruments—guitars, banjos, Nashville-tuned guitars, and dobros—all bounced down to one glorious mono track! In the center the main melody is played on my JS6. This was the way Andy would work. He would invent and innovate and tweak and have me play things over and over and over until he felt that we'd arrived at something magical. His studio technique was very unique, and together he and John Cuniberti created the sound that is the *Extremist* album.

> **Andy Johns:** Joe is as close to a genius as [Cream founding member] Jack Bruce. He's a very clever man, and centered—meaning when he makes his mind up to play, he just leads you from one moment to another, and that is more than admirable. But along with being very soulful, which he definitely is, no question, he also has this technique; his knowledge is bigger, and more than anyone I've ever worked with. And when you ask him, "Why did you play that?" he'll literally answer, "Well, the pentatonic scale leads me to believe this; therefore, when I bend this note I can go back into the fruition of the resolving F . . ." 'cause he actually really knows. With some people, it's bullshit; with Joe, it's a fact.

I remember being especially excited when "Summer Song" finally started to come together. Going back in time a bit, the writing of that song is actually a very interesting story. When I was out doing radio promotion with David Counter, a promotion rep from Relativity's L.A. office, we used to have great conversations about songs and life. And as I was getting ready to start work on *The Extremist*, he said, "You know, the next record is gonna be huge. It's gonna be fantastic"—he was talking like a radio guy—and he continued, "All I need is that one song . . . I need a *summer song*." And as soon as he said it, I thought, "'Summer Song' . . ." I loved the sound of it. I wrote it down on a slip of paper, and later on, sitting in my San Francisco apartment practicing, I'd just stare at that piece of paper as I played. I don't know why. I just thought that torn little piece of paper had some mojo on it, so I just never discarded it. I would go into my little studio room and I would just stare at that thing and play and play, and I kept thinking about all the good times I had over summer vacations growing up in New York.

Slowly the song started to emerge. When I sense inspiration

coming on, I have learned over the years to do whatever I can to clear a path so I can get it written down or recorded as soon as possible before the glorious moment fades and it becomes only an intellectual memory. It's always good to finish writing it, or at least get most of it down, while you're in the first throes of the inspiration. With "Summer Song," I started out by writing the first two chords, and I would sit there and play that pattern for like three hours a night and just imagine a soundtrack to my summertime memories. Making it a song was going to depend on that melody, and the melody was going to have to be very long because the chord pattern was very short. It's just a little two chord/four bar pattern, so I'd ask myself, "How am I going to tell my summer story over these two chords? How am I going to make it compelling and have drama?" Slowly I got to the point where I thought, "Okay, here's this nice, long melody, but I still need more," and I'd never really written a "guitar" song where I could play two verses back to back, and maybe take the second verse an octave higher. I was beginning to wonder, "Wow, how does a guitar instrumental get away with that?" It would be more common to just write one verse, one chorus, one set of solos—that kind of thing.

I decided "Summer Song" was going to feature one dominant guitar sound from beginning to end playing the melody and solo. This was a new approach for me, and it wasn't like "Surfing," where I'd had all these different guitar sounds trading off. When the song got into Andy's hands he imagined something entirely different for the rhythm section, and as a result created a very unique canvas for my guitar. I have to say, it's not pop rock and it's not heavy metal, but the energy level is so high and sustained that that's what he achieved. And even though the main guitar parts were recorded a year earlier by me and John in San Francisco, it all turned out great in the end, ultimately producing what became my biggest international radio hit to date.

Andy was really great at capturing energy, not only sonically, but I think in personal performance. So as we would go out and do takes, he would run out from the control room and tell Gregg, "Try 'boom, boom, bop bop boom' when you get to this part," and he'd say, "Hey, Matt, would you try using this other string when you go to that part?" Then later on, when we were overdubbing guitars, he'd have me play things over and over again until he thought it captured this thing he was after. When he was mixing "Summer Song," it was the same thing: He was trying to create this sound that was a very high-energy sound, which is NOT just turning things up louder or making them sound aggressive. It has to do with the ambience and bringing out the energy of each musician's performance, which is a very difficult thing to do. We all struggled with it for a very long time, and when we started mixing it was driving Andy crazy, literally driving him crazy! I remember he was getting very frustrated, and a couple of times he'd leave the studio for hours just because he didn't think it was working.

The breakthrough came in a perfect example of his ability to be totally creative with something by starting from scratch, and he would do that all the time. He would sit there and pull all the faders down, then start from scratch and throw them back up. And it would freak me out to do that because it would be so hard for me to get back to where I was. But I think all good mix engineers, Andy and John included, have no fear of breaking down a mix and starting from scratch and looking at a mix from all different angles. I remember early one morning Andy called me at my hotel to say, "When you get to the studio, press PLAY. I've got a mix up. I don't know if I've totally ruined your career or if this is the greatest mix ever? I've tried something radically different from what we've been trying for the last couple days." So when I got to the studio, I pushed PLAY and turned it up loud and couldn't believe how great it sounded!

First, the rhythm section was huge and rockin', and there was this delay effect he created for the harmonics in the beginning, which turned that little performance into a true hook and some delicious ear candy, too. He was looking for something more with those harmonics, and I had never heard it that way; I had always heard it just played straight without any of the delays on it. But Andy had made it work with this ping-pong delay effect. And then he got rid of one of the rhythm guitars, too, using only one of the original rhythms with one of the new rhythms, and split them left and right. This was a big deal because we were now in that age where people had started to double, triple, quadruple guitar tracks, playing the exact same thing left and right, and it was something Andy never liked. So he was always looking for smaller-sounding guitars that were playing differently. We had that double-track thing going on from the very beginning and he was just working with it for months until his breakthrough idea was to get rid of it! It made more room for the bass and drums and helped propel the natural rhythm of the track.

The final thing Andy focused on was my melody guitar line, which he fed into a combination of Prime Time chorusing, reverb, and compression and brought its return back on a separate fader. By creating this unique space for the sound he was able to give it a depth that allowed you to find it instantly without it having to be loud and in your face. He would ride that fader during the mix to create a changing "space" for the main guitar. That solved the problem of placing the wah-wah guitar sound in the mix, and it was a brilliant idea.

Andy Johns: Joe came into the control room the next day and listened to what I had in mind, and I remember he turned around to me and gave me a very nice compliment when he said, "I didn't know you were doing all that, man. I've never heard myself sound like that. That's absolutely fabulous."

One of my other favorite songs from that record is "Friends," which is a difficult one to describe stylistically. I remember the idea for the song came to me one afternoon when my mother and sisters were over visiting us in Berkeley, and we were all going to go to lunch. And I said, "You know what? I'm going to stay home. I feel like I'm gonna write a song, so I'd like to just hang out for a few hours." So they all left me alone in the apartment, and I had a photo book that Rubina had brought home with the smiling faces of children from around the world. I remember looking through the pages, and I came across a page of some six- or eight-year-old kids, maybe somewhere in Africa, just beaming and smiling into the camera. So I left that page open and wrote the song on bass while I was staring at that picture. It was just one of those things that was very easy and fun to write. It's a celebratory song, and I'll never forget the excitement when we heard our first take of "Friends" played back for us at Ocean Way. Everyone was wondering beforehand, "What's this going to sound like? Andy's a crazy guy . . ." He'd called us in and said, "I think you guys should come in and listen to this." I don't think any of us had ever heard anything so big and beautiful, ever! Hearing it made us want to run out there and play all day long, because each one of us was saying, "My instrument sounds bigger than it has ever sounded before. It's finally captured in all its glory!" We were just so psyched about it.

Gregg Bissonette: With that song, Joe and Matt and I hit it off because we wanted the same thing: We wanted Joe to have an album that he was proud of. So whether he'd ask me to play a beat forward or backward, if it's something you want, and you're paying me to play on your record, and we can succeed in getting the sound you want, that's the greatest gift ever.

I was excited about "New Blues" as well. The melody and chord sequence of the chorus section was new and exciting territory for me, and we had a lot of fun tracking the song back in Bearsville. The rhythm guitar in that song was done live, and it's all two-hand tapping. Funny thing is, when the album came out, nobody asked me about that, and I realized that no one had ever done that before, working two-hand tapping into the structure of a real song where the technique wasn't the "showboat element" of the song. It wasn't meant to be, "Hey, look at me, I'm tapping!" It was part of the ensemble and it went over everybody's head, so part of me patted myself on the back and said, "You did your job. That's what you wanted to do, to show the validity of two-hand tapping as part of the ensemble." But the other part of me said, "How come no one patted me on the back for pulling that off?" Ha! I guess I did it too well, and it just went under the radar. That's part of the art of arranging and composing: You don't want to reveal the structure and distract people like that all the time. It's really about the music, not about the technique. And I truly loved that song, as it brought a lot of my jazz roots to the record.

"Crying" was a difficult song to record because it was about my father's passing and my grieving process. When writing the song, I guess I was at that point where I was focusing on the good memories and trying to carry on. So each time I would go to work on the song there'd be this emotional intensity, but I would have to be professional about it as I tried to get people to play it. It was also a bit heartbreaking during the sessions when I couldn't get people to play it the way I wanted them to. It was always difficult for me to get into the proper head space, because you either open the floodgates or you keep them closed—you can't just open the door a little bit and think you're going to get a great performance and keep your act together. If you're producing a track, you can't be an emotional wreck. So I arrived at the last sessions with the Bissonette brothers to once again try to do this track. I was thinking, "I've gotta give the definitive performance on this song, get this cathartic thing recorded and carry on." The emotional roller coaster of working on the song was wearing me out.

I remember being in the control room with Andy while Gregg and Matt were out in the music room, and we did this take that turned out remarkably well. Andy turned around and said to me, "Amazing! That was the take! What are you plugged into?" It wasn't supposed to be "the take" for me; it was supposed to be a guide track for Matt and Gregg. I wanted this to be my ultimate emotive performance on the album, and we recorded it almost by accident!

Andy Johns: He actually made me cry because he was playing like a bird. His elegance in the melancholy moment, you can hear the man thinking, and when he was done, and I listened, of course I shed tears. And he has this absolutely astounding technique, which isn't just rich on purpose, it's to emote. I admire that so very much. I really do think one of the things on that record that blew me away most was the song "Crying," because he did play that through a box, and I thought, "This is a very soulful thing. I'm going to leave the room and let him get it on his own." When I came back in, he played this spectacular thing and it made me cry, and I took it home when the record was finished, and I and my wife got a couple bottles of Champagne—as she does whenever I finish an album—and I put it on my system, which is a pretty good one, and I turned around and one of my kids also had tears running down his face. So Joe's take definitely had the desired effect upon people.

When I finished playing it, I was relieved, because I had carried that performance in me for years. When I finally heard the playback I thought, "That's it. That's what I've been waiting to perform," and I didn't care that I had put my guitar through a Zoom headphone amp and not a "proper" amp. Just, "Thank God we have a recording of it."

I had an unusual experience writing "War." I was in a local supermarket in San Francisco, where we'd just moved from Berkeley. I remember I was doing some shopping, and the news was on about the war that was getting started in Iraq. And I just remember thinking, "War is hell. People should avoid war at all times. It never turns out good," and I started writing that riff right there in my head. Anytime that happens to me, I get very excited about finishing something—if I've created something that sounds so easy and yet the structure of it is so bizarre, I get very excited by it. When I got home, I picked up the guitar and started to flesh out the song, and there were a lot of things about it that were important to me. Harmonically I thought it was a very interesting way to suspend tension and hold off resolution. This served the meaning of the song well. The chord combination in the chorus was unique, too: D minor to D minor (add) 9 followed by A flat 6/9/Major 7th (#11). I thought to myself that nobody had tried that before.

It's one of those things nobody ever noticed or asked me about, but I loved it! I never heard, "Man, what's up with that chord progression?" and I'm happy I didn't in one respect, because that means I did my job very well. I didn't make them think about the structure, in other words; all they're doing is reacting to the music, which is what I wanted. But at the same time, part of me was saying, "I just wish one musician would come up to me and say, 'Wow, the bass line drops a flatted fifth while the upper partials are suspended second chords dropping by a whole step . . .'" Those are the things that, when I'm composing, I go, "Wow, look at that harmonic structure, and look how I can play a melody on top of it that sounds so powerful and yet is so simple." That's what creates the tension and resolution. That's what tells the story. That's where the art form of harmony can really be put to work. I love that—that's what I've devoted myself to in part as a composer, to unlock the secrets of compositional harmony.

Cliff Cultreri: Joe came up with the title for the album, *The Extremist*, while he was visiting me down at my house in Hermosa Beach, actually at a cookout at the house of a neighbor friend of mine. He was grilling some fish on the barbecue and doing his wonderful gourmet thing, and we were talking about the concept, batting around different ideas for the title, and Joe was talking about going from the precise drum machine—everything perfect, every beat here and there—to the question of "How do we do live in the studio?" And I always favored that, because I didn't just want a live-in-the-studio album, but

> I wanted something that was almost a little bit chaotic in a way. I wanted some energy—let's see what happens when things aren't all mapped out and going by the numbers—because I would always cite certain albums and how they were recorded, and Joe was on the same page. So as we're talking about doing this, my friend Philippe says, "Joe, you're crazy, you're such an *extremist*." And that's where the album title came from, my neighbor calling Joe an *extremist* because of the way he wanted to work and push these new boundaries! I think it allowed him to finish it by using the title as kind of an inspiration.

By the time our focus began to turn toward the mixing stage, we'd been working on "stage three" of the project for almost too long. I had been living in a hotel room in L.A. for four or five months by then, and I was beginning to go crazy. I wanted to go home. I didn't want to hang out in L.A. by myself anymore. *The Extremist* was very much a throwback record to celebrate classic rock—it just came out at the perfectly *wrong time*! I really didn't know what was going on outside of my world until I packed up my car in L.A. after mastering and started driving home. And on that seven- or eight-hour drive home, listening to the radio, I thought, "Oh my God, what radio station will play anything off of this record?"

I realized now they were playing Nirvana and Soundgarden, and there was no room for my record; I was too young to be on the classic rock stations, and I wasn't young and grungy enough to be on the active rock stations. I remember going on MTV's *Headbangers Ball* and Riki Rachtman saying to me, on television, "Some of this stuff could be very New-Agey," and I almost killed him right there on television. I couldn't figure out where he was coming from . . . It's a funny thing to think about, because I wasn't thinking of it like that while I was tracking. I was just trying to make the best recording of the best performances of what I thought were my best songs at the time. So I didn't know what we were going to do about it.

When the record came out, I knew that there was a lot going against it because of the trends at the time. Here in America it met resistance to some degree because it was very straight ahead. Outside of the U.S., it was received more openly, for what it was. Within the U.S., however, we had what was proving to be a bit of a problem . . . until Sony used "Summer Song" in a Walkman commercial, which re-broke the album for us!

Mick Brigden: Joe by this point was a star worldwide, and BIG worldwide, because on the *Flying* tour that preceded Joe's returning to the studio to make *The Extremist*. We had toured A LOT of shows in Europe where we were headlining theatres and going to arenas in France. In the U.S., we had gotten to amphitheaters and multiple theater runs. That's where we were by the early 90s. Now Joe's touring and record-selling market is the world, not just the U.S. That's something that I knew from working with Carlos Santana, that a guitar player with great melodic songs can be very successful outside the U.S., and Joe had built a worldwide market and he had toured those markets and had great songs.

Cliff Cultreri: Once the *Extremist* album was in stores, we knew we had a lot of momentum behind Joe, and his live performances were just perfection. There are not too many musicians who have done or who could do what Joe does live, and you can probably count them on one hand: Steve Vai is there, Jeff Beck is there, certainly Hendrix, but you're talking about a very elite few who really, really could deliver like that. By that point, he had already reached the status of living legend because he was a cut above the rest—and not in an egotistical way or anything, but his listeners recognized that. He was really something special, a very special artist.

The *Extremist* tour was fun. I had Gregg and Matt Bissonette on drums and bass, and Phil Ashley on keys. It was a great band and we were able to record some good live shows, too. We all began wondering if it was the right time for a live record, so I began brainstorming this idea to do a live album that would have a retrospective component. We could use the recent live recordings as well as older live stuff along with studio outtakes, and so forth . . . So I started to pull out all of my DATs, listening to everything in my archives. By this time, I knew that I wanted to call this album *Time Machine*, though I still had to sell the idea to the label, and Cliff was very helpful with that. Thankfully, when we pitched it to Relativity, they were totally behind the idea.

Me and my Ibanez JS "Tele" prototype at a video shoot in '93

PHOTO BY JOHN CUNIBERTI

The work that went into the record was extensive, though. John had to compile all the live and studio music, mix it, and get it properly mastered; the art department at Relativity, which was fantastic, worked with photographer Michael Llewellyn, who shot and designed the awesome cover; the label pressed vinyl versions of the album in addition to releasing it on cassette and CD; Matt Resnicoff wrote the extensive bio and liner notes; we had to get permissions from all the photographers, who provided a wonderful batch of photos, and so on . . . Everyone involved pulled together to make it a great project. For an instrumental guitar player to be able to put out a package like that on an independent label was very, very cool. And the fans loved it!

Ultimately, all these things you do when you release records, they stay around forever—they really do. Your music stays there year after year after year, gaining new audiences, and at the time we were right to push for *Time Machine*'s release, because it turned out to be a hit. The album was essential for my future; it allowed people to better understand what I was all about, where I came from, and where I was headed. In other words, I wanted them to know about all the different kinds of music I was into. I felt that it really was an important artistic statement and that it was going to help my career keep moving forward.

CHAPTER 13 ★★

Eponymous—1995

> *"Home (is) . . . exactly where we find Satriani on his latest offering,* Joe Satriani*. On it, visions of the raw, screaming electric blues of Jimi Hendrix, Jeff Beck and Jimmy Page permeate the album, which some have called Satriani's* Blow By Blow*. Produced by veteran helmsman Glyn Johns (*Rolling Stones, Led Zeppelin, The Who*),* Joe Satriani *abandons the guitarist's trademark overdubbed, highly produced guitar attack in favor of a more honest, jammy, live feel that's fully entrenched in the magical vibe of the late Sixties/early Seventies. The result is an album that sparkles with some of the most soulful and moving guitar playing of Satch's career."*
>
> —*Guitar World* magazine

When I first picked up the guitar, I started with the blues. My primary influences were Jimi Hendrix, Jimmy Page, Jeff Beck, and Eric Clapton, and through them their heroes: Robert Johnson, Buddy Guy, Albert King, and everybody in between. When it came time to record the last installment of the *Joe Satriani* LP, I wanted to honor those blues roots of mine, but in a new way.

Something important to remember here is that we were doing this in 1995, so it was not the early 1990s anymore. This was a different era; there had been, I think, a cathartic process happening in the music business, and by the time we got together in 1995 for these sessions, people were *running* from the late-eighties/early-nineties thing.

So the feeling was, "Boy, we gotta do something raw, but different."

When producer Glyn Johns and I first got together, I was looking for him to guide me during this process by weaning me from my old way of making records and put me in a new position that all of my heroes had been in before. Glyn had recorded many of the guitar players who make up my roots: Keith Richards, Jimmy Page, Eric Clapton, Pete Townshend, and Steve Miller, to name a few. He understood how to put an artist in a situation where he would have to rise to the occasion and create a record that could potentially affect a generation.

Mick Brigden: As soon as we put the two of them together and they sat and listened to Joe's demos, Glyn became an instant fan, which is the way it should be. Glyn is not the kind of guy who you would ever be able to convince to make a record if he didn't like the musician or the music—he's not that kind of guy. Better than that, he thought, "This is a challenge. I've never made a record like this," and Joe gave him so much support in helping him put together how they were going to make the record, which meant putting an album together in a way Joe was not used to making.

Glyn Johns: Joe was very respectful to me. I was a rather odd choice because Joe's normal method of recording is completely different from mine. But he was open to the idea of making a record in the way that I do and went along with it. I just wanted to give him a different environment that allowed him to just play and not have the responsibility of every other aspect of making the record. I definitely wanted to give him a bit of a challenge, though, because it seemed that was what he needed. The record he'd made with my brother Andy, *The Extremist*, I thought was a phenomenal record; I'd heard that, and thought it was a remarkable album on many levels. I think my brother is probably the finest engineer of that type of music that there is, and I think that record is a really good example of his abilities. But I wanted to put [Joe] in a room with people who would react to music in a positive way and for him not to tell them what to play, basically, so that it would just leave him to play the guitar and be the artist, but not necessarily have the minute control, which apparently he normally had. I'm not knocking that approach—it had been extremely successful for him—but my object was to try to put him in a situation with musicians who were as competent as he was. My understanding had been that he'd already obviously worked with really good guys, but I think his tendency had been to tell them pretty much note for note what to play.

We assembled an all-star backing band that represented the crème de la crème of the world's finest session musicians, including drummer Manu Katché (who played with Peter Gabriel), bassist Nathan East (Stevie Wonder, Eric Clapton), and rhythm guitarist Andy Fairweather Low (Eric Clapton, Roger Waters). Unfamiliarity might have proved a handicap in the hands of a lesser group of world-class musicians, but this band instead thrived in the face of considerable pressure.

Nathan East, me, Andy Fairweather Low, and Manu Katché at The Site in '95

Photo by Michael Kirk

These guys were very expensive. I could only afford them for a total of fourteen days, two of which I missed. So we basically had twelve days to make the record and there was no time for preproduction rehearsals. We would gather at The Site studio about eleven in the morning, listen to a track, do about three takes, break for lunch, come back, and listen to see if we could do it any better, and that was it. Sometimes we would come back and listen, and both Glyn and I would be just knocked out by the intensity of the performance. Other times, everybody would learn something, and Andy or Manu would come up with a suggestion and then we would go and see if it worked. Since everybody was learning and developing their parts at the same time, we felt that it was the right thing to do to allow them to come up with ideas of their own. Being the great producer that he is, Glyn was fantastic at managing us.

Glyn Johns: My method of recording and producing a record is exactly the same as it was in the late sixties. My approach in setting a band up and recording them is exactly the same. I'm not the least bit interested in doing composites, or changing the tuning on something, or other things you can do with Pro Tools. There was very little overdubbing. Joe might have put an additional guitar on the odd thing, and of course there's a vocal on one track he overdubbed, but most of it was done live. Pro Tools is totally meaningless to me. I still mix a record without a computer and personally don't see the necessity if you've got really good musicians, and I tend to work with really good musicians. Most of the legendary guitar players I've worked with—Keith Richards, Eric Clapton, Pete Townshend—have been "feel" players, obviously all entirely different from each other and from Joe, and Joe's style of very fast, fluid, extraordinary bit of gymnastics on the guitar is not my normal listening pleasure. But I was astounded by his ability. He's an extraordinary musician; there's no question about it. I think he has two huge assets: He has an extraordinary ability to write very listenable instrumental music, which very few people in that genre do; and technically, he's a genius. It's extraordinary what he can physically accomplish.

For this album I had to learn a different way of recording that was completely opposite from my usual method. Glyn wanted everything played live. With John Cuniberti or Andy Johns, we would usually overdub melodies and solos, and would brainstorm guitar sounds after we had our basic tracks. We would work on those tones for hours until we came up with something we thought was really fun and unexpected, and then we would go about overdubbing a performance. Instead, here I am in a live room with a couple of effects pedals plugged into a small amp setup, and Glyn saying, "Do it all live." I tried to explain that wasn't how I did things, but Glyn's idea was, "Give me the whole Joe, all at once." He didn't want me to sit there and work on it because he felt it didn't need any more work. He felt there was no need to polish anything beyond the first or second take. So, I had to come up with something on the fly for each song. On "S.M.F." I had to play my guitar and harmonica simultaneously, live! That was a first for me.

Glyn saw what I was going through. Every song that we finished would turn out so different from what I had expected. I kept waiting for that solo moment like in "Surfing" or "Ice 9" or "Summer Song," and it wasn't happening. We were making an entirely different kind of record.

Glyn took me aside once and said, "It's not your job to decide what people will like. It's your job to play your guitar." So while there were times when we would celebrate what we got in the studio, there were definitely other times when he had to pull me aside to keep me motivated. He'd say, "Believe me—it's going well. You're doing great. It's going to happen. Just keep moving forward. Don't rely on what you used to do."

Glyn would encourage me to go even further away from where I'd been, to work further from my comfort zone, because he saw something else in me. He saw the method of me overdubbing, and critiquing myself, then doing another twenty takes on a track as an obstacle to artistic growth. He'd say, "You've done it. You've already done these stunning albums that will be great forever. All these records, why do them again? Now you need to move on and do something else that will be equally outrageous, and the only way to do it is to do it." It's the most obvious piece of advice, but it is very often the hardest thing for an artist to fully embrace: to do something completely different. No artist wants to stumble, certainly not in front of their audience, but sometimes that's what it takes.

Glyn Johns: Hearing Joe play was jaw-dropping! The one thing that I remembered more than anything is that we would do a take that we would all feel completely stunned and blown away by, and Joe would come in and hear in his own performance—not necessarily in anybody else's—all kinds of things he wasn't happy with, but to me it was all completely stunning. That was a little bit frustrating from my point of view; however, obviously I bowed to his better knowing—it was his record and he was judging his own performance. I might argue with him and point out that we all thought it was really good, but if he wasn't happy with something, of course we'd go and do another take. It wouldn't be a matter of him replacing his part; it would be a matter of everybody going out and doing another take. There's no problem with that. You never know, and you have nothing to lose.

Each time we played, Glyn got unique performances out of each of us. We were improvising and thinking fast on our feet. We had to react to changes that the other musicians or Glyn would throw at us, which happened a lot. We'd finish a performance, and someone would say, "Are you going to play that? Because if you do, then I'm going to change my part like this," and Glyn would come out sometimes and say, "It sounds great, you've done it, let's move on," or he'd say, "I'm not happy. Where else can you guys take it?"

With "Down, Down, Down" for instance, we did three heartbreaking takes, then broke for lunch. It was an emotionally heavy song to dig into and perform repeatedly. When we came back and listened to what we had played, everyone was like, "Wow." That was the first time I turned to Glyn and said, "I had no idea I could ever sound like that." There's so much personality in the performance, yet it's so naked and unadorned with effects of any kind. It's my JS Black Dog going into a Wells amp coming out of a Marshall bottom. That's it. Originally I was thinking of a more produced version, but Glyn saw the heart and soul of the song and said, "Do it stripped down and at a slower tempo. It will be more emotionally powerful that way." He was right.

The first ten days of recording, we did "Cool #9," "Down, Down Down," "S.M.F.," "Home," "Moroccan Sunset," "Slow Down Blues," "Sittin' 'Round" and "Killer Bee Bop." They were amazing sessions. As I listened back to the music, I heard some great moments where it felt like I'd grown light-years, right there on the tape. On every song, I heard a new side of my playing, a new facet to my musicianship.

I had actually started the record a year earlier with engineer/producer/drummer Eric Valentine. After returning from a tour playing with Deep Purple in the summer of '94, Eric and I recorded the beginnings of "Cool #9," "Look My Way," and "Luminous Flesh Giants," and finished a song called "Time." "Time" was a big, sprawling composition that John Cuniberti and I had started recording during the *Surfing* sessions back in '87! Eric and I finally finished and mixed it at The Site in 1994, but Glyn wasn't keen on including it on the record because he thought it didn't fit stylistically. I thought it was the best thing I'd ever done! Oh well . . . It eventually found a home on the *Crystal Planet* album, where it fit perfectly.

A second set of sessions with John Cuniberti in early '95 would yield "You're My World," "Look My Way," "Z.Z.'s Song," the start of "Home," part one of "Slow Down Blues," melodies and solos for "Luminous Flesh Giants" and "Cool #9" (version one), and some other pieces that would take even more time to mature. So by the time the project landed in Glyn's lap he had a lot of material to sort out.

When we started the last set of sessions, Glyn said that when we were done recording, he wanted me to write one last song that summarized my experience making the album. I wrote "If" as I was driving to The Site for the last band session. When I got to the studio I sat down with guitar, pencil, and paper, sketched out the song, showed the band, and then we recorded it on the spot. I'd never done that before! It was all part of Glyn's plan.

Eric Valentine mixing "Time" at The Site in '94
PHOTO BY JOE SATRIANI

When Glyn was mixing the record, I remember being shocked: only seven or eight active faders on the desk, and none were labeled! Nothing labeled "Kick drum," "Guitar," "Bass," et cetera . . . Only Glyn knew where everything was. Aside from the few faders, he operated a little reverb/delay unit sitting on his lap, and that was it. That's how he mixed the record! It was both fascinating and frightening. To be honest, mixing that record was one of those things I couldn't be there for. After mixing records with John and Andy, meticulously adjusting tracks and effects for hours, moving things up 2 dB here and 1.5 dB there, I was ready to step outside the studio while Glyn mixed because I was getting a little toasty around the edges. I can see it when I watch *Reel Satriani*, the documentary we filmed about recording *Joe Satriani*. By then, I was just beaten down by the whole experience.

Still, the way that the recording sounded coming through the speakers was a revelation to me. What I had heard from Glyn's work with all of my guitar heroes was the artist's performance exploding full of personality, and he brought that to this record. The process of making the broader album was in fact a growing period for me, and that's exactly what Glyn had promised. He was trying to get me out of my old skin and into a new place, and he was always confident that when I landed there, I was going to want to make that new thing part of who I was.

Glyn Johns: I was very happy with the record when it was finished. As far as I remember, he was very pleased with it when it was done. He didn't seem particularly enamored with it while we were doing it, but at the end of the process, when we'd actually finished, he was very pleased. I think Joe liked the record when we finished it, but let's put it this way—he's never gone back to that way of recording.

Each time I record, it's not like I've got a band that I'm always touring with that can just pop into the studio for a week. The process of going in and recording live before we've had a chance to play the music, and before I've played with those musicians, didn't make any sense to me at the time.

Unfortunately, the documentary *Reel Satriani* captured only the last two days of recording at The Site. It made for a good, gritty, *Let It Be* type of film, but it hardly scratched the surface when it came to telling the whole story. The album actually contained work and performances from four different producers and four different rhythm sections, and took a year of recording at three different studios! In the end, though, it was well worth it.

The week that the *Joe Satriani* album was released, my longtime label, Relativity, was absorbed and then dismantled by Sony, and we struggled to get the word out on the new record. Retail would call for a box of *Joe Satriani* records and there was literally no one answering the phone. It was a disaster because it was a very important record for me and I got no support from the label in the States. Still, in places like the United Kingdom, the record was a smash. We played London's Wembley Arena on the record's subsequent tour! I think anyone would feel validated playing a place that size. I felt overwhelmed that a record that was such a risk to make was being embraced by a new wave of fans around the world.

A funny side note: Mick Jagger came to hang out and watch the Wembley show in the fall of '95. While we were playing "Moroccan Sunset," he moved from watching us at the mixing desk to the side of the stage, and during the song's breakdown I actually got him to strum my guitar a few times, and it rang through the house as we reentered the song. No one saw it. It was a cool, private moment in a very public setting. Mick was strumming my guitar, and it was reverberating through the arena. It was one of those "Oh, wow" moments for me: "Mick Jagger is strumming my guitar on 'Moroccan Sunset.' How did I get *here*?"

CHAPTER 14 ★★

G3/*Crystal Planet*—1997

"A dream come true for guitar fanatics."
—*Billboard* magazine

Even after all the success I was enjoying as a solo artist, I was beginning to feel a bit isolated from my peers. I had to remedy the situation, and from that simple desire to play with other guitarists, G3, my own little mini-festival, was born. In a phone call to my manager, Mick Brigden, I asked, "What if I toured with two other guitarists, then jammed with those two players at the end of each show?" That way I'd get to jam every night with players that I'd handpicked! Why three players together on one bill? If we had seven guitar players, we'd never find a promoter to take on that many guitarists playing on one night, and no artist would sign on to the tour to play for only ten or fifteen minutes, so we had to figure out what length of time would be attractive for the artists. Forty-five minute sets for each band was key to making the show work to everyone's advantage, especially the fans'. You'd also have to leave time for a jam, because the audience is really waiting for that. That's the big climax. Mick soon came up with the name G3, and then the real work started.

Once we'd settled on the concept of three stars, Mick asked me, "Okay, who do you want it to be?" and I instantly said, "It's got to be Steve Vai and Eric Johnson." The role of getting players to sign on fell to me. I had to call Steve and Eric up directly and talk to them over and over again about why it was a great idea. We worked on them for months. It took a very long time to convince them, their management, and the record labels that competition would not be an issue, but I knew in my gut that the audience would love this show. I'm sure Mick spent just as much time talking to their managers trying to get those guys to agree, because up to that point, there was a very well-organized music machine with rules like "don't play with your competition."

Concert promoters were a bit reticent to have three headliners play on one night, in one venue. Not only was it expensive, but it put a lot of their eggs in one basket. They felt audiences would prefer to see me in March, Steve Vai in April, and Eric Johnson in May. That way the audience would buy tickets to every show, and if there were a problem, they'd have spread out the risk on three different nights rather than one night. It would have been a dream for me to see Jimi Hendrix, Jeff Beck, and Jimmy Page all on one stage together in a G3-like setting. It would never have changed my mind about who was better or whom I liked more. So we had to convince everyone to forget all the rules about competition and risk, and take a leap of faith.

Me, Steve, and Eric at a photo shoot at the Capitol Records building in L.A., '96

Photo by Neil Zlozower

The other cool thing about G3 was that we weren't out there just promoting our new albums and playing our new singles. It felt more like a rock 'n' roll victory lap, celebrating our musicianship, our camaraderie, and the genre itself. And at the end of every show, the audience responded so positively to the fact that we were all just standing there on the same stage together and trading solos back and forth, improvising with our guards down. We felt their excitement and it made every show better and better.

Steve Vai: G3 is a celebration of the beautiful guitar by people who love the instrument and have devoted their lives to it. Joe has put great care and attention into making sure that the musicians who take part in a G3 tour have something valuable to offer an audience that loves the instrument. I feel tremendously grateful for its success!

Mick Brigden: There's no way any of our promoters knew what the results would be; they were going off our energy to tell them to trust us. Plus Joe was strong enough on his own to be able to put numbers down where we weren't going to come out looking bad either way. But its success actually went way beyond what we thought. I absolutely have to say, I would NOT have been able to imagine that what happened that first fall of '96 was going to be as successful as it was. The very first shows of the tour sold out right away, so we were blown away!

Standing next to other guitarists playing really well night after night, you can't help but notice similarities and differences with your own playing. You marvel at what they do and also realize how different you are as a guitarist. I think I began to know more about myself as a player as I was going through those first six weeks of the G3 tour.

Back in the States, after our G3 Euro Tour, I was now signed to Epic/Sony and had John Kalodner, the legendary A&R man, as part of my team, along with Mike Fraser, my new engineer/producer. Kalodner had worked with Mike quite a bit, and he brought him in for the *G3: Live in Concert* project. John was very keen on us using Mike for the next studio record, too, and since we already liked working with him, it seemed like a good idea. I was excited to see where this new producer was going to take me.

Digital editor Eric Caudieux checking a mix from the G3 live show

PHOTO BY JOE SATRIANI

Mike Fraser: Joe and I go back to the eighties, when we had first talked about doing a record together. It just didn't work out timing-wise for us. Then we ran into each other again at a live show, and said, "Hey, we should do something together." Joe explained his G3 concert, so I went out and recorded and mixed it, which sort of launched us into working together on *Crystal Planet*. We just wanted to make a really good band record and bring him back to his instrumental roots. Up to that point, he'd experimented a lot with singing and vocals. *CP* was one of the first records in a while where he'd returned to the instrumental part of it without worrying about vocals. The focus was on getting a really solid band thing with Jeff Campitelli and Stu Hamm, a three-piece thing, and later on we added the keyboards and all that. But essentially, the nucleus of it was a three-piece.

Although not a musician himself, Mike Fraser is very musical and good at coming up with melodic, harmonic, or rhythmic suggestions. He might say, "Maybe a higher harmony," or "Maybe a more relaxed groove." His ideas are based on his own natural musicality.

As my new producer, Mike was looking back over my catalog and said, "I'm going to respect what you've done before, but what can we do that will move you into a new territory? Why don't we see what we can do with capturing more energy?" He was really keen on capturing the energy and creativity of the unit—me, Jeff, and Stu—and then bringing in my overdub ideas on top of that. I was trying to create live melody and solo performances that were keepers, too, and the effects were really part of each song's personality, so I had to treat it like a live show as we were tracking. When we got into the studio, we were able to set up like a live trio, and we would do just six or seven takes at a time. Everyone was encouraged to expand their own performances with each take to see just how interesting we could get.

Playing Chrome Boy at The Plant in '97
PHOTO BY NEIL ZLOZOWER

The influence of my son, ZZ, was everywhere on *Crystal Planet*, starting with "Z.Z.'s Song." I recorded that particular piece of music back during the previous record's sessions, which turned out to be the eponymous album.

On that session I had all of my amps set up in a line in Fantasy's Studio C. There must have been eight or ten amps set up, and I think I was plugged into a JC-120, a Marshall 6100, and my Wells amp. In the end, John wound up using the Wells amp, and the JC-120 in stereo for ambience. It's just a live recording of me playing, with John miking everything up. Technically, it was a very delicate but fun piece to perform. I used to play it for ZZ through headphones I would place on my wife's belly before he was born. I don't know whether he liked it or not, but we used to feel him kicking!

We moved into our new house on the day ZZ turned four. A few days later we were on the G3 U.S. tour. That was his first time going on tour. My wife was with us, too, so the three of us were traveling together as a family. I shared so many experiences with ZZ on that tour that it was natural his influence would be felt on *Crystal Planet*. One day we were looking out the window at a series of clouds. ZZ pointed up and said, "It looks like a *train of angels*." I remember thinking, "That's just the coolest phrase I have ever heard," and I wrote it down.

Kids that age say stuff like that every day. One day, when asked if he needed anything to drink, he said, "I just need a *piece of liquid*." I felt like if I was going to use "A Piece of Liquid," "A Train of Angels," and "Psycho Monkey" (another of his offerings) as song titles on the record, I should give him proper writing credit. It really is like a never-ending muse when you see a child with his or her mind developing in leaps and bounds—it's fascinating and at times funny the way they put things together as they learn how to express themselves.

The title track of *Crystal Planet* came from a book I was reading to him. It was a science book and in the first paragraph, it said something like, "We live on a crystal planet." I remember looking at that phrase and thinking, "That is a great way to express what it is

I've been thinking," because this new record was going to be about the underlying structure and the beauty of music, but I just hadn't quite thought of the title yet. I hesitated to use the phrase for a while because I thought people would think it was another album from me about aliens or outer space, but to me, it suggested something much more organic and down-to-earth.

I started writing more material for the next record after the G3 tour. I keep notebooks from all my previous albums of all the music and production ideas. Everything's written down, even where to put sound effects.

One thing I did differently for *Crystal Planet* was to not make any recorded demos. When I sat down to write, I had my guitar (though it wasn't always plugged in), a metronome to get the tempos and keep me focused, a notepad, and a pencil. Then I'd write out the song and the chord sequence, writing little notes about what I thought the song could sound like. So the first time Mike Fraser and the band heard the songs in full form was when we played them live at rehearsal. I didn't want them to be influenced by a drum machine demo. I thought that maybe that was what had been so difficult on previous sessions, getting musicians to make that leap from the demo to what a song should sound like when a band plays it.

Mike and I thought it would be a great idea if we rehearsed first, and I wanted to see if he could capture our sound the way he did on the G3 recordings. So for a week, Stu Hamm, Jeff Campitelli, and I rehearsed *Crystal Planet*, and everybody got to take tapes home. By the time we pulled into The Plant to record the album, we were well rehearsed and ready to rock.

Stu Hamm: Making *Crystal Planet* was a good creative process, I had some great bass tones involved in that, and great grooves, and we'd been on the road for a while, so it was good to get in the studio together. I think it's great to bring in different musicians to motivate and inspire you, and after a while, Joe knew so many different musicians and what they did that he was able to write for specific players. He knew that in this or that particular song, a musician's going to be able to come in and add what he was looking for to get a spark, and maybe find something in a song that he hadn't heard initially. We would always record as a band for *Crystal Planet*—that's the essence of any rock record, because, believe me, in the final product, you can hear when there's a rhythm section actually playing and working up a sweat and looking at each other and communicating, versus studio musicians trying to play the part effectively and correctly according to the chart.

Jeff Campitelli, me, and Stuart Hamm at The Plant in '97
PHOTO BY NEIL ZLOZOWER

For *Crystal Planet*, my original Peavey 5150 amp got the most use, along with my Marshall 6100, a Zoom headphone amp, and the rack-mounted SansAmp. My Ibanez Chrome Boy, Black Dog, and assorted JS1000s saw the most action in the guitar department. On a few songs we would add a vintage '58 Stratocaster, a '58 Les Paul Jr., my '58 Esquire, or even a Flying V, just to expand the sonics a bit.

Mike Fraser: I usually mic each of Joe's cabinets with a 57 and a 421, and then I'll put a 414 just somewhere nearby the cabinet, but in the room, just to kind of capture some of the room sound. With Joe, I'm working to get sort of silkier guitar sounds as opposed to aggressive, brash, rocky guitar sounds—they have to be a little bit more fluid sounding, which requires a slightly different approach. I still mic him generally the same as everything else, but it comes down ultimately to what Joe's playing—if he's running it through some chorusing effects or some delays, we will change his amps up a bit to get his tone singing a little more as opposed to jumping at you.

Producer/engineer Mike Fraser at the console, The Plant, '97
Photo by Neil Zlozower

With Joe's sound, you have to take a little bit more care with things, because a lot of that sound we're looking for would come from the amps, so we'd start there and play around with how much distortion he wanted to have on the note. Because obviously, the more gain you have, the better the sustain, but then the note gets a little bit crunchier, so it's not as silky. So there was a lot of balancing between how much gain to get that sustain, but at the same time we kept the sound smooth and easy and would play around with different levels of mid-range, boost, and all that stuff. And then sometimes I'd have to go and adjust my mic placement a little bit so it's not right on the cone of the speaker, which would get a harsher sound. Then if you pulled it off the cone, it got kind of a more mellow sound, so it was a matter of finding that combination. But once we found what would work great within a track, depending on how thick that track was with other parts, it went pretty smooth. We knew where we had to go with the amp settings to get this tone, and Joe would add maybe a couple of pedals on to help push that tone to that direction.

Joe would usually say, "Okay, let's try this out," and at the end of the first pass, sometimes I'd say, "Hey, in the second verse there, why don't we try doing this?" and he'd give it a try, and as we tried that, we might stop and agree, "Yeah, that didn't work. Let's go back to how you originally did it." So that process was ongoing as we were working on the album, versus being something that was sort of preplanned. Joe's open-minded to any suggestions, but he does have an idea of tones and how he wants a particular guitar to speak and what voice it has. He had a pretty good idea of what personality he wanted in there as it related to effects, but he's always been open to ideas on how to best create that.

Working with an artist like Joe, who doesn't have a singer, your role as a producer changes in terms of what you pay attention to because there's a lot more guitar layering. So there will be some rhythm parts put on there, and then the melody/lead guitar sort of becomes the vocal. We had to make sure with each sound of the guitars that they were not going to keep building up the sound on top of each other. To do that, we had to make sure they left room and space for the other guitar parts to work, and for that melody guitar to come up in the middle, front end of the mix and still really sing.

It is my method to create a unique voice to play the melody. If a singer had a radically different song he was about to sing, an engineer would use a different kind of microphone, or surround the vocal performance with a unique set of equalization, limiting, compression, reverb, delays, and so forth . . . It all creates a vibe that eventually transports the listener and delivers that extra magic. The sound of the vocal also carries with it a message. Since I don't have lyrics, I need to put more emphasis on that sound to create a kind of "voice." Every song's melody winds up with its own voice that is not duplicated on any other song on the album. I'm searching for that perfect tone that allows me to tell the song's unique story.

A good example of that process in play on *Crystal Planet* would be "Love Thing," because the lengths that we went to just to record that beautiful love song were insane. It took months, four or five different recordings, using different key signatures, and different musicians and instrumentation. We finally ended up using three acoustic guitars for the rhythms, all tuned to an open E. I used my 1948 Martin 000-21 that had had its intonation adjusted by Buzz Feiten, specifically for the open-E tuning.

Another new approach we explored on *Crystal Planet* was digital editor Eric Caudieux's involvement in the tracking. Since I was trying to add "techno" elements to the sound and feel of the record, I asked Eric to work up some techno versions of the songs using loops and that sort of thing. We then would monitor those backing tracks in our headphones as we recorded our "real" performances. Crazy idea, but it worked: We were energized by hearing all that extra musical information in our ears as we explored each take. Eventually, we used a very small amount of those modern textures in the final mixes, but their effect was evident in our performances. The song "Raspberry Jam Delta-V" is a good example of the synergy we accomplished with this approach.

As we wrapped up tracking on "Crystal Planet," John Cuniberti had just finished refitting the new Coast Recording studio, which was a large facility originally operating as the San Francisco Recording Academy. John put a Neve console in the control room and it sounded so beautiful! Upon returning from our G3 Euro Tour we were able to book time in the studio and commence mixing. The studio itself had a lot to do with the sound of the album—it's very fat and "Neve" sounding. I told Mike I wanted this album to sound really great on headphones, too, so we were listening to every mix carefully through speakers as well as using the headphone amp in the Neve console, which was a fun way to mix.

No matter what the techniques I've highlighted on a studio album, I've always done my best to keep them fresh and updated. When I look back on *Crystal Planet* now, of course, it's 2014 and I just can't believe we got it done! And I'm so happy we stuck to our artistic guns, so to speak, didn't change anything, and just followed our creative impulses and made the record we wanted to make. Because when all the dust settled and the anxiety of the moment was behind us, the record stood tall on its own artistic integrity.

I should also mention that in early 1996, I decided to shave my head while we were on the *Joe Satriani* tour. I'd appeared that way on the subsequent G3 live DVD, but the *Crystal Planet* album cover was my first studio project to be promoted with that new, bold look. It was a moment of reinvention, and an interesting way to announce the next stage of my career.

CHAPTER 15 ★★

Engines of Creation—2000

> "Engines of Creation . . . *blended electronica with rock guitar elements without losing that characteristic Satriani sound."*
>
> —*Premier Guitar* magazine

After *Crystal Planet*, I was coming out of a whole period where there had been a lot of live work, so I was personally feeling, "Okay, after all that, I've been about as live as I want to get for a while. What can I do that's totally different?" I wanted my next record to represent the ULTIMATE radical shift in terms of how my audience heard my music.

The millennium was coming and the big question was, "What's going to happen?" I saw that society was shifting to an online life in a HUGE way, and I wanted to do something where I felt like I was jumping into the future, and part of that had to do with thinking that I shouldn't record in a studio or even with a band. I approached Epic/Sony with three ideas for the next album: a "classical" record with my guitar on top of an orchestra, a straight-ahead rock 'n' roll record, or a techno record. I had enough material written to get moving on any one of those ideas.

Sony said, "We'd LOVE a techno record," and that felt like the right direction to head in to me as well. My new coproducer/engineer, Eric Caudieux, and I decided as part of that departure to record this album entirely "in the box." In other words, we'd do it all on Pro Tools in his living room: no studio, no other musicians, we were going to do it all ourselves. It was exciting! First of all, Eric was a fantastic guitar player and a composer himself, so it was really great to work with a musician of his caliber who could understand exactly what I was going through, from my fingertips all the way to what I was aiming for compositionally and conceptually with the technology.

Eric Caudieux: When Joe and I started writing together for *Engines of Creation*, there weren't many loops involved, so I composed the beats that you hear on the record. It was pretty much Joe's music that dictated what I did, and the ideas for the beats would come when Joe played me his demos or something live in my living room. For instance, with the title track, I remember Joe played me the arpeggio part on the guitar live, and I came up with the rest based off what he played.

A good example of our writing process for that album is the song "Borg Sex." I gave Eric a drum groove with a completely atonal keyboard improvisation on top. There was no guitar on the demo! "This is about a female and a male borg having sex," I said to Eric. "This is like conversation, foreplay." That was all I had. Eric said, "Whoa, how do we get this thing going?"

Eric Caudieux: That song became one of my favorites from the record, and was probably one of the first one or two that we did as well. When we started that track, we had no clue where we were going, because it hadn't been done before as far as I can recall, for a rock musician to do a song like that. With "Borg Sex," I remember Joe gave me a melody line, and I remember just taking that and doubling, quadrupling it, putting it out of phase and then putting it back till that melody line opens wide and makes you feel funny in the stomach. I knew I wanted a ton of dynamics, because usually you hear machine music and it's just one

That's me in late '70 or early '71 in bassist Steve Muller's basement. Guitarist John Riccio's amp towers above me in the back.

Photo by Steve Muller

John Riccio; me; my brother, John (sitting); and bassist John Gordon jamming in my backyard in '71

Photo by Satriani Family Archives

My first band's business card. We never played a gig! I'm not sure who came up with the name. My sister Carol provided the lettering.

Photo by Joe Satriani

Rock - Hard Rock Group

MICHUOCAN

Parties
Social Affairs

Tom - 334 - 8122
John - 333 - 5250

This was the business card for the first "real" band I played with back in high school

Photo by Joe Satriani

My '68 Fender Telecaster and Univox amp in my room in late '71

Photo by Joe Satriani

Me in my Westbury, Long Island, basement on New Year's Eve '71

Photo by Satriani Family Archives

Just getting started in Berkeley, CA, '79

Photo by Katherine Satriani

The Squares after a Berkeley Square show in '81
PHOTO BY SAUL GRABIA

The Squares at Berkeley Square in '81
PHOTO BY JEFF HOLT

The Squares backstage at the Keystone Berkeley club circa '82

Photo by Rubina Satriani

Teaching at Second Hand Guitars, Berkeley, CA, circa '85

Photo by Rubina Satriani

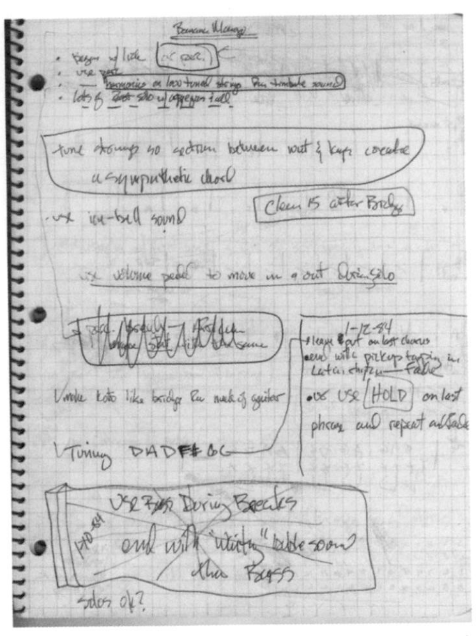

A page from my Joe Satriani *EP notebook for "Banana Mango"*

Photo by Joe Satriani

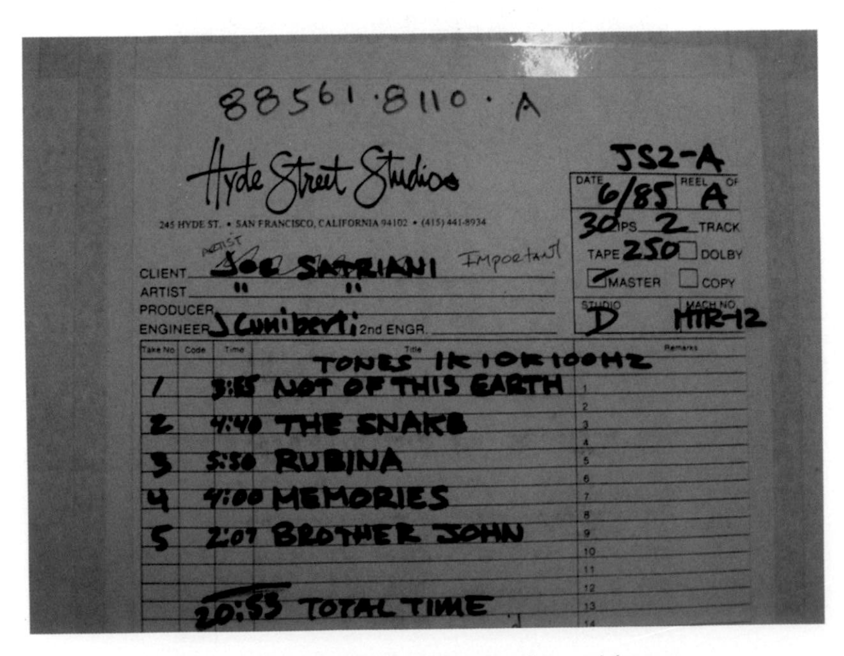

Not of This Earth *2-inch tape box, side one*

Photo by Joe Satriani

88561 . 8110 . B

Hyde Street Studios

245 HYDE ST. • SAN FRANCISCO, CALIFORNIA 94102 • (415) 441-8934

JS2-B

DATE 6/85 REEL B

30 IPS 2 TRACK

TAPE 250 DOLBY

MASTER COPY

STUDIO D MACH NO MTR-12

CLIENT JOE SATRIANI

ARTIST

PRODUCER

ENGINEER 2nd ENGR

Take No	Time	Title
1.	3:25	THE ENIGMATIC
2.	3:30	DRIVING AT NIGHT
3.	4:55	HORDES OF LOCUSTS
4.	3:56	NEW DAY
5.	1:50	THE HEADLESS HORSEMAN
	17:45	TOTAL TIME

Not of This Earth 2-inch tape box, side two

Photo by Joe Satriani

That's me at a Bamboo rehearsal in S.F., most likely in '85

Photo by Chris Witt Ketner

Surfing with The Alien *mix reels*

PHOTO BY JOHN CUNIBERTI

At Hyde Street's Studio C with my Black Dog in hand in '87

PHOTO BY JOHN SIEVERT

Jeff Campitelli hamming it up for the camera in Hyde Street's Studio C in '87

PHOTO BY JOHN CUNIBERTI

Me and Steve Vai backstage at The Limelight, Chicago, July of '87

PHOTO BY ROBERT HAKALSKI

Me and Mick Jagger at S.I.R. Studios, New York City, rehearsing for his solo tour on February 20, 1988

Photo by Ebet Roberts

Manager Bill Graham and me backstage in '88

Photo by Neil Zlozower

Me and Kirk Hammett backstage, S.F., in '88. Note my new braces!

Photo by Pat Johnson

John Cuniberti and me in Studio C at Hyde Street, S.F., '89

Photo by Ken Friedman

Sunset down by the water in Berkeley, CA, in '89

Photo by Mark Leialoha

Steve Vai and me after a long photo session with Neil Zlozower in L.A. in '89

Photo by Neil Zlozower

Me and Stuart Hamm on the Flying *tour, 1990*

Photo by Mark Leialoha

On tour in '90 playing acoustic

Photo by Larry DiMarzio

My tech Mike Manning tuning guitars on the road in ’90

Photo by Joe Satriani

*1990 Ibanez/*Flying in a Blue Dream *ad*

Photo by Robert Hakalski

Doug Wimbish, Phil Ashley, Simon Phillips, and me at Bearsville, late '90

Photo by John Cuniberti

Sitting at the Bearsville console in late '90

Photo by John Cuniberti

Andy Johns, Matt and Gregg Bissonette, and me at Ocean Way Studios, L.A., '92

Photo by Lori Stoll

That's me with Gregg and Matt Bissonette in the Ocean Way control room, with Andy Johns coming up behind us. L.A., '92.

Photo by Lori Stoll

Performing on the Extremist *tour in '92*

Photo by Neil Zlozower

Me with an Ibanez JS/Tele-ish prototype guitar at a video shoot for "All Alone" in '93

Photo by John Cuniberti

Glyn Johns and me at The Site, 6/14/1995
Photo by Jay Blakesberg

Recording at The Site in '95
Photo by Jay Blakesberg

Eric Johnson, me (shirtless!), Jeff Campitelli, Stuart Hamm, and Steve Vai at G3 rehearsals in Arizona in '96

Photo by Neil Zlozower

My home studio in panorama circa '01

Photo by Jon Luini

Eric Caudieux at The Plant for the SBM record in '02

Photo by Joe Satriani

Matt Bissonette recording with my '64 P-Bass at The Plant in '02

Photo by John Cuniberti

Mike Manning tunes a JS1000 painted by Nicholas Del Drago at The Plant in '03

Photo by Joe Satriani

Robert Fripp having a bit of fun with ZZ's skateboard after a G3 show in Spain in '04

Photo by Joe Satriani

Me and Les Paul after his ninetieth birthday party show at Carnegie Hall, New York in '05

Photo by Dave Allocca

Producer Mike Fraser, me, and Jeff Campitelli with wigs, posing like rockstars at Armoury Studios in Vancouver in '05

Photo by Armoury Studios

Jeff Campitelli at Armoury Studios in Vancouver for the Super Colossal *sessions in '05*

PHOTO BY RONN DUNNETT

Listening back to a solo at The Plant during the Satchafunkilus *sessions in '07*

PHOTO BY JOHN CUNIBERTI

Chickenfoot at Sammy's studio in '08

Photo by LeAnn Meuller

Andy Johns and John Cuniberti at Sammy's studio during the Chickenfoot I *sessions in '08*

Photo by John Cuniberti/Jamie Durr

After some Chickenfoot mayhem at Shepherd's Bush, in London in '09

Photo by Rubina Satriani

Sammy and me at Shepherd's Bush with Chickenfoot in '09

Photo by Christie Goodwin

Chickenfoot at Shepherd's Bush in '09

Photo by Christie Goodwin

Jeff Campitelli, Mike Keneally, me, and Allen Whitman in hazmat suits at Skywalker Studios in '10

Photo by Arthur Rosato

That's me with my lightsaber using "the Force" at Skywalker in '13

Photo by Arthur Rosato

Me and Mike Fraser taking a break from the Unstoppable Momentum *sessions at Skywalker in '13*

Photo by Arthur Rosato

Vinnie Colaiuta, Chris Chaney, Mike Keneally, and me at Skywalker

Photo by Vinnie Colaiuta

Vinnie took this shot of me at Skywalker during a short break in the action in '13

Photo by Vinnie Colaiuta

Warming up backstage before a show in Bucharest during the first week of the Unstoppable Momentum *tour in '13*

Photo by Rubina Satriani

The Unstoppable Momentum *live band with the Steve Morse band, backstage in '13*

Photo by Bob Mussell Photo

JOE
SATRIANI

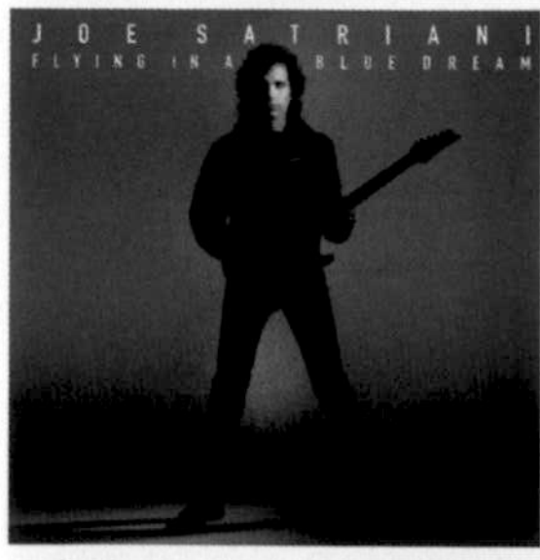

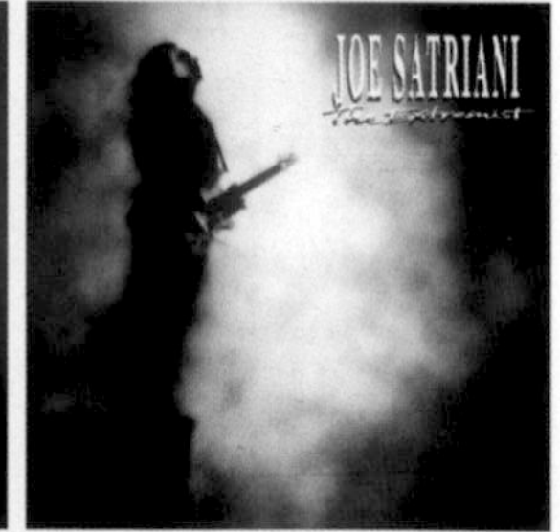

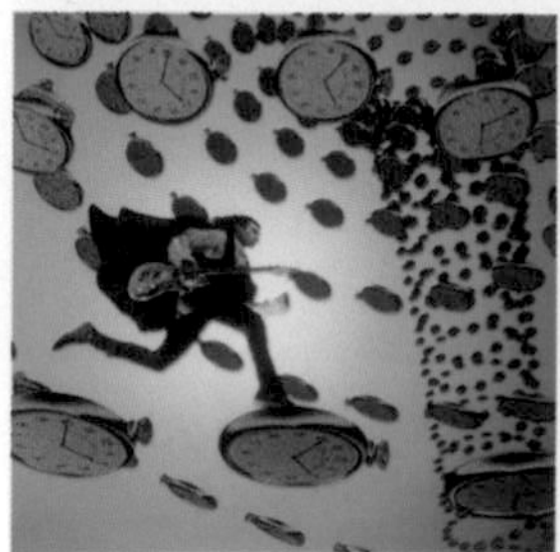

joe satriani
crystal planet

joe satriani
ENGINES OF CREATION

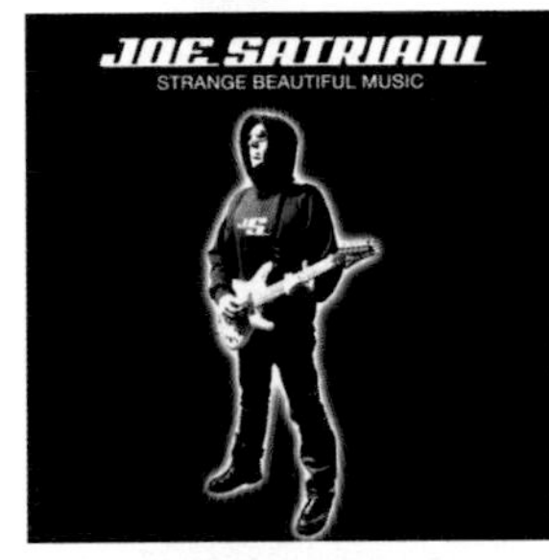
JOE SATRIANI
STRANGE BEAUTIFUL MUSIC

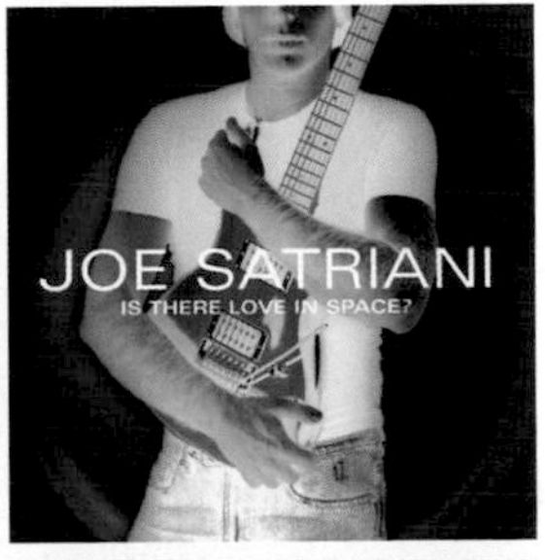
JOE SATRIANI
IS THERE LOVE IN SPACE?

JOE SATRIANI SUPER COLOSSAL

JOE SATRIANI
Professor Satchafunkilus and the Musterion of Rock

CHICKENFOOT

JOE SATRIANI

CHICKENFOOT

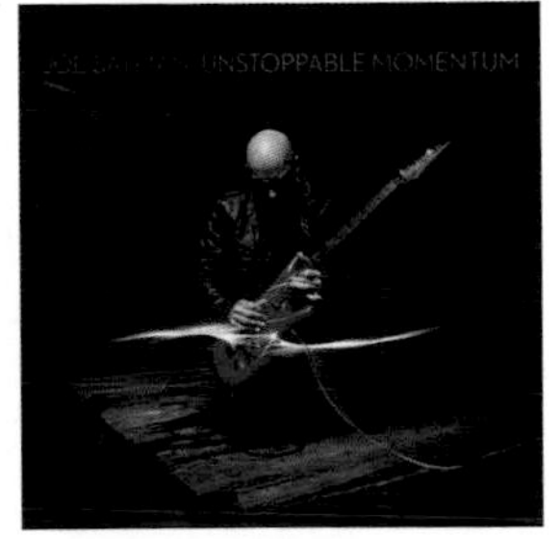
UNSTOPPABLE MOMENTUM

Live in the UK in '13

Photo by Christie Goodwin

thing that goes from top to finish, and that's about it. So I wanted basically a machine record that sounded live, and I had so much fun with that one.

The studio was in a house right in Laurel Canyon. There was a gigantic living room with crazy tall ceilings where I put all my gear and setup. There was a tracking room for the drums upstairs, which we didn't use because everything was machines, and I had a tracking room for the amps, which we didn't use because again it was all in the box, but we worked in the living room primarily. I had set it up that way because I'd always thought the problem with any studio for anybody who collects gear is not having the gear right there: when you can't look at it, you forget about it. I also remember I'd gone out to IKEA and they had a shitload of shoe racks, small ones for small shoes and big ones for big-ass boots. Since we had small pedals and big pedals, I placed them accordingly so you could literally look at them all, grab whatever pedal you wanted, and try it at any time. It worked great, and there were loads of amplifiers used, just no speakers—we had amplifiers galore.

I remember Eric's living room was completely taken over by every kind of amp and pedal you could think of. He had purchased a couple of hanging shoe racks, except instead of shoes there were effects pedals inside each compartment. I was like a kid in a candy store! This alternative recording environment gave a boost to our creative approach to each song. On "Borg Sex," for example, we put together the strangest combination of effects pedals just to see if we could get the guitar to be the "male borg." Then we'd set up another configuration to be the "female borg." We were making it up as we went along, with Eric encouraging me to just freely improvise. Anything I played was going to be saved and we could manipulate it in any way we wanted. If anything, we had a bit too much freedom, but we were sort of intoxicated with this idea that we were not recording a conventional album. We were fully embracing the idea of recording and mixing "in the box" without any other musicians, in a living room in Laurel Canyon.

The sessions were so different from the way I usually worked. Sometimes we'd create right in the moment, and with other songs, Eric would ask me to leave him alone for three days so he could construct the drums, bass, keyboards, create original samples—anything we had discussed that was going to be the "band" around my guitar performances. He encouraged me to trust the process because he knew my history was to record in a more conventional manner. He kept telling me, "It's gonna work, you'll see."

Eric Caudieux's Studio City living room filled with amps, guitars, and keyboards in '99

Photo by Joe Satriani

Because Eric was a musician, he could listen to a demo of a song, then create a version of that song electronically. That's when he was ready for me to listen. I'd fly down, plug in my guitar, and start to record over his grooves, keyboard pads, and bass lines. We had Neve preamps, a GML mic pre, and a '64 Fender Bassman head that wound up being used 50 percent of the time. My guitar went into an amp, which would then go into a Palmer speaker simulator, and from there into a Neve mic pre, and from *there* right into Pro Tools. Sometimes we'd use a Hafler Triple Giant, which was a 4-channel guitar preamp. You hear a lot of that on "Borg Sex" in the intensity of the distortion.

Most of the time, I used my JS Chrome Boy and Black Dog guitars. We also used a '58 Fender Strat quite a bit. As far as pedals, we were using the Electro-Harmonix Micro Synth, Dunlop Cry Baby wah-wah pedals, Fulltone pedals, and the DigiTech Whammy pedal quite often.

As we started seeing these ideas come to life, I started to realize how much flexibility is inherent in that kind of creative process. It changed my whole approach to tracking. For instance, there was no reason to put down guides like you usually would for a drummer or bass player, just to give them an idea of what's going on in the song. I realized that I could make it up as I went along. I would come up with twelve different performances in one afternoon and each could be going in a new direction. We could have a Brazilian approach, a techno approach, a heavy rock approach, and a blues approach, and we could just sit back, relax, and pick or combine the ones we thought sounded the most interesting. The difference was, when you have a band in a studio and it's costing you $4,000 or $5,000 a day, you'd better have your mind made up about what you want people to play. Here we had removed the element of time and money from the recording process, so I wasn't paying to record an album by the hour. I didn't have to settle on a band's performance each afternoon. We could build the tracks over a period of months, changing them and letting them evolve, which was fantastic.

Compositionally, each song was built differently. I'd decided to work with a new piece of gear this time around, the Kurzweil K2000, a digital audio workstation (DAW) keyboard with these beautiful sounds in it. I'm not a keyboard player primarily, but whenever the mood struck me, I would turn that keyboard on, push RECORD, and just improvise. The DAW made it so easy and fun, so I started to use the keyboard as a writing tool for some of the songs, especially

"Borg Sex," "Until We Say Goodbye," "Champagne?," "Attack," and "Slow and Easy." Some of those keyboard performances wound up on the final recordings, too. Once I realized how simple it was, I could email Eric a MIDI file that he could open up and assign almost any sound to it he wanted. I could also send Eric a little audio file to cue him to the kind of sounds I was looking for.

The album's title, *Engines of Creation*, came from skimming an article in *Time* magazine. At one point, the writer paraphrased K. Eric Drexler's book title, *Engines of Creation*, in his piece. Unaware that it was Drexler's book title, I wrote it down in one of my production books. Months later I came upon it and realized I had to write a song around it. I just thought it was such a beautiful phrase, and it was the perfect title to represent this trance/techno record I was working on.

Eric Caudieux: I composed beats for the record based off the moods of Joe's original compositions, so if a song was more joyful, then the beat would be more that kind of upbeat thing; if it was a little more mournful, then we'd go more for that kind of vibe. With that album, we did all the little tricks you could do in the box at that time: doubling, tripling, quadrupling, anything you could get to create the thickness, the detuning stuff, sticking it left/right, and creating that weird out-of-phase what-the-hell-is-going-on kind of vibe!

When we were putting beats together for the record, I was experimenting with different ways of getting rhythmically inspired. We were using Eric's own loops a lot and I was also experimenting with the sequencing software program Reason. We took advantage of digital editing to get away from the sound of just a guy playing his guitar in a studio. Everything had to sound edited to a degree. So if I was going to play rhythm guitar, Eric was not going to ask me to play something for an hour; he would instead ask me to play something for thirty seconds and then we'd go and make our own sample from my performance. That way, the repetition would have an effect on the overall sound and vibe. Then I would perform the solos and the melodies in the traditional way. Those would be the live elements, but we wanted the background tracks to have that sort of cut-and-paste, looped quality to them.

"Devil's Slide" was a great example of machine gun–style synergy between the rhythm track and guitars. On a rock record, the ensemble parts would be a lot looser, but I wanted to make it sound completely automated. So Eric would trim and edit each guitar harmony part, so together they would be completely diabolical sounding. We wanted the guitars to be one with the automated loops. That meant everything had to get chopped into pieces so it sounded very robotic.

With "Attack," the entire track was recorded on my K2000 first, and then the architecture of it and some of the sounds were transferred to the master template in Eric's Pro Tools session. We'd synched Pro Tools and Logic together on two separate machines. The challenge for us was to see how we could create a guitar sound that could mimic the keyboard sound. We used a Moog Moogerfooger filter pedal for the main effect, then used either the SansAmp, the '64 Fender Bassman, or the Hafler Triple Giant. It was something that was just an entirely different way of saying, "This is a melody—dig *this*!" The juxtaposition of the song's sections is quite unusual in that I'd written this dreamy breakdown piece that was used for the solo. I was thinking that in the middle of a fierce battle, there's a moment when time seems to stop, or go into slow motion, and the warrior is having a moment of clarity, a moment of spiritual searching of some kind. I wanted that breakdown to suggest some sort of dream state.

In a completely different way, with "The Power Cosmic 2000—Part II," my approach in that solo was something that mystified even Eric at the time. "What are you doing?" he asked me. "I can't follow this." There was a chord progression in my head, but I didn't want anybody to hear it! I kept changing the scales that revolved around the key note of C that had this techno-bass thing going. I was playing five or six different scales but changing them deliberately at certain times. That was something I hadn't heard anybody do before in the context of a trance/techno song, and certainly I hadn't done anything like it on any of my records before.

The idea behind having "Parts I and II" was to complete something I'd recorded for a *Guitar Player* Soundpage back in 1987. The original "Part I" contained the main chord progression played as cascading, eleven-note arpeggios, with no melody on top. I updated it and composed a melody to be played over the main chord progression. I wanted to write a more futuristic-sounding "Part II," so I started with a loop on Reason and sent that off to Eric. We then used the loop as the driving force underneath the melody and chord sequence of "Part II." Once Eric had laid out the song's master template, we "flew in" my cassette demo's melody, recorded with a Zoom, for the new "Part I," then added melody and solo guitars over the new sections. The new guitar sounds on that were created using a Fulltone Ultimate Octave pedal, and two Whammy pedals as well, one going an octave lower and one an octave higher. It's one of my favorite guitar tones. It's just so beautiful and complex.

Eric Caudieux: "Power Cosmic Part I" was different from the rest of the album because the melody was on a cassette that Joe gave me. The big challenge with this one was that he told me he could never repeat it, with the sound he'd used. I took the cassette, cleaned it up a little, and just programmed some stuff around it for "Part I." For "Part II," we were working with a different challenge entirely, because the solo was three different parts that he played all at once: one Whammy up, one Whammy down, all going through Neve mic pres, and the guitar going directly distorted through a Neve mic pre. For the solo in "Part II," he played one solo, then another. By the time we got to solo number twenty-five, we wound up listening back to the first solo he'd laid down, and it was beautiful and wound up being the keeper take.

Throughout the recording of *Engines*, what we were doing was manipulating in the box all those guitars and whatever sounds we had. That was basically the cleanest path to be able to work with the sounds that Joe was giving me, going DI, or in the case of the amps, we'd go to the load box, into a mic pre, into the computer, and that would give me the cleanest path to basically go either to a synth—the Korg MS-20 or Minimoog—or into the computer to affect it even more with several plug-ins I had to completely change the sound. So that's why it was so important to have the sound as direct and pure as we could.

I was very happy with the album as we were finishing up. I felt we had really made something "new" and creative. But I knew once we took it out on the road to play for people around the world, a big transformation was going to have to happen. I had no intention of going out with a DJ or something like that, but I thought the album would serve as a springboard for doing something totally different with the songs live, which was eventually captured on *Live in San Francisco*. We did rock-band versions of the songs "Until We Say Goodbye," "Devil's Slide," and "Borg Sex," and they became "new" again, and were just fantastically fun to play in front of an audience.

Eric Caudieux: Once we hit the road, the transition to the live stage was really, really easy. What we had to decide was: Do we want to recreate the stuff we did in the studio, or do we want to play as a band? And once the decision was made that we wanted to play as a band, it was easy because everybody played their part and that's just about it. Obviously the bass played the bass line, and Jeff [Campitelli] had to figure out what the vibe of each song was, and since it was just one guitar, bass, piano/keyboards, and drums, we just played the parts that were needed naturally, so it was far easier than you might think or expect.

One I'll never, ever tire of is "Engines of Creation," because Joe stays—from a musical standpoint—basically on one note that still has so many different melodic and

> harmonic variations on that one drum-bass note. Also, if you listen to it, you go through the cycle, but there's never any conclusion to it, you just want it to go on and on and repeat itself. And every time it comes back, it makes you feel happy—you know it's coming back and you want it to—it grabs me. The music itself really, really grabs me. He plays those arpeggios over and over, and it doesn't resolve—that's what it is, I LOVE music that doesn't resolve!

When *Engines* finally came out, there were techno fans who started listening to me for the first time, with this record. When they went back and listened to *Surfing* or *Flying*, they'd go, "Ooh, what the hell is that? I like this *Engines of Creation* guy, whoever he is . . ." And it was very interesting. The same thing happened with the 1995 eponymous release—some people thought, "Finally, he's made something I can listen to," and others thought, "Hey, it's not *Surfing with the Alien* or *Flying in a Blue Dream* . . ." *The Extremist* did that to a certain degree as well, in that some people missed the drum machines from the earlier records, and others said, "Finally, a record of Joe's with real drums on it."

What I learned from *Engines* is the same thing I knew other artists had learned when they changed directions: You gain some new fans, you lose some old ones, and there's a dedicated core that appreciates how cool it is that you tried something they weren't expecting. An artist is not supposed to second-guess his or her audience. It really leads to disaster. Just do what you do. Be happy when they like it and move on when they don't.

CHAPTER 16 ★★

Strange Beautiful Music—2002

"This album is one of his best."

—UltimateGuitar.com

Strange Beautiful Music was the first record I made using Pro Tools at home. This allowed me to overcome specific problems I had with demos made on cassettes and laptops, or just writing things on paper. It was a creative renaissance for me. By demoing straight into the computer I could easily pull up and listen to every session I was working on for the record in a matter of seconds. This gave me a clearer understanding of where I was heading with my new music, and it was so much fun! On top of that, each performance could be a potential "keeper" track.

My producer, John Cuniberti, set me up with the Millennia Media Origin SST-1 mic pre, which included an optical compressor and a parametric EQ. This allowed me the flexibility to record keyboards and bass, along with direct guitar, and to reroute stuff that was done directly. If I wanted to use a real guitar amp, I would run it through a Palmer speaker simulator instead of a speaker cabinet, and sometimes I would run it through the Millennia for effect, too. Other times, I would just go directly into Pro Tools.

This may sound too technical for some, but for me it's exciting to share how much more flexibility Pro Tools gave me. I could finally record music all by myself and work without looking at the studio clock, thinking, "Damn, I have to move on to record the bass now." Or not being able to spend any more time on the guitar because the budget won't allow it. The biggest upside of recording at home without a schedule was that if I sat down to do a solo and was not into it, I could just put the guitar down and walk away.

On another level altogether, my home studio offered an important refuge from all the chaos going on in the music business at that time. I remember a lot of people were fired from Sony during the *Strange Beautiful Music* sessions, and being able to record whenever I wanted at home helped me focus just on the music itself. Not having to worry about a budget also let me be so much more creative in how I constructed each song.

I could sit in my studio and keep working on the music, go outside and mow the lawn, go to the market, for a run, or to the beach, then come back and work on the song some more. I could record it in the middle of the night, early in the morning, in the middle of the day; musicians could come by and listen, and I could make my own rough mixes. There was no time and money hanging over my head, and I think that allowed my creativity to be truly unchained.

While this approach made recording a lot more flexible and freed up money for other things, it also created challenges. My job in the studio was now to function as the record's producer and engineer as well as the artist. Before, the way it would have worked is I would sit there recording a melody, and maybe John would have said, "Okay, that's the best you got, Joe. We're done." Then we'd move on to the next song, never to return. Now I could literally record a million performances and never have to throw anything away.

Digital recording isn't just about making something perfect, though. It encourages spontaneity, which in turn can lead to capturing "once in a lifetime" performances, and it did so throughout *Strange Beautiful Music*. A great example of that process was "You Saved My Life." I was focusing on my wife and my son, thinking, "Where would I be without these loved ones in my life?" And from there, I was deeply inspired and started composing and tracking right there at home. The end result was an ensemble of guitars playing the melody with changing harmonies. I had never done anything like it before, but it perfectly represented the story I wanted to tell. Having the home studio setup allowed me to be creative on a new, deeper level.

Eric Caudieux explores early VR technology.
PHOTO BY JON LUINI

"Oriental Melody" is a song that has an interesting history. Back in the mid-nineties, I had a black-and-white Apple laptop that had a recording feature on it using its own microphone. I wasn't very computer savvy yet at that point, so I thought this feature was pretty unique! So back then, if I was in a hotel room without my recording gear and got an idea, I recorded it on the laptop. One day when I was working on modes, I played one I just loved, and I wondered why I hadn't written anything around it. So I came up with a riff and recorded just the riff by itself on that laptop. It was a small clip, just eleven seconds, but this little file followed me around with every new computer I had for the next six or seven years. I finally heard the clip years later and realized it used the Oriental scale, so I set about writing an entire song around that short piece of music and "Oriental Melody" was born.

John Cuniberti: *Strange Beautiful Music* was the first all-Pro Tools session I had done, and the first time Joe and I had made a record that was entirely in digital. I was faced as an engineer with how to manage twenty tracks of guitars once Joe brought them in. That, I think, was the challenge of this record, managing what he had recorded at home. Once Joe was ready to transition into the live studio, we set up at The Plant in Sausalito and structured the recording like the old days, where we would spend two weeks cutting drums and bass and rhythm guitars, and then Joe and I would spend another two or three weeks together doing whatever guitar overdubs he hadn't recorded at home that were still left to track.

John has always been perceptive enough to notice when I've written a song that's close to my heart. His approach would be, "What can I do to help enhance this creative experience?" When I'd bring in these unusual performances and tell him, "It may not be the guitar-through-an-amp with a Shure 57 on it in the big room that you want, but it is a performance I will never be able to reproduce," he would understand and respect that. That spirit was on every track of *SBM* and was part of what made it so different from the records we'd made together up to that point.

Matt Bissonette: When Joe called me up to come and play with him and Jeff Campitelli on this record, I of course said "Yes!" right away, and brought all my stuff up in my van from

L.A. The day before we started, I remember being in downtown San Francisco, and I had fifteen basses in my van, just loaded up, and I turned to get up to the Golden Gate Bridge and my transmission blew out! So I had to be towed over the bridge and buy a new car the day we started, and I just remember thinking, "You gotta be kidding me . . ."

Before that album, I'd never paired Jeff with Matt before, so I didn't know how it was going to turn out, but once they started jamming together, they discovered they both felt time very much in the same way, which was a great relief. They share a lot of the same influences, too. On *Strange Beautiful Music*, I gave them the freedom to improvise quite a bit, and that was very important to the feel of the record. I've always found that tapping into a player's creative nature is where all the good stuff is. A good example of that is "Oriental Melody," where, once again, starting out there were a lot of tracks I'd written and already recorded at home: the keyboards and all the guitars, I believe, and some pretty distorted, funky-sounding guitars. John, Jeff, and Matt really liked the song, though, and really made it shine with their unique ideas and live performances in the studio.

John Cuniberti: As well as this process was working overall for Joe, I remember we didn't know if we had the record until we mixed it. Back in the 24-track days, once you got done recording on a song, you could have a rough mix in front of you and everyone could go home with it for the night. Today, if we spent all day recording thirty or forty tracks of guitars on Pro Tools, the last thing any of us wanted to do was sit down and start weeding through all the performances just to get a rough mix. You might get a rough mix of something but not really even know what it was. When we were limited to four or five guitar tracks, at the end of the session we could go, "Let's just use tracks thirteen and fifteen." By contrast, if you have ten guitar tracks, which two do you want to use? How representative will this be of the final product? It really did create in its own way a whole host of new problems, but I know it gave Joe a lot of benefits as well, having the time to create performances he was really happy with when he brought them in for the band to work on.

Listening back through the songs during mixing, I realized that each represented a special moment in my life. "Starry Night," "What Breaks a Heart," "Mind Storm," "Sleepwalk" with Robert Fripp—*all songs very close to my heart.* I was also thrilled with songs like "Hill Groove," which had a fresh, funky attitude. It was also the first time I had used a MIDI–guitar interface to record the "organ" performance. It sounds like a funky guy on a B3, but it's really me improvising on guitar plugged into a Roland MIDI controller with an organ patch dialed up.

John Cuniberti: I enjoyed making that record partially because of the fact that Joe had a new air of confidence about him—he was more philosophical in his approach to recording. At that point in his career, it seemed like it was more about expression and having fun, and didn't take on the importance that his earlier records seemed to have. During the earlier records, he was really trying to establish himself, build a career, pay his bills, not be rejected by the music community, and by the time we got around to doing this record, he was a rock star. So it was more fun, it was more relaxed, and I really enjoyed making the record as a result. I think Joe was very happy with the album when we were done—it was very different, very powerful, and I think it was a smart move to make the album he did.

CHAPTER 17 ★★

Is There Love in Space?—2004

> *"One need not know a thing about guitar to appreciate the man's sense of melody, and that's really his biggest gift. He may possess flying fingers of gold, but what grabs most ears is the deft way he handles moving songs forward without vocal accompaniment."*
>
> —BlogCritics.org

Before reuniting with John Cuniberti, Matt Bissonette, and Jeff Campitelli to record *Is There Love in Space?*, I started recording the new songs at Studio 21, my home studio, trying once again to break my own style down and rebuild it into something new. I was deeper into Pro Tools now and having much more success and fun with it. The new record would feature quite a bit of compositional variety, with lyrical-sounding melodies and more angular-sounding solos—and two vocal tracks!

At Studio 21, I was using a Korg Triton DAW keyboard, Universal Audio 1176 and LA-2A compressor/limiters, an Empirical Labs EL8S, old API EQs, the Millennia Media STT-1 mic pre, and Palmer speaker simulators. For guitar amps I had an interesting collection: Soldano, Mesa Boogie, Cornford, Vox, Wells, and several vintage Marshalls. Added to that group was my new Peavey JSX prototype head. Everything just started to sound better!

I was getting into pairing differently tuned or stringed guitars together and creating arrangements that featured the unique nature of those pairings. "Up in Flames," for instance, was a six-string JS1000 with a drop-D tuning, into a Cornford/JS prototype amp, pretty raw and in your face sounding. "Hands in the Air" was a couple of seven-string guitars paired with twelve-string electrics and some slide guitar. "The Souls of Distortion" and "Searching" were also seven-string-based songs.

With "Souls of Distortion" I wanted to see if I could create a song where the distortion *itself* had a life of its own. I was trying to imagine a piece of music that when played on piano would sound beautifully simple, but when played on seven-string guitars and plugged into distorted amps would have its sonic message become more mysterious and compelling because of the complex nature of the distortion itself.

The title track was inspired by a painting that my son, ZZ, had done of what looked like an alien staring straight at you. It was hanging in my studio and I would look at it every time I sat at my keyboard. One day, I was wondering if the concept of love that we know so well here on Earth is recognized elsewhere in the universe. So I looked at ZZ's alien drawing and wondered how I would describe love to an alien who had no concept of the emotion.

"Bamboo" was a song I recorded primarily by myself at home, although the idea for the song had first come to me years earlier on the road. I wrote the body of the song while on the *Flying in a Blue Dream* tour. I was really into doing those two-handed tapping pieces at the time, but the piece never really went anywhere. Years later, I'd come up with this other two-handed tapped arpeggio technique, which you hear as little flourishes in the beginning of the song, but at the time I didn't know what to do with that either. Finally, during the making of this album, I was inspired to take those two elements, put them together, and create a song around them. That included enlisting ZZ one afternoon to use a violin bow on a five-string bass to record the bridge section's big bass tones. The only thing I didn't record at home was that really strange/beautiful octave-jumping chorus melody. That was done live in the studio using a '64 Fender Bassman amp with my JS1000 going through a Whammy pedal.

The song still needed the right ending. One morning, when Jeff Campitelli had just come into the studio, I said, "Just go out there and be funky." So next thing you know, he gave us this slinky, funky performance that brought the whole song together and gave it a proper ending, too. After that, we added a backward guitar solo I had recorded at home, and it all just grooved together beautifully. It was the perfect last song for the record.

At the start of the album, I knew I wanted to sing on "I Like the Rain." Lyrically, this song was inspired by Billy Gibbons of ZZ Top. I imagined myself playing a character who likes what everybody else doesn't. Billy has changed the way people view the composition of rock music. ZZ Top is an institution, its own genre, and Billy's playing style is likewise unique. He's really elevated the art of blues-rock songwriting. No one really comes close. When Jimi Hendrix heard Billy Gibbons back in the day, he said Billy was "the future of music." He got that right!

Every time I bring a vocal song into the studio, there's always the chance that it's just not going to work. I need some sort of trick to get me in the mood, so I sang "I Like the Rain" with a sense of humor, and in character, as I did on "Big Bad Moon." One afternoon my tech, Mike Manning, was pulling up to the studio on his Harley, and I thought how great it'd be to record Mike on his bike for the start of the song. We had him ride up to the side door of The Plant and stuck some microphones out there. He started up the bike, revved it up, and pulled away. That's what you hear at the start of the song. No samples used there!

"Lifestyle," the other vocal track on the record, goes back to '85 for me. I recorded a demo of the song at Jeff Holt's Likewise Productions with the idea of "placing" it. Specifically, I thought it would be a great song for Steve Miller. It featured me singing in harmony, imitating Steve's cool way of triple tracking himself, and a crazy, vibrato-bar, multitrack riff that was the song's instrumental hook. I never did get it to Steve, but I always thought it was worth a second look. As I write this I'm thinking, "I wonder if Steve would consider doing a version of this now?"

Jeff Campitelli and his drums, The Plant, '03
PHOTO BY JON LUINI

I thought that as an engineer, John would appreciate the creative approach to this album. He liked the variety of stuff I would bring in, such as something live like "Searching" followed by something unusual like "Bamboo." I think he liked the outrageous nature of some of the songs and was really up to trying to capture me getting more and more creative. I knew this was a project he would really enjoy sonically as well. Like all engineers, he would have preferred it if I did everything in the studio, with him in control, but by this point in time most engineers were used to artists bringing in projects where half of the album or more was already recorded. That's just where the world was going.

John Cuniberti: At heart, I wanted to do a live analog record. Instead we ended up doing the record in digital because by this point, Joe was doing a lot of recording himself at home on Pro Tools. This was a new process. On our first day of recording, Joe walked through the front door with a hard drive filled with hundreds of guitar parts! *Is There Love in Space?* was recorded in digital, but I decided to go retro on Joe for the song "Searching." To try to keep the live vibe going with the band, I rented a 16-track head stack for a Studer 2-inch tape recorder, and we recorded analog. I told them I didn't need more than 16 tracks to record the three of them. Since this was live, I allowed a couple of overdubs. I wanted Joe, Jeff, and Matt to go out there, practice this song, and then I'd record it, and we'd just keep recording it till we had something really wonderful. And that's what happened. My hands were full just handling the engineering chores and making sure everything was recorded properly. Joe, as a producer, was really guiding Matt and Jeff through the process of getting good takes. When we were done recording the album, Joe decided to bring in Mike Fraser to mix it. There was a trend at that time for records to be recorded by one guy and mixed by another guy. Mike did a perfectly fine job mixing this record.

When principal tracking was over, we decided to bring in Mike Fraser to mix the album. We had a feeling that Mike would add a big, round quality to the sound, along with some new ideas. John and I had talked about bringing in a mix engineer for just about every other record we'd ever done, but we'd avoided it because we didn't want other people to "screw up" our records. Sometimes, though, you want what another mix engineer might add to a project. Such was the case with this record.

Mike mixed that album at The Plant, in the same room we recorded it in. When it was finished, John and Mike together produced a really beautiful-sounding album for me.

Mike Fraser: John and I got along great, and I don't think on either side of us there's ever any jealousy or competition or anything like that. Joe will do a record with me, then a record or two with John, then be back working with me again. It's whatever personality is going to help him create what he's looking for on that specific project.

With some songs, it's very difficult to unlock their secrets in the studio, while with others it's like an unlocked door opening up into a whole new world. "Searching" was one of those "whole new world" experiences for us. I had never before presented an opportunity to the band like that: go in with a song in mind, show it to the band, improvise the arrangement on the fly, and record it as a trio, live to 2-inch tape. They all wanted eight more songs like that! I liked the way the material on *Is There Love in Space?* was balanced. It was similar to Hendrix's *Electric Ladyland*, where you had some songs that were meticulously worked out, and then you had others that were obviously jams in the studio. I like that kind of variety on a record. From "Gnaahh" to "Lifestyle" to "If I Could Fly" to "Searching" to "Bamboo," we achieved a creative mix of songwriting, recording techniques, and performances that gave the record its own unique balance.

Matt Bissonette and his bass, The Plant, '03
PHOTO BY JON LUINI

A while after the album's release, it gained new notice because it contained the song "If I Could Fly." I had started writing that song on 1990's *Flying* tour, and it had taken me over ten years to finish it! I felt it was the most lyrical-sounding message of love I had ever written up to that point. The recording captured an innocence, too, an honest, straight-from-the-heart quality. The song also achieved quite a bit of attention for an unintended reason, about which I can only say, "No comment." It remains a fan favorite and always brings a smile to my face when I hear it.

CHAPTER 18 ★★

Super Colossal—2006

> *"Some of the most technically accomplished guitar music ever written."*
>
> —*BBC News*

When I'm writing for a new record, I write freely without my inner critic getting in the way. For instance, I don't start writing a slow song, then stop myself and say, "This should be an up-tempo number like 'Summer Song.'" I just write until I'm finished with a piece and then I start writing another one. So I keep an artist's point of view right to the end. There's usually a month or two where I know that I've got some kind of a deadline to demo up. That's when I gather together all the new song ideas on little scraps of paper written in hotel rooms, tour buses, backstage, and all around the house. I put those together with the full songs I've written in manuscript, on Pro Tools, on my laptop, or on my phone. I usually take between forty and fifty songs into this review period. Then I decide which songs I'm going to pursue and which I'll save for a future record. I usually end up with twelve to sixteen cuts that I think will be fun, challenging, cohesive, and interesting to work on.

Once I have those tracks, I look to see if there's a trend that ties certain songs together. Early on I realized that "A Cool New Way," "One Robot's Dream," "The Meaning of Love," and "Made of Tears" were a group that could be tied together, almost like their own separate chapter. I approached drummer Simon Phillips with an idea: "I'll send you four tracks, sans drums, and you record yourself at your own studio playing whatever you feel like playing." It turned out great. He gave me memorable performances that swung and grooved just like they needed to, and his recording technique was very hip, too. The rest of the album's tracks would feature Jeff Campitelli's drumming, which we recorded up at Armoury Studios in Vancouver, British Columbia.

Once I had written the title track, it gave me a direction for the album as a whole. I felt like this album's cornerstone was going to be this daydream about a 100-foot-tall guitar player. The song hinged on a simple riff turned gigantic by way of an Electro-Harmonix POG pedal. I ordered it online from Musictoyz.com, got it in two days, opened the box, plugged it in, and wrote "Super Colossal" in about ten minutes! Sometimes it's just that easy and fun.

Writing music for the record, I was getting really excited about using my JS1200, too. It has such a unique sound to it, and there's a lot of it on the album. We had just put in this new DiMarzio PAF Joe pickup in the neck position, and as for the guitar itself, I could swear that the sound on it was different just based on the candy-apple-red paint job it had! I was really getting into the sound of using the neck pickup and was also getting a good DI sound with Pro Tools. By this time I was using a "real" HD Pro Tools rig, which was a big improvement from my earlier home studio setups. I also had the Marshall SE100 speaker simulator, which improved the signal path from my amp to Pro Tools as well.

I had a better, more balanced-sounding environment now, so when it came, for instance, to recording "Made of Tears," it inspired me to play harmonics on two electric twelve-strings with delays paired with a bass guitar to create a new atmosphere for my melodies. The tone of the album's songs, like the title track or "Redshift Riders"—where there have to be about eight guitars—was really *big*, but the clarity in my studio allowed me to stack those things up and still get a really powerful sound. So when I brought those tracks up to Mike Fraser in Vancouver, it was easy for him to incorporate live drums and make the guitar, bass, and synth tracks all work together.

Mike's strength, aside from his being completely unflappable, is that he can be creative and bring all his technical knowledge into play no matter where or when you bring him into a project. It could be something where he's involved from the ground up, like *Chickenfoot III*, or something that's halfway finished, like *Super Colossal*. Nothing fazes him. He always excels!

Mike Fraser: When Joe and I record, there's not too many outsiders. There may be a weekend where some of his friends come through with his wife to say hi, but they're brief moments. He's pretty focused in the studio. If somebody else is in doing keyboard overdubs or something like that, Joe will be sitting on the back couch doing his email or whatever, but he's always kind of got an ear to what's going on. He'll give his opinion, so he's always involved. Even when his parts are done, he doesn't leave: he's there the whole time. He oversees the production from A to Z.

Joe was always in the control room for his overdubs and solos, but for rhythm tracks Joe's out with the band because there's a lot more energy and more of an eye contact thing that you just can't get with him in the control room—especially for endings and stops. It's hard to do that without looking at each other. We put him off in a little booth out on the floor, because with the drums, you really have to crank your earphones up to hear anything. So he'll sometimes stand in a little iso-booth area, which at least cuts down on the thunder of the drums, and he can keep his headphones down a little quieter. That said, recording Joe is pretty much the same every time: set it up and turn it up!

The kind of songs I was putting on this album were a huge leap forward for me artistically, so making *Super Colossal* was great fun! With "A Cool New Way" specifically, I thought that song was aptly titled because it was a new side of me that I'd never really showed people. The pacing of the song was much longer and more spread out than other pieces of music I'd done on previous albums. It had this structure that was just so open and groove oriented, while on the melodic side, there were these different melodies on top of repeating chord structures that traded off until the song's chorus. Then there was the use of the harmonies and the unisons, which were quite different than what I'd done before. There's also a jazz and R&B element at play there, too. I love that song and I love playing it live. It's very cathartic playing that piece of music live because I'm going all the way back to my bebop lessons with Lennie Tristano and just pulling out music that I heard from my childhood when I was listening to my parents' jazz records.

My home studio during preproduction in '05
PHOTO BY JOE SATRIANI

"Redshift Riders" was another song that I had so much fun recording. The idea of it came from my thinking about the property of *redshift*. As I understand it, around large, celestial bodies, there's a warping of space-time because of their gravitational force. From that I came up with my own theory that perhaps people traveling through space, with technology we don't yet have, would be able to use this warping of space-time as a kind of slingshot to travel faster and farther. I envisioned that maybe as part of my sci-fi daydream there would be a select few space travelers who had figured this out. My questions were, "What would their adventures be?" and "How do I represent vast distances and warping of time and space musically?"

When it came time to compose the melody, I knew that I needed to use large spaces between the notes, big intervals to create that feeling of open space and that slingshot effect I imagined.

Mike Fraser: Joe's game for all styles and he's quite eager to try new things. Even though he's in a genre and you can tell it's Joe Satriani right away, he works pretty hard at trying to switch up melodies, do different tones and different effect-y things on his guitars to make each song more interesting, and "Redshift Riders" was a great example of that off of *SC*. Usually when we're in the studio, we have three or four guitar setups, and once we're finished with drums and everything, you gain a lot of your board back and can use those channels. Among our guitar setups, we had one really loud, rocky setup, one that was sort of a melody-type setup, and a solo sound, and then we'd have cleaner, smaller amp guitar setups. It's probably about a day's process for each song to lay some of the overdub guitars down, and maybe even at the end of that day you may or may not have a solo yet.

"It's So Good" is a great example of one of those songs where the experience in my studio was so wonderful compared to previous records. That's got to be the most gorgeous-sounding recording on the album. How Mike Fraser mixed it is amazing and how Jeff played on it was just beyond my expectations. It's not flashy like "Satch Boogie" and there's nothing on there that would make a list of the top twenty most outrageous guitar performances, but it feels like a huge step over that hurdle that separates guitar-nerd music from the music that everybody else in the world listens to. When that song comes on, I feel like everybody can enjoy this, because it's not bogged down by guitar-centric ideas and agendas. Everything about that song sounded perfect. The clean guitar sounds were so beautiful, and I can't remember a bass sound I've liked more on any track I've ever done. I feel the same way about "Just Like Lightnin'," which has got one of Jeff Campitelli's biggest and fattest grooves.

For many years I've tried doing a call-and-response thing with the audience, but the problem seemed to be that they weren't comfortable improvising. I set out to solve this dilemma with the song "Crowd Chant." Whether you're in Spain, India, Sweden, or the U.S.A., audiences like to participate in the show and sing along with whatever you might ask them to. Sometimes, though, you get a lot of empty, blank-looking faces, or people just randomly yelling. The problem, as I saw it, was that these fans didn't know *what* to sing. I thought if they knew what they were supposed to sing ahead of time, maybe they would really want to participate. I wanted to put a call-and-response song on an album that wasn't a "live" recording from a show, but asked myself, "Could I really do that? Is that too cheesy?" I decided to try and see.

When I sat down to do it, I combined the elements of an opening riff, a few call-and-response sections, and a deep, melodic section. I'd been playing with the "Pavane" piece written in 1887 by Gabriel Fauré for a few years, and while I'd already written another song around it, I thought this would be a good counterpoint. My idea was to have a very simple, blues-rock call-and-response thing with a big, heavy riff and then shift to this classical piece in the middle, and you could have people sing this beautiful melody at the end. I imagined it would be like a great juxtaposition of music all behind a big, concert pulse that Jeff was going to provide.

Next, I mapped out the song in sections, and then recorded the main riff. I then recorded between twenty and thirty "calls," then sat back and listened through them all, asking, "If I was in the audience, what would be fun for me to 'respond' to? Which lick has too many notes? Which lick is too simple? Which are the most inspiring licks?" From there I picked what I thought were the winners, and then arranged them until I got to what I thought was an uplifting and powerful song. This is an example of a song that took a lot of listening back to in different environments, because I kept thinking the song would be unconvincing if it was arranged the wrong way. And I also thought, "If I don't put some humor in there to balance out the seriousness of the Fauré classical piece, the audience may not get it."

When I showed the song to Mike, I said, "I've got this unusual song—here's what it sounds like with a drum machine, here are all the keyboards and all the guitars, now how are we going to get a group of people in a studio to sound like an arena full of people chanting?"

Mike Fraser: I don't think either of us knew if it was going to work until the night we recorded it. That one was a standout and one of the things coming in that Joe really wanted to establish on this record, so that when he played it live, the crowd would sing along. First we had to authentically pull that off on record in the studio. For the big call and response, I called up a bunch of singer friends of mine, and we all had a good night at the studio there to track that. I used 87s for that song to record the crowd.

I still didn't know if it was going to work until we were there that night. After recording the singers on ten consecutive passes, Mike heard the playback and said, "It's too big. We don't even need half of what we recorded." When we sat back and listened to it, we realized this was going to work. It wasn't corny. It was really powerful. It's such an important part of my live performances now, because we put it on the record *first*. The whole concept of it worked, and Mike brought it to a higher level, higher than I ever thought it could go.

Mike Fraser at Armoury Studios, Vancouver, '05
PHOTO BY RONN DUNNETT

You can tell if an album really makes a difference when, years later, any songs from it *always* have to be on the set list. "Flying in a Blue Dream," which was never picked to be a single, wound up being a song we *have* to do live. The audience decides for you what songs get played from an album long after it's released. "Crowd Chant" was a song I wrote specifically with a live audience in mind, and the audience has thankfully decided it's a track we *have* to play. Now, every time we play somewhere, we've always got one song where everybody in the audience knows exactly what to do.

CHAPTER 19 ★★

Professor Satchafunkilus and the Musterion of Rock—2008

> *"Satriani shines in his ability to hold back and write tasteful verse/chorus songs with memorable hooks. Like the majority of his songs in his ever growing catalog, most of these are technically impressive numbers that never go overboard with the showboating and rely on a sense of feeling rather than virtuoso technique."*
>
> —MTV/AllMusicGuide.com

For many years I've owned a beautiful-sounding Petrof upright piano made in the Czech Republic, and it's been very good to me. Whenever I sit down early in the morning and start playing, a song comes out. One day, I sat down and wrote an intriguing chord sequence and quickly jotted it down on a piece of paper with the title "It's a Mystery." That word *mystery* kept haunting me, so I looked up the word's etymology online. The word *musterion* came up, which led me to a very interesting story about the Apostle Paul traveling to Greece to spread the word of his Messiah, Jesus. According to the story, Paul took the Greek word *musterion*, which actually had a negative connotation to it, and flipped it around to suit his purposes. He would tell prospective followers, "You can't understand these stories I'm telling you now because you've not yet received the *musterion*. Once you've received the *musterion*, then the secret of God's message will be revealed to you." When the English translation for the King James Bible was done, the translators had no word for *musterion*, so they translated it as *mystery*.

Top row: Mike Manning, Jeff Campitelli, Eric Caudieux, Matt Bissonette, and Mike Boden. Bottom row: Me and John Cuniberti. The Plant, '07.

PHOTO BY JON LUINI

Today we say, "The mystery of faith," but that's completely misconstruing what Paul's original message was. Having grown up Roman Catholic, I thought the story was outrageous. How come I never learned this in Catholic school? But what really interested me was how a word could be so powerful. I knew then that I wanted to use the phrase "Musterion of Rock" in the next album title and, in a humorous way, suggest that you have to receive a musician's "musterion" to be able to hear the real message behind their music. I was also toying with the idea of using "Professor Satchafunkilus" as the title, but in the end found the two titles together were better than either one alone.

I saw *Professor Satchafunkilus and the Musterion of Rock* as an opportunity to try different things. Some of that had to do with performing in different parts of the world on tour. For instance, we wound up in Istanbul for four days and our promoters were so kind as to guide us through the city, showing us the best of what it had to offer. One of the promoters gave me some Âşık Veysel records because he had a feeling I'd love his music. I'd never heard of him, but when I played those CDs back home, I remember thinking how beautiful this music was. It's folk music from the Turkish countryside sung in the old Anatolian language. I didn't know what the words meant, but that freed me up to just associate with the songs in a more musical way. I came up with a story imagining that Veysel would have traveled to Spain at some point and would have been influenced by Andalusian music as well as some heavy rock, too. I tried to keep it in the harmonic framework that his music often centers on, the Dorian mode. The guitar performance on the album was recorded in one take at my home studio. Jeff and Matt improvised around it later on when we got together at The Plant studios.

For "I Just Wanna Rock," I got an idea about a robot that starts to gain consciousness, goes out for a walk, and comes across a small rock concert happening in a park. The robot asks people at the show what their purpose is because he literally doesn't understand what's happening. Everyone in the audience tells the robot, "I just wanna rock." As he learns more about the process, he finally sings, "I wanna learn how to rock with you," but his voice changes from his distorted robot voice to one with a more humanlike quality. I know that sounds crazy, but it's just how I think about these things when I'm writing!

I recorded the vocals using an old 57 microphone I had at home that I put through Low-Fi, Sci-Fi, and SansAmp plug-ins. I recorded myself maybe three times and stacked the vocals so it would sound tight. When I brought it into the studio, the plan was to record it with better equipment so it would sound *better*. I spent about an hour in front of a great microphone doing the same thing I'd done at home, but we could not get it to sound anywhere near as good, so we went with the takes I'd recorded at home.

I originally wrote "Out of the Sunrise" years earlier for the *Crystal Planet* record. It started out on a piece of paper because I didn't demo anything when I wrote for that album. I hadn't written enough of it, but I remember just loving the whole vibe of the piece. It was about trying to capture that moment when you stay up all night and watch the sunrise. Very often it's a cathartic experience where you gain some sort of insight about who you are and your life in general.

"Professor Satchafunkilus" came about while I was driving ZZ to a friend's house. We were listening to the hip-hop artist Mos Def when ZZ said, "You should try doing something like this sometime." From there, we started talking about how interesting it is that some artists like Mos Def have this cool feel that just sounds so musical, even outside of the lyrical message that he's giving. We talked about how different the song would be if you removed that special personality from the track—it wouldn't really hold up. From there the conversation turned into "How would I, as a guitar instrumentalist, approach this style of song and add some compositional weight to replace that special personality?" In that scenario, you wouldn't have lyrics or the attitude and message of the rapper. So the idea started from a brief conversation as we were driving in the car, listening, and having a good time, but it made a big impression on me, because I immediately drove home after I dropped ZZ off and started to record what became "Professor Satchafunkilus."

I'd already recorded most of "Professor Satchafunkilus" by the time ZZ got home later that evening. I played some of it for him and then suggested, "I think you should play sax on this." He was just learning how to play the instrument with the high school jazz band, so one night after he finished his homework, I set up a mic in my studio and said, "Just play some random riffs for me, whatever you want, and keep it in this particular kind of a key, and then I'm going to fly it in later." So he just started blowing some licks. I wound up using one or two and placed them at the beginning of the song and put some delays on it, and I had him do it again later in the song. Then he gave me a long, foghorn kind of a tone for the breakdown section. He's so used to me making music every day that there's no ceremony around making music at home. He just walked over from his skate ramps, through the door into my studio, picked up his sax, and played.

After I got ZZ on there, it was interesting because the song itself had a long jam at the end with this electric piano part, and I remember thinking, "Oh, it would be great to have this long improvisation at the end where more of the 'familiar' Joe starts to come out." Then we worked on it for an hour or so, and although I put down a bunch of solos, I remember just not liking it and decided to edit it out of the song entirely. We just cut the whole third solo section out, and suddenly the song really didn't have a solo at all. Instead, it ended with ZZ playing a few riffs, and when he heard it, John thought, "Wow, that's really weird. He's got to have a guitar solo in it 'cause it's Joe," but I was thinking, "No, this is really what Professor Satchafunkilus would do, because he's already made his statement. His statement is the entire funky-guitar ensemble throughout the song—he doesn't need a solo!"

Matt Bissonette: It seems natural that ZZ would be playing on Joe's albums, and making albums with Joe was really becoming a family affair by this point. We got closer and closer after another record and another tour, and all the drama that comes with the road, and becoming closer friends through dealing together with all the good and bad of that kind of life. So you just kind of realize that you've become a friend where you know somebody's personality, the good side and bad side, and know what to do. With certain people I've played on records with over the years as a hired gun, you don't really get to know that side of them, but with Joe, as time went on, I kind of knew what he was going after and what was going to work and what wasn't going to work on a record.

John Cuniberti: Shortly after the *Strange Beautiful Music* album, the whole atmosphere started changing. Joe started recording more stuff at home and using less and less studio time, which dramatically cut down on his overhead. I would say it was 75 percent for artistic reasons, but if he records 50 percent of his guitars at home, he's probably saved $20,000. For that kind of money, you can buy some pretty sweet gear, versus coming to the studio and paying a thousand dollars a day. We'd had discussions even before then about how he could take the $20,000 we'd need to record those guitars and go buy three great mic preamps and some EQs, and then sit at home working for a month on the parts, or as long as he needed. When he started to make that Pro Tools transition, it was kind of a no-brainer for him.

I had a guy come in and tune his room with an equalizer to get it more sonically together. In reorienting him in his room, we redid the acoustics of the room and I had the room retuned for him, which was probably the biggest change we made because acoustically, one of the problems in his project room was, first, it wasn't a big room to begin with. He had a lot of gear in there, of course, and he had his platinum and gold records hanging on the walls, photographs, all these highly reflective surfaces. Joe was never really happy with the way the room sounded, and I told him, "We have to really get this room acoustically better, because you're never going to get it right with all these reflective surfaces."

He asked me to come up with a plan, so I went in and measured the room and came up with a solution for both absorption and reflective types of treatments. We put bass traps into all the corners, and we took down all the reflective surfaces. There was a large window on one side that we covered, and because the room is a rectangle, I changed his orientation so the length of the room was to his back now, and put him one-third of the way into the room—which mathematically is what you're supposed to do for the best acoustics.

When an artist goes into the studio, everything is about time and money. The musicians you hired need direction right then and there, because if you have a band, they want to know what to play. Every hour you're there is more than what seems logical, and every day when you walk out of the studio, you know you've just spent thousands of dollars. You wonder if you got anything that you're actually going to use. Now, things have gotten to the point where you can tweak a room in your home so that it sounds almost as good as an actual recording studio.

Right before I started the project, I had a local engineer, Leff Lefferts from Cutting Edge Audio Group, come in and tell me what upgrades I needed to make. He's worked at The Plant, and currently works at Skywalker Sound as a sound designer for Lucasfilm, so he knows his stuff. When Pro Tools made the leap into HD, I changed my system. I also had my studio tweaked by Manny LaCarrubba from Sausalito Audio, who analyzed the room's sound with computer programs and then adjusted it and made suggestions. I was still using my Genelec speakers, which are highly detailed and polished sounding. They're the opposite of, let's say, NS10s, which throw out a lot of midrange.

I was using an old Marshall SE100 as my main speaker simulator, which meant I was going guitar into amplifier into Marshall SE100 into Pro Tools directly, or through the STT-1 if I wanted to shape it with some EQ or optical compressor. Additionally, the SE100 has some really clever ways of simulating a microphone being right at the cone, at a slight angle, or at a big angle. I like using the 30- and 60-degree angles—off axis, they call it—and it worked pretty well. It really does sound like an amp being miked up by a 57, so that setup worked in my room. As far as guitars, I was using the Ibanez JS1200 and the JS1000 most of the time. What mattered more than the equipment by that point was that another two years had gone by where I continued getting more proficient at recording with Pro Tools in general.

John Cuniberti: Joe's become such a competent sound engineer in his own right that there's a lot less pressure on him during recording. When I go over to Joe's studio and see how he's got his system hooked up, it's an interesting way of doing it because he's not coming from a technical background. He's more experimental with the way he goes about it. He can walk into the studio with performances that have been edited and feel and sound the way he envisioned them. Back when the studio clock was running, we could go two or three days and not get a guitar performance and/or sound that he was really happy with. So he's eliminated all that by doing it at home, and he's feeling more comfortable and confident about his parts. There's not this anxiety about it, because the problem was that if he wasn't playing something the way he believed it should be played, the band would be playing to that subpar performance. Then if Joe decided to throw his parts out, what the other guys played with him had to be scrapped, too. So whenever we're making a record, he's kind of splitting roles, and it's got to be tough producing your own instrumental guitar record, because that's a ridiculous amount of pressure that I personally wouldn't want to have.

When you're producing, you've got to make some decisions ahead of time just to try to get things done, but when you're out there with your instrument strapped on, you just feel like it's more natural to change direction based on what you feel in your gut is the right thing to do at the time.

Matt Bissonette: Joe does a lot of the legwork, and like any great producer has always been remarkably composed and relaxed under the circumstances. As we recorded *Professor Satch* live in the studio, I remember there was more time spent screwing around because we were getting the work done faster. It takes the pressure off when you're on a budget to know the songs are in the bag, and he got more relaxed and was not so much stressing about the little stuff, and just kind of grew like everybody grows, and knew what to sweat and what not to sweat. So toward the end, Jeff and I were just dying laughing half the time about whatever the situation was, and it was just really relaxed. That said, Joe throughout the years has always definitely known what he wants, and he's got no qualms about telling you if something isn't working. As a producer he'll let you know, and that's his job.

The lines Matt creates between chord changes are just very unique. He's a great bass player for all the obvious reasons, but I think the particular thing that always struck me as very unique to Matt Bissonette is his actual creativity in writing connective bass lines. He won't necessarily look at a chord and then put notes in between. That would be your average bass player's approach. Instead, Matt will somehow look to the third, the fourth, the sixth chord down the line, and he'll make a determination as to what is the real important landing point. Then he'll create a bass line that arcs over a few chords and lands on one you weren't expecting. He continually surprises me as a player.

John Cuniberti: The kind of music Joe wants to make is highly technical yet has to have a feeling and soul to it. How do you put soul into something so technical? He's been able to walk that fine line. When Joe's working with a band, he wants to know what each of these guys is going to do to make this a better record.

A good example of that interplay was the recording of "Andalusia," where the acoustic rhythm guitars that begin and go all the way through the song were recorded at home via DI. The solo at the beginning was played on a Sexauer Pernambuco acoustic guitar, and was recorded at The Plant. The song's electric solo required an unusual approach—I already had "Asik Veysel," which was a first take of this total compositional solo kind of thing, and then when I got to "Andalusia," I thought, "Well, okay, this is similar in the way that it's another long song that's got another long solo in it, so I need to come up with a different way of doing it." The guys had a demo solo that they were listening to while tracking that gave them the idea of the arc of the piece, how long it would last, and the intensity of it. Then I had an idea.

When I got to the studio one morning around 11 A.M., John was already there with assistant Mike Boden and editor Eric Caudieux, and I said, "Here's my plan: I want to record ten solos. However, the song is seven minutes long, so if you think about it, to do ten solos and tune up in between each one, we're talking an hour and a half of constant playing." So then I suggested, "I'm going to play these ten solos in a row and then I'm going to leave for a few hours. You guys listen to the solos, and if you hear one you like or want to 'comp' a few of them together, you can do that. Just don't tell me what you did."

So I just went crazy, ten solos: BAM, BAM, BAM, BAM, tuning up in between takes, and when I finished, my left hand and arm felt like they were going to fall off! So I left for a couple hours and when I got back, they were all looking at me funny, like, "Oh, you're going to love this." So they played me the whole solo, and I thought, "That is really great," but I literally did NOT remember what I'd played. So it almost sounded like someone else had played it, some other "Joe." I just knew that I went in there and sort of went crazy ten times in a row. I think they may have comped the solo, but I can't really tell you what bits from which takes they took. In the end, though, it was a successful experiment in producing myself, and we got a very emotional and powerful solo out of it.

I've never recorded acoustic guitars with microphones at home—I'm always plugged in. There's a lot of extraneous noise at home: phones, dogs, street noise, and the risk that somebody could walk in right as you're playing your best stuff. Also, to use a mic at home is pointless because I can't hear the sound the way my producer, John, can hear it while standing right in front of me. That's the way you need to be miked, by someone who's standing in front of you, not someone who's leaning over the guitar. Another thing we did differently with this record compared with past band-oriented records was mix the entire record "in the box," not using the studio console.

John Cuniberti: The beauty of my home setup by that point was that when Joe called me and said something like, "Hey, can you bring my solo on 'Out of the Sunrise' down a dB?," I could do that for him in ten minutes. Then I could send him back that mix within an hour for him to approve. By contrast, if he'd wanted to do that on a console, I would have had to call The Plant, book a session, be sure that everything was thoroughly documented—all the outboard gear in the room, all the patch points, all the cabling—recall everything in the console, which would take me and the assistant engineer probably an hour to do. Then once we got the mix up, we'd need to compare it to the first mix, then continually work on it until we'd gotten it as close as we could to the original, but in truth, it's never going to be exactly the same. Only then could I make the change for him. Not only is that a pain, but it costs $2,000. Joe loved this new immediacy, being able to just pick up the phone, and so mixing the whole record here at home for him was an easy sell. When he came to my studio and sat down with me on my system, we were doing just fine-tuning. It was fairly painless and effortless.

Songs like "Asik Veysel," "Andalusia," "Revelation," "I Just Wanna Rock," and "Musterion" all felt fresh to me in terms of how they came together, but there's one song that brought out the composer nerd in me. The chorus in "Ghosts," which wound up being a digital-exclusive bonus track, was a series of minor keys strung out in a particular order I'd never heard used before. I came up with a melody that used two whole-tone scales over these two minor keys. When I was writing it, I was so excited about how they worked together. It was one of those moments when I was so intrigued by the compositional architecture of it, and later on I couldn't believe no one had picked up on it. It was definitely one of those times when you're reminded that the rest of the world does not hear music like you do. Ultimately, the kind of feeling I get when I'm working on a new record is one I love: I just want everybody to hear it because it's a new version of my creativity.

CHAPTER 20 ★★

Chickenfoot I—2009

> *"Satriani, rock's leading instrumentalist and hero of a thousand guitar magazine covers, has joined forces with rock's most irrepressible front man and his monumental rhythm section."*
>
> —*San Francisco Chronicle*

I was just getting ready to master *Professor Satchafunkilus* when I got a call from Sammy Hagar inviting me to Las Vegas for a celebrity jam with Chad Smith and Michael Anthony. I didn't know Sammy that well, but it seemed like a fun thing to do. As it turned out, the twenty minutes we played together was so much fun, we decided to become a band!

Sammy Hagar: I'm okay with the "supergroup" label, because we are: We're super players. We're superstars in our own right who got together, but we didn't do it for the supergroup reason. We did it for all the RIGHT reasons. We're doing it because we want to play this kind of music together and with no fame-and-fortune business attached. We just wanted to do it and it's so unique because this is like Van Halen without the business end for me.

Chad Smith, drummer, Red Hot Chili Peppers: I'm the founder of Chickenfoot. I'm sure Sam will probably dispute that [laughs]. It started with us both living in Cabo San Lucas. I moved down there in 2002, and Sam of course is like the mayor down there. I first met Sam when I went down to his club one night for a birthday bash concert he was throwing. When I pulled up, there was a line out the door, and on the street there was a big screen with Sammy playing with Jerry Cantrell, Tommy Lee—all these guys are down there, right in the middle of this little weird Mexican town! We hit it off immediately. He loved the Chili Peppers and I was a big Montrose fan growing up. We had a shot of tequila together, and fifteen minutes later he said, "Come on, let's jam!" We became fast friends and whenever he would go down there, which was a lot, he would call me up. We'd hang out in his club and just play whatever—James Brown, Zeppelin, the Doors—whatever we wanted. It was really fun.

Producer/engineer Andy Johns at Sammy's studio for Chickenfoot I *sessions in '08*

Photo by John Cuniberti

Michael Anthony, former bassist, Van Halen: Sammy came up with the name Chickenfoot. It's like the three talons on a chicken's foot.

Sammy Hagar: When we were Chickenfoot without Joe, we were jamming and playing other people's songs: Led Zeppelin, Cream, the Who, whatever. Chad was the one who said, "Let's get together and make a record." I said I wouldn't do it unless we had a great guitar player because I just wanted to sing. I cannot be a great guitar player and a great singer. Chad's too good of a drummer, Mikey's too good of a bass player, and we needed a guitar player as good as those guys. Chad asked, "Who are you thinking?" and my immediate reply was, "Joe Satriani's my favorite guitar player."

Chad Smith: In 2007, the Chili Peppers were taking our first real break for at least a year, and we hadn't done that in ten years. I told Sam, "Hey, I got some time off if you want to do something. Let's do it now." Sammy said, "I'm going to get a real guitar player. I'll call Joe!" I asked, "Joe?" Sammy said, "Yeah, Joe Satriani!" I was a little reluctant to believe Joe would really be into it. A month or so later, Sammy called me up about a Super Bowl party he was playing in Vegas and said, "I called Satriani up and he said he wants to come and jam. Let's get up for the encore!"

Michael Anthony: You never really know what to expect when you are live onstage. It could have been, like, five minutes of jamming the blues, then "See you later." There's a magic and chemistry that can happen, though, and for me, it's happened three times. Once when I joined Van Halen, the second time when Sammy joined Van Halen, and the third time when Chickenfoot jammed for the first time. We were having such a good time onstage, and it was great because after all the crap you go through—and that I went through in my career in Van Halen—to get together with some guys and not even have to think about anything but purely jamming with some buddies and having fun is the best feeling that there is. That's basically why we all decided to get together and keep this thing going. There was no talk of, "Hey, let's get together and form a supergroup." It was more like, "Wow, that was so much fun!" I remember when we were up there at that very first jam, we'd played through two or three songs, and Chad yelled to the crowd, "You want to hear more?" They just went wild, and he started Zeppelin's "Rock and Roll." Chad wasn't ready to leave the stage that night and neither were the rest of us.

At Skywalker for Chickenfoot I *sessions*
PHOTO BY BRYAN ADAMS

I think the central idea for Chickenfoot's stylistic direction was like an early-seventies rock band. Underneath that, it's obviously the blues. We were celebrating the very early stage of classic rock. That was a surprise to us, but it just seemed to be where we naturally went. Chad didn't just bring his Chili Peppers stuff to the band, I didn't bring all my solo guitar stuff, and Mike and Sam weren't trying to be Van Halen. I think that's what surprised us and what's kept us together as a group. We created a fifth element that we all loved and were surprised by, and that really *is* the sound of the band. So as a group, as a four-piece, we performed really well, but it was amazing how much bigger we were than just four guys when we got together. There was something extra that came out of us, and that's what we decided to call "Chickenfoot"—that extra thing.

Sammy Hagar: It was very bold because the music we were playing was very unfashionable, and it still is. We're playing brand-new classic rock. We're bringing fresh songs to that format. The only thing we discussed before we started was, "Let's play the music we like to play." We didn't know what we were doing because we were on the front line, just digging the hole and stepping in it at the same time. We weren't looking to be something else that we're not.

The only learning curve was being confident around one another and feeling comfortable to show your ass. When you play music—especially when you're writing and nobody knows exactly what they're doing just yet—it can be uncomfortable around people you don't know or trust to really go for it. A lot of guys—mainly singers—will kick everybody out of the room when they're doing vocals or won't sing in front of people. We don't do it that way—we fucking just go for it. I just make HUGE bad notes before I know what I'm singing sometimes. That's the only learning curve, getting to that point where I could say, "Joe's not gonna make fun of me, though Chad's gonna make fun of me," but that's okay because that's what he does. If Mikey makes a mistake, he knows we're gonna go, "What the fuck were you playing?" We joke with each other but we're not there to intimidate anyone or make anyone feel like they need to tighten their shit up. We really get loose around one another.

Joe in his pre-Chickenfoot incarnation wasn't really a jam kind of guy. Joe is a perfectionist. I know he can jam but his songs and his shows were usually ones where every lick was worked out precisely to end at a certain time. That's kind of how he did things when we started because he wanted it to be perfect every time, and when you jam, things aren't perfect. So me and Chad really turned Joe out because Chad and I had been jamming together for at least five or six years before he came in the picture—Mikey too, but mainly me and Chad. We're brave souls and we're not afraid to show our asses. We're not afraid to make a mistake and go for it and try anything. Joe loved that, and he got so into it that he fell right into the same attitude. So as Chickenfoot started playing more together as a band, I could feel him getting off the hook and loosening up. I'm always telling him that "We turned you out," which is like we took a virgin and made him a whore [laughs]. And he fell in love with it, too, knowing he didn't have to be perfect.

Our chemistry was surprising to us. It didn't feel like something that was manufactured. This was not a record company–brainstormed band, this was just four guys who got together, surprised one another, and just went with it in a natural way. We would write and record, sit back and listen, and if we liked it, we'd release it. Both Chickenfoot albums have been do-it-yourself projects, with no label involved until we were absolutely finished, so artistically it's our own thing.

Chad Smith: Once we knew we wanted to make a full album together, someone said, "Let's get Andy Johns to produce us!" Joe had worked with Andy on *The Extremist* and with Sammy and Mike on *For Unlawful Carnal Knowledge*. I'd never worked with Andy but knew he'd been an engineer on *Led Zeppelin IV*. Here was a chance to work with a guy who worked on "When the Levee Breaks"! YEAH, I'll work with that guy!

Sammy Hagar: Andy's brilliant, and musically, he'll sit and fucking work five hours straight on something with you, trying to get one note right. When you put your drums in a room and Andy starts listening, he starts moving mics around, putting mics here and mics there. He comes up with some great live rockin' sounds!

Andy Johns: In the studio, we understand each other very well. They know what I'm thinking and I know what they're thinking. When I got the call for Chickenfoot, we worked at Sammy's first and did some demos, and I had quite a bit to do with how that went. Sammy was all on fire and eager. We continued recording at George Lucas's Skywalker Ranch and it went really well.

Chad Smith: The studio was really big—obviously orchestras record in there—and it was very comfortable. We actually didn't really utilize the live room; we used about a quarter of it with baffles during tracking.

Sammy Hagar: When Joe and I first got together, in one session we wrote "Sexy Little Thing." Within a day or two, we had three or four songs written. "Learning to Fall" and "Turnin' Left" both came out of that and I knew it was working!

With "Sexy Little Thing," I was playing a friend's '63 Stratocaster in my upstairs music room, looking out into the backyard. When I started writing it, I recorded it on a laptop and called it "Trekking Song." It sounded like an esoteric little instrumental. It had a Celtic feel to it, but I didn't really know what was going to happen with it until I brought it downstairs into the studio and listened to it a few times. I thought it could be a very accessible song. It didn't necessarily have to be some unusual Mixolydian-based instrumental. I think I'd written it before the Chickenfoot thing came together, but once Chickenfoot happened, I realized I had to write a bunch of songs before I went on tour. I started thinking for the first time, "What would I want Sammy Hagar to sound like if I had a chance to point him in a new direction?" My feeling was that he could dip into blues, sing in a lower register, and add elements of the Faces and Humble Pie and the Rolling Stones, and all that early-seventies rock stuff. I just had a sense that he would click with that. Going into our first writing session, all I had was the music and the title "She's a Sexy Little Thing."

It was enough to inspire him to create a story and melody line and a whole arrangement.

Sammy Hagar: With all the other songs outside of those we wrote in that first session together, Joe would bring me the music, and I would hear a melody first. Ninety-nine point nine percent of the time, I hear a melody to every piece of music and I just start singing. And 99.9 percent of the time, I end up keeping my first melody idea. I may have to tweak it, change a line, or make a phrase a little better, but that's it. Then I write lyrics to my melody. My melody is usually what dictates the individual lyrics, but it's Joe's music that usually dictates the title. So, for instance, with "Oh Yeah," I just immediately started singing that for the chorus, and knew it was going to be the title. With that song, I didn't know what I was going to talk about in the verses. I could have written that one about a thousand different subjects. So for most of them, I came up with a title based off Joe's initial idea—like with "Sexy Little Thing"—and then I just started writing the most tongue-in-cheek, dirty, sexy lyrics I could think of.

Sam has a great amount of experience being a successful writer of hits, and because he's a singer and a really great communicator, he has an innate sense about how to communicate an idea vocally. That's not my strong point, so when I bring ideas in, I'm always looking for something that's a little bit left of center and strange, because that's the kind of stuff I like to listen to over and over again. When Sam gets some of my ideas, I think he tries to figure out "What is Joe getting at?" and he tries to *bring it to the people*. He tries to make it something you can actually grasp. "Sexy Little Thing" is a good example of where he took something that, if I had written it, I would have made it a little bit odd and not as accessible. Since he's the guy standing in front of the band holding the mic, looking at everybody in the audience, his thing is to reach the biggest number of people and get them to understand this idea. His gift is to cut through my weird guitar stuff and then figure out what to sing about and how to sing it so that everybody can relate to it.

Chad Smith: Joe would come up with the riffs and the basic song ideas and he'd email them to us. We'd say, "Yeah, I like that one. That's a cool riff," and Sam would say, "I got something for that." It was real relaxed. Then Mike and I flew up one weekend, and we all got in Sam's studio and demoed six or seven songs. Probably five of them wound up on the album. You know what's really cool and rare is when you get together and play with someone, and think it sounds cool, and then go in the control room of the studio, listen to a playback, and go, "Fuck, that sounds better than I thought it was when we were playing it!" Microphones don't lie. They're naked and you can't get away with shit.

You can't worry about appearances when you're working on music. You have to go with what ultimately makes the song better. When I'm in Chickenfoot, where I'm playing with other players who are very creative and extremely capable and always ready to deliver, I always remind myself that I haven't hired these guys and they haven't hired me. We're all giving ourselves latitude. No one tells anyone what to play or not play. I love collaborating and I recognize that although it can be difficult when you're in the middle of it, the end result is worth it, and usually far better than you would have done on your own.

Chad Smith: It was great in the studio because nobody was telling anybody what to play. Everyone was just doing their thing, just eye contact and "play." It was really free. Of course, everybody's a songwriting pro with building bridges and choruses and solos and shit, but we didn't want to overthink everything, and I love that, personally. I think that's lacking in music today because Pro Tools makes it so easy to be so perfect. We just got in a room and played with no clicks, no editing. It was just an old-school band playing like the guys we'd all grown up loving.

Michael Anthony: I remember Chad and I talking to Andy quite a lot about our desire to really keep this thing fresh and loose and not try to get too precise on takes. In Van Halen, even if there was a little slipup, we'd leave it in. It's just the energy of it, you know. I've been in so many situations with Van Halen where you beat a song to death, and even though it sounds great, you listen to it and go, "Man, it just wasn't like when we first picked up the instruments." We wanted to keep that excitement there with Chickenfoot because that's what it was all about!

The band in Skywalker's control room for Chickenfoot I *sessions*
PHOTO BY BRYAN ADAMS

During recording we'd play a song several times and let everybody kind of experiment a bit. Then slowly we'd say, "I liked when you did this more than that." It's a process of being allowed to experiment, all of us throwing out options, new ideas, and suggestions for how how to improve something. We'd do that from about noon until three o'clock, when we'd decide we were finished with a song and wanted to lock it down. The important thing is that musicians can deliver a performance after taking in criticism. It's easy to agree with criticism and to acknowledge new ideas, but to actually implement those ideas takes a whole higher level of musician. Sometimes you're in a situation where you say, "Make it funkier," and then the band says, "Yeah, we understand. Let's do it," and it turns out that they can't. They just don't possess the talent. With Chickenfoot, we always seem to be able to move in the direction that we agree on as a group because we're fortunate that we've got a lot of ability in the band to change direction on a dime and take advantage of any inspiration that pops up out of our unique synergy.

"My Kinda Girl" was one of those kinds of songs. I had a riff, and when I first played it for everybody, it had more of a metal/heavy rock crunch to it. As Chad, Mike, and I worked on the arrangement, it started to get more Stones-y sounding and we liked it better. Chad is not a fan of metal music at all, so anytime I brought something in that had hints of metal, he would slowly veer in the other direction. Where we wound up was with something we all really liked, so then we just had to come up with another little section where I had to write a solo and riff kind of thing. Then the three of us arranged the whole song as we were going along!

Sammy Hagar: "Future in the Past" was something we wrote as the last song for the album, and it is one of the greatest things I've ever been involved in writing in my life. That song in concert has just turned into this special thing. I brought in the first riff for it—believe it or not, that was a musical piece I was working on. Joe took it and made it the greatest thing ever. When that song was done we went in and listened to that vocal. I always let the band pick which track to use, so out of twenty takes, they said, "We like take seventeen." I sang it live every time because I was working out my lyrics and my phrasing. I took that take home, listened to it, and came back the next day and said, "I don't want to re-sing this. I don't want to fix anything or do anything to it.

This is the one." Everybody had goose bumps on their arms. That's a magical thing that only happens once in a while. It happened with "Love Walks In" and "Cabo Wabo" with Van Halen—one take, reading the lyrics, boom, it's done. No reason to sing that again!

Sammy had this idea of what "Future in the Past" would sound like in the beginning, and then how we would use that chorus at the end to be this big crescendo and big ending. I took those chords and his two verses and shortened them to about a quarter of their length. I then combined the two verses into one, to make it a bit stronger, and presented it to him with the idea being that we would start very quietly with what had been his chorus thing, but then go into my miniaturized version of his original two verses. Then at the end of the song we could bring back his opening thing and play it loud and combine guitar and vocals with it. We needed another part, though, so I came up with this little funky piece with drop-D-tuning on the spot. I asked Mike, "Does that sound cool? Do you want to do that?" Then Chad came in the room, and as a band we arranged it and recorded it. It was *that fast*. We went from Sammy just strumming the chords to having a finished take in maybe three hours!

Chad Smith: I didn't really know how the other guys had worked, but for me, with rock 'n' roll, if everyone can play—and everyone can play in this band—we just get in a room and play off each other. Sam would sing, but a lot of times he didn't have all the words yet, so the vocals weren't kept. He was in there for the vibe, though, which is really important, and we'd keep what was on the bass and guitars. It wasn't like we ever said, "We need to completely redo the bass," or "We need to completely redo a guitar." All the basics were kept.

I remember Glyn Johns used to tell me, "You can never go back to a party that's over." Back when we were doing the *Joe Satriani* record in 1995, he wanted me to play all my parts live. I told him I was an overdub guy. He replied, "Now's the time to change. Once the party's over, good luck trying to overdub the main parts on this stuff." He was right. It's very difficult with a live band because it's not a matter of just being in time. It's that the swing of the moment is almost impossible to get back to.

The basis for all Chickenfoot records is the band playing live. Then we add stuff to it. Everything recorded was always with the group, either at Sam's studio or at Skywalker. The performances are always slightly ragged because they're not layered perfectly with computers. Everything's done without a click so it's just raw performances, with overdub bits applied later. We do it this way because those live sessions always pull us in some new direction from where we thought the song was going or where the demo was heading.

Sammy Hagar: The sound Joe gets is always WAY beyond me. I would have accepted the first sound he had plugging his guitar directly into the amp. I would have said, "Wow, that sounds great," but he'd always say, "No, no," and then he changes it and changes amps and changes guitars and ends up with this AMAZING sound. THEN he starts playing his parts. His first solo on the live take always sounds incredible. I ask him, "You're gonna keep that, right?" He says, "Oh, I don't know." I come back a few days later and he's changed it and it's better, and he says, "I want to do a couple more little things." I mean, he just thinks SO FAR beyond my satisfaction range. That's why I'm not the lead guitar player in Chickenfoot, because Joe can take it so much further. Why eat a hamburger when there's a steak sitting there? Joe's also one of the greatest rhythm guitar players ever. You don't think of Joe Satriani as a rhythm guitar player. When I'm singing a song and he's playing a rhythm part behind me, oh my God, you don't even need a drummer. I know right where the pocket is. Joe is in the pocket, and I REALLY noticed it right out of the box because I'm a guitar player! He's so clever and it's something that people would never know unless they played with him.

When I started playing guitar, along with trying to play like Hendrix, I was intrigued by the blues. My older brother John played blues harp, so I was exposed to John Lee Hooker and players like that during that whole period. I knew Jimi Hendrix was into Buddy Guy and that they all listened to Muddy Waters and Jimmy Reed. I remember as a young player sitting down and playing the blues very slowly, trying to get to that space, and realizing it was something special that I wanted to make part of my playing. When I became a successful solo artist, people defined me by songs like "Surfing with the Alien," "Always with Me, Always with You," "Summer Song," and "Flying in a Blue Dream." They didn't associate me with my blues playing, although it was a big part of my style and background. Chickenfoot was the first band where I had a natural place for all my blues influences, and I think that drew out similar elements from Sammy as well.

Andy Johns: I think Joe in Chickenfoot was more confident in his own ability, not that he'd lacked confidence before. He was just a little more experienced and a little more relaxed about stuff. He laughs a lot more than he used to. Joe's quite aware of how good he is—there's only one Joe Satriani, like I said before. He can play anything he hears in his head and can fucking do it perfectly. If you ask him to do a certain kind of thing, boom, there it is. He's very easy to work with. Joe and I got very involved on the overdubs. That's the fun part because you never quite know what Joe's going to come up with. Joe had pedals and I got him to use the wah-wah a few times. Joe is just all-around fucking unbelievable and I'm very lucky to have been able to work with him. I'm not just saying that. I really believe that. I'm very lucky to have worked with that man!

Michael Anthony: Andy would always have a great story at the end of the day. We'd all be sitting around bullshitting and us guys in the band would look like little kids sitting around the campfire. Andy would be telling us stories about Zeppelin or someone else that he'd worked with. He always had a great story about his past that would have us captivated.

Sammy Hagar: When the album was done we all loved it a lot and were very proud of it. We couldn't WAIT till our generation of rockers and people who like this kind of music heard it. They were gonna freak out! I expected it to be successful because of the name value, because our backgrounds professionally are pretty steady—we'd always delivered something good for our fans, so none of us were trying to make a comeback here, but we weren't expecting to sell out arenas. As it happens, Chickenfoot was one of twelve records to go gold that year. Fuck!

Michael Anthony: In this day and age, you have people who put together these so-called supergroups, and fans don't really take the supergroup type of thing too seriously. It's like, "Okay, these guys are getting together to make a bunch of money and get a bunch of publicity, go out and tour, shake hands, say good-bye and that's it." By contrast, our approach to everything that was happening was rooted around the reason we first got together, which was that we wanted to do something that wasn't ego or money driven. We all had money and had done what we'd done in the past, and so we wanted to do this purely for the sake of playing music and having fun. In Chickenfoot, we knew we had something there, that we all had a connection. And the songs, I thought, were fucking great! But you never know what to expect when you're getting ready to release it. I know going top five was a big surprise to all of us. It was like, "Crack the Champagne," because after Van Halen, you've been in one big band, you realize something like that rarely ever happens again in someone's career. And here it was happening to us! So all this stuff was happening while we were on the tour. All of a sudden, we're getting gold albums. What a trip!

Chad Smith: Our decision to go with the Best Buy label was smart of us because they really promoted it a lot at their stores. Gary Arnold loved our band, was out on the road with us, was passionate about the album, and that really made a difference. Also, we're not competing with the Lady Gagas and Rihannas of the world. We're, like, old fucking rock dudes. We did have a certain amount of hype, "supergroup" this and that, and I thought our first record was strong and a good record. Going gold with no hit singles and with MTV gone, I was impressed.

Sammy Hagar: Once we got out there and started playing in front of people, Joe got really loose playing on the road. I'm telling you, this band's been so good for Joe, because he plays so different in this band than he does as an instrumentalist.

Just a few months before my mother passed away, Chickenfoot was playing at the Beacon Theatre in New York City. She was a great supporter of mine. Growing up during the Depression in New York, she understood how hard you had to work to get anything out of life. She had a great work ethic and understood why I practiced like crazy and never gave up. When I was a young kid, she never tried to stop me from playing and always encouraged me to keep going.

My mother had seen me perform at the Beacon at least ten times, but for some reason that night she decided to sit on the side of the stage. She had never done that before. During "Future in the Past," where Sammy and I are doing a very long intro together, Chad walked her out onstage. I knew she was having a hard time walking so I told him, "You cannot let go of her." She LOVED being onstage. My mother and Sammy had a good conversation with the audience for about a minute while I repeated the song's intro, then Chad came over and very gently led my mother offstage. It was very much a part of my mother's personality to feel totally comfortable walking out in front of three thousand people and saying, "Hello, I'm Joe's mother!"

CHAPTER 21 ★★

Black Swans and Wormhole Wizards—2010

"Apparently his time in Chickenfoot made Joe Satriani want to get back to where he once belonged, so he goes retro on 2010's Black Swans and Wormhole Wizards. *About as far away from the heavy-footed party rock of Chickenfoot as possible,* Black Swans *is pure guitar prog, filled with compressed boogies, sci-fi synths, exotic flourishes, and all of Satch's phasers and flangers in full-tilt overdrive."*

—*Billboard* magazine

Between the Chickenfoot record and tour and then the Experience Hendrix tour—where I was playing with quite a few other musicians in a kind of revue—I'd racked up a lot of live and studio experience that was very different from playing solo. I wanted to isolate what was good about those experiences, what would bring me forward artistically, and use it as a positive influence for the next solo record.

Mike Fraser: Joe wanted a "band feel" on this record as opposed to a studio-manufactured record. His intent wasn't to make a live record, but he wanted a band-feel record, and that's done by everybody playing together. Our focus this time around was on getting the takes where we could keep most of the performances without having to come back and redo them. We didn't want to sort of chop it all up, put it on a grid, and make it all proper. He just wanted a little bit more of that ebb and flow that a real band playing gets.

Tracking at Skywalker Sound in '10
PHOTO BY ARTHUR ROSATO

When I was writing for this record, one of my favorite memories of that process is of "Littleworth Lane," which is an actual street in Sea Cliff, Long Island, where my mother owned a house up until she passed away. The house had been built in the late 1600s and was very unique by American standards. I wanted to start that cathartic process of writing about my mother's life and her influence on me and the rest of the family. I thought I needed to write something that reflected the kind of music she would relate to. She was into jazz and soulful music and had expressed to me many times over the years the kind of music she wanted at her funeral. One night, driving away from the house, I wrote this song in my head and I kept it there until one afternoon, backstage after a sound check. There was a piano in the dressing room and I realized I was ready to play this thing, so I took out my iPhone and did a quick recording of it. That wound up being the demo of "Littleworth Lane" that I sent to the band.

With "Solitude," I was thinking about how I often require time to be alone, much as my parents did, and I coupled that with my mother's absence from her house once she passed. It was so profound, I couldn't put it into words. I was working on a song called "Heartbeats" at my home studio one afternoon when the inspiration came. I was thinking "Heartbeats" needed some kind of introduction, but instead I started writing a piece that was much bigger. It was a song about my moments of solitude, and the lonely feeling in my mother's house now that her spirit had moved on. It eventually found a home on the record right before "Littleworth Lane." I played my JS1000 direct into my STT-1 for that recording.

The idea for the title "Pyrrhic Victoria" came from a story about King Pyrrhus, who defeated the Romans in battle but lost 99 percent of his army doing so. He is quoted as proclaiming, "If we are victorious in one more battle with the Romans, we shall be utterly ruined." That's where we get the term *Pyrrhic victory*. This is a tune where the flexibility that I had at home working with Pro Tools and software synthesizers allowed the song to grow. It started in the most organic way: I was in my studio, plugged into a JS customized Two-Rock amplifier, just having fun improvising. My studio room is relatively small, which can overemphasize the low end, but it makes the guitar sound and feel 100 feet tall. I recorded the improv using QuickTime Pro on my laptop before going out to dinner. When I returned home and listened to it, I thought, "That is REALLY cool! Now let's add an orchestra!"

"Dream Song" was a song that literally came to me in a dream. When I woke up I had the entire song in my head. I thought for sure I'd been listening to music until I realized I'd been asleep and it was dead quiet in the room. I spent the next three hours recording what I remembered from my dream before the memory of it faded. The organ arpeggios and all the wah-wah guitars were done in my home studio—as a matter of fact, all the guitars on that particular song are from home. They just seemed to tell the story the way it needed to be told.

With "Wormhole Wizards," I had been reading about black holes and theories about parallel universes and people traveling faster than the speed of light. Around that time I was speaking to Jeff Campitelli about the number of songs that I had finished, their tempos and time signatures, and I mentioned that I had a fast song inside of me ready to come out. Sure enough, that night I got inspired to put something together. Instead of using BFD to start my drum track, I wanted to use another program for the drums that had more of a drum-machine feel to it. I created the bass line on keyboards using a cool Fender Rhodes plug-in, and then I could see where the song was going. It turned into a spacey but driving soundtrack about traveling through wormholes in space.

I didn't want this record to be a radical departure from the last one because I'd done that before. *The Extremist*, *Joe Satriani*, and *Engines of Creation* were all radical shifts, but I didn't want to rock the boat that much this time. A lot of the record was already tracked, and I was learning how to record myself in a more transparent manner. Ultimately, the vibe of the album would depend on the personality of the musicians and coproducer, so I took a chance that Mike Fraser would click with the other band members: Mike Keneally, Allen Whitman, and Jeff Campitelli.

Black Swans was all about unique band performances—interactions between Allen, Mike, Jeff, and myself. We needed a studio like Skywalker Sound because I felt both Allen and Mike needed lots of space. Allen's a big guy with a big personality and I thought he would blossom if he was given not only musical space but physical space. Mike is a super-talented multi-instrumentalist and it was great to offer him two grand pianos, a B3, and a Wurlitzer that we were allowed to keep set up, so he could freely experiment. I wanted the guitar, bass, and drums close enough but not too close, so we could interact with one another while not being bombarded with one another's sound.

For this album, the process wasn't about working out every arrangement detail and forcing people to play it. Sometimes that works, but other times you have to throw the music at the musicians, let them explore it on their own, and then capture that exploration.

Mike Fraser: For the *Black Swans* record, I remember I set the drums up in the middle of the room and baffled them off a little bit because it was almost a little bit too roomy. I had Joe's cabinets off in another little iso booth and Allen Whitman's bass off in a nice little room, and then Mike Keneally came in and played keyboards on the basic tracking. That's something new that I've done with Joe, to have the full band tracking. It's usually just bass and drums. That added a lot to this record, as did the input of keyboardist Mike Keneally. He'd say, "Hey, let's put a Rhodes in this part" or "Let's distort this Rhodes and put it through this pedal." He was cool with that kind of stuff, and Joe was open to those suggestions.

It was important to have the time we gave ourselves during tracking because you're looking for unusual performances. You might do seven to ten takes each time and in between each performance, the band's members are all talking to one another. Someone might say, "Would you mind if I went from the organ to the piano?" Or, "I want to change my entire drum kit." Fraser was also there to guide us along and tell us how the music was popping out in the control room. Because we were all in the studio together, we could change direction on a dime if that's what felt good. Then we had the luxury of sitting back and listening to all of our performances to see which ones were really making the song most exciting.

"God Is Crying" was originally supposed to be on *Professor Satchafunkilus*, but there was a day in the studio when I asked everybody in the band, "What two songs would you like to stop working on?" I was totally shocked when they voted it off, but it turned out to be the right call. When I brought it back, this band was much more excited about playing it, and they brought a whole new feeling to it. Mike Fraser was encouraging us to jam right up until we counted the song off, and we eventually used one of those jams for the intro. I think it was Mike's design all along to trick us into basically creating a new part for the song!

Mike Fraser: With Joe and the band, as we tracked these songs, everybody played off each other a little more, which was the intent all along. So there were times when, for instance, we decided that instead of doing a part of Joe's as an overdub, we said, "Well, he's such a great player, let's just do it live and see what we can grab." Recording Joe's solos was quite an easy process because he's so good at coming up with great melodies. With singers, you have to make sure the lyrics are right, and he's singing in tune and all that, but with Joe, it goes pretty easy. Sometimes you give your opinion on what direction that one run was leading, but Joe always comes in with everything sort of preplanned in his mind, and he knows what he wants and what's going to work. Sometimes he just needs somebody to bounce ideas off of. When you listen to *Black Swans*, the tracks are all different, which is amazing because how many instrumental songs can you keep doing and they're still all different and interesting? It's a process I find quite fascinating because he's got such a great grasp on his musicality and on what notes are gonna make that song flow. I'm always baffled every time I watch him play. He makes it look so easy.

This time I told Mike Fraser that I wanted to reach people more deeply with my guitar playing. I said, "If you're watching me do a solo over and over again, the one that I want you to keep is the one where you feel I'm really reaching people."

While recording "The Golden Room," a song about protecting

yourself from negative spirits, I wanted it to be as improvisational as possible while working around a basic structure and melody. A prime example of this approach at work is the keyboard introduction, just something Mike Keneally had played at the end of one take. Fraser loved it so much he grabbed it and popped it into the beginning as an intro. He asked us, "What do you guys think?" and we all agreed we had to use it. It's a good example of how it's not just the band that is part of the creative process. Your engineer/coproducer is also listening, taking notes in the control room, and keeping track of things that you're just throwing out there but perhaps not remembering. Unless the musicians think they really nailed it, they forget half the gems that they're offering up.

Mike Keneally playing multiple keyboards during the BSWW sessions at Skywalker in '10
PHOTO BY JON LUINI

Mike Keneally pulled the same trick with "Wormhole Wizards." We found a sound on the Korg and started recording. People were coming in and out of the room, there was food out on the table, and we were all joking out loud about it because we weren't recording with microphones. Mike just kept sitting there improvising, riff after riff, arpeggio after arpeggio, and each thing he played was more brilliant than the last. He did that piano part in ONE improvised take from the beginning of the song all the way to the end. When he was done, I said, "Okay, Mike, see you later! Your job's done!"

Guitar cases lined up at Skywalker, '10
Photo by Jon Luini

CHAPTER 22 ★★

Chickenfoot III—2011/2012

> *"Joe Satriani's imprint on the musical world extends far beyond his own ethereal talents. Now, with Chickenfoot, Satriani fans can see him rip into leads with the same singer as Ronnie Montrose and Eddie Van Halen."*
>
> —*Huffington Post*

The most exciting part about being in a band with great energy and chemistry is that you're all inspired as performers and writers. When you get an idea about a song with a grand arrangement, you're encouraged to imagine all the possibilities because you know that these guys can make that song a reality. I know Michael Anthony is going to come up with some bass line that's going to be thunderous behind these chords. I know Sam's going to come up with some incredible and unique vocal. I know that Chad's going to exert his influence as an arranger on it and come up with an exciting drum part like he always does. With Chickenfoot, you always feel inspired and encouraged to move forward and bring ideas in.

There was no preproduction for our second album between when we finished touring for *Chickenfoot* and the next time I saw the guys again in the studio. It had been over a year, and it was extra rushed because with Chad's Chili Peppers commitments, we only had him for about ten days. I realized early on in recording that we had to move at a very fast clip, make decisions as we went, and stick with them because there was no going back.

On the first tour, we'd done a lot of spontaneous writing backstage every night before shows. For instance, the second track on *III*, "Alright Alright," is from an improv we did backstage.

Chickenfoot with 3-D glasses in Sam's control room, '11
PHOTO BY JON HILL

Sammy Hagar: "Alright Alright" was a great example of what can happen in this band when you're goofing off jamming. You'll start doing something stupid like shouting, "Alright, alright, alright, alright!" like I'm yelling at my old lady, "Alright, alright already!" It was just kind of a spoof or joke against this punky kind of Clash-y riff Joe was playing. I remember we were in Atlanta backstage filming our first DVD. It didn't come out good so we did it again in Phoenix, Arizona. We were there all day, so we were getting a little stir-crazy backstage, and that's when that song came alive. From there we played it all the time, that whole tour, and then it came together in Europe when I finally came up with some lyrics and a verse idea, and all that stuff in Switzerland at the Montreux Jazz Fest. I told Joe, "Just do a jump break, and I'll sing against the doo-doo-gaa-gaah beat," and "I just need a vocal break and a place where I can just yell some belligerent shit, then you can play, then me and the drums." That really came together in Montreux, and the song was done. Joe really came through.

That song is definitely reflective of the kind of stuff that makes its way from tour to a record, because I don't think a song like that would have come about in a planned way. It was just one of those silly things where you start playing some chords, and everybody starts singing a chorus that's just kind of odd enough to be catchy. So we had lots of moments like that where there were interesting little nuggets, and if they didn't actually suggest a song, they would suggest to one or all of us a kind of style of playing or something we wanted to take advantage of. Once we get started, Mikey, Chad, and I are like a freight train, so I made a note in my musical mind to make sure to write songs that had big, heavy riffs where we played together as an ensemble.

Sammy Hagar: Joe and I are the band's songwriting team, but Joe is the musical foundation of this band. On the second record, I think Joe had the confidence to put his opinion out there and really kind of lead the band musically. I'm the spiritual motivator and front guy, the mouth you might say, but Joe's really like Jimmy Page in Led Zeppelin. I'm the spark plug, no question about it, but Joe's music dictates everything. I love writing lyrics and melodies and singing to his music. It's like when Van Halen was good—I loved it. It was the same thing, before Eddie and I hit rock bottom. Of course, it's no fun being creative with a guy that you're not getting along with. That's a hard gig, brother. But Joe and I aren't there and hopefully we'll never get there.

He's really a fun guy to create with, and he comes through with his part. For instance, if I say, "Maybe we'll write this song kind of like a midtempo groove, like "Every Breath You Take"—you know, just throwing a title of a song out there that is vibe-y like that, or a Pink Floyd thing—Joe comes through. The next day, he'll come back with a piece of music that's beyond what I was talking about and is definitely not ripping anybody off. He just goes in his heart, or what I like to call his little safe of music, and comes out with stuff that is ALWAYS great. I just love that. Like I said, he's the musical dynamic behind this band.

We made a really strong effort on this LP to try to get into some unknown territory. I kept telling Sam, "I know you're powerful in this area. We've just got to write songs to let you get there," and he really delivered! I love the way that Sammy sings on *III*.

Sammy Hagar: Heading into the second record, I remember I told Joe, "I wanna do something different. I want to sing some way I've never sung before," and Joe went, "Wow, that's really what I want from you." So I said, "Okay, write me some music that makes me want to do that!" He came through, and I came through with "Something Going Wrong," which is a huge stretch for me. Another one I think's a pretty damn good stretch is "Come Closer." I'm touching on R&B gospel on that bridge, man, but the verses are kind of almost talking. I love it. The hardest thing to do as a singer is to stretch yourself, because it's so personal, and if you do something stupid, you feel embarrassed. It's embarrassing to sing, is really what it is, but having Joe around just makes it so much more comfortable. A lot of times I'm real insecure about doing it and so on the edge trying to stay on key, and it's just hard to do something new. But when I finish it and hear it back and go, "Wow, I'm so proud of that," I look at Joe. We high-fived MANY times because of "Something Going Wrong" and "Closer." They were stretches.

On this record, I really wanted to capture our power, and with a song like "Something Going Wrong" that captures our creativity, we're able to do things like that. But I think the band is about songs like "Soap on a Rope" and "Oh Yeah" and power. Because for four guys live, we can put off some POWER coming off the stage. So when it's rockin' like that, from "Turnin' Left" to "Future in the Past," there's a lot of bands, man, who can't bring that power without a bunch of overdubs and backing tracks. We're raw, straight-up live!

Michael Anthony: Obviously from all that time playing and hanging out on the first tour we found—I don't know if I'd call it *the* Chickenfoot sound—but more of the niche of what Chickenfoot really is.

As excited as the band was about the new songs, it was still difficult to get together in one place with our competing schedules, so the challenge as always was that we didn't have much time. We were picking a song in the morning, working on an arrangement, recording it for the album right then and there, then moving on a few hours later before we even knew what the song was going to be about. The plus side is all the spontaneity and energy that you get. That is the benefit of moving at a fast clip in the studio. No one gets bogged down and none of the recordings suffer from being overworked. They were all *underworked*.

Me and luthier Gary Brawer at Real Guitars, S.F., getting guitars ready for Chickenfoot III *sessions. Gary has worked on my guitars for decades; he's the best.*

PHOTO BY ALLEN WHITMAN

The Chickenfoot experience is extreme. There's always a lot of joking around and a super amount of energy. Personally, though, it was a challenging transition. For my solo records, I take two months to work on my songs, then bring them into the studio with guys who've had the demos and learned their parts, and then we very carefully go about recording stuff. Then we go out on tour and play these meticulously rehearsed arrangements. Then I jump from that right into Chickenfoot, where it's completely the opposite approach.

Michael Anthony: The one thing that I wish we had was more time just to work the songs up. In Van Halen, we'd play a song, God, a hundred times before we decided to record it. With Chickenfoot, when we all got in the studio, and we were all on a pretty heavy time schedule because Chad was getting ready to pick back up with the Chili Peppers, we were recording from the time we picked our guitars up to the time we put our instruments down. We were recording the whole time!

Here's the way it usually worked: Sam would say, "Let's cut a verse or add a verse." Then Mikey and Chad would say, "Can we do it a little faster or slower? Can we get rid of, or extend, this part?" All four of us are always exerting that influence and that helps make the band work. Everybody truly respects one another, how they play, and their musicianship. That's what makes the sessions work. We're all listening to one another and nobody tells the other person what to play. Sometimes all four of us would write something new and record it right away, like with "Down the Drain" or "Alright Alright."

Sammy Hagar: Chad's always fucking around on the drums or on guitar and Joe would be playing drums, or I'd be playing guitar and Joe'd be playing bass. We were always goofing, and when you're goofing, things come out of you that you normally wouldn't do, that you'd keep hidden.

Chad Smith: All of us are good with ideas on arrangements and what works, but Joe's *really* good at that. Once Sam gets melody and words on top of it, that really helps. I know at some point that frustrates Joe. He'll say, "I don't know what to put down here because I don't know what Sam's going to sing yet." Sometimes Sammy would have something halfway but not fleshed out at all, and for Joe, who plays a melodic instrument, you have to know what the singer is doing. You can put down a bonehead riff, but why? Somebody like Joe needs more info, so that was the only thing that kind of held up the second record. But it all worked out. I thought it was great!

Sammy Hagar: My writing process for the band's music is unique. In every song there's usually something different, but it's the same way I wrote with Eddie, and the same way I'd write with any guitar player, where I say, "You write the music. I'll write the lyrics." We only did it one time differently on *Chickenfoot III* with "Come Closer." I'd written those lyrics and really liked them, and I said, "Joe, would you take these lyrics and write music to them?" He said, "Absolutely, let me try that," which excited me because that's what Elton John and Bernie Taupin do. The song is one of my favorites I've ever written. I write lyrics that fit in those holes, and it's hard and stresses me out. It fucking beats me to death because every word's got to have rhythmical power first, and then it's also got to say something, so I paint myself into a real bad corner there, but I can't help it. I was a little embarrassed to sing a song like "Come Closer" because I meant that lyric. It's about my wife and I—we've been together a long time, and I don't want that to happen, where we start to lose that love, and I spoke about it in that song.

"Come Closer" was really quite unique in how it was written because Sammy sent me lyrics first. There were two pages of lyrics with four verses and a whole bunch of choruses. I sat down at my piano one morning and wrote a very moody piece of music to what

I felt was a very dark kind of song coming from Sam. I emailed him a recording of it that very morning before going into the studio, and when I got there, he said he wanted to do it right away. Of course the other guys hadn't heard it yet, so I sat down and played it for them on piano. The consensus right off was, "Let's do it." The problem was I'd never played it on guitar, and I'm not the greatest piano player, so I was afraid that if we tried to track it with me playing piano we wouldn't get a good take. So while Mike and Chad worked up bass and drum parts, I taught myself how to play the song on guitar. We cut it within about an hour and that was it.

Michael Anthony: I was really surprised at how well the second album came together. The music was clicking so well that I remember Sammy coming to the studio, we'd tell him, "Hey, we laid another one down," and he'd say, "Hey, slow down. I don't even have any fucking lyrics for this shit yet!"

Sammy Hagar: The idea for "Three and a Half Letters" first came to me from a sign I saw on the side of the road. There was a little nine-year-old homeless kid, and it broke my heart. I thought "What the fuck?," so I asked Joe to play the most belligerent music he'd ever played in his life, and I was going to try to talk over it. I get these letters constantly from people with hard-luck stories, so I was going to read four or five letters on the song. We wound up with three. Normally, I don't want to dive into politics. I don't want to be judged for it and I don't want to really say what I think because there's always somebody who's going to say, "Fuck you, I feel different." I wanted to do that song and I wanted to make the statement. I'm more of an up-tempo guy. But every now and then, I gotta make my statement. Then I'm done with it and want to make people happy again.

On this album, I had started to make the full transition to playing my twenty-four-fret JS guitar almost exclusively, which was a new model for us, the Ibanez JS2400. Believe it or not, when you suddenly add two frets, you've got to rethink some of your playing. By the time I got to recording *Chickenfoot III*, I was fully comfortable with it. I had also started developing my own acoustic guitar with Ibanez, which was used on the album and in the *Satchurated* 3-D movie, too. The amplifier that did 99 percent of the guitar work on this record was the prototype for my signature Marshall amp, the JVM410HJS.

Wrapping up the first Chickenfoot record had been rather traumatic, because toward the end, our producer, Andy Johns, had to be hospitalized and ultimately couldn't finish the production. So we decided for the second album that Mike Fraser, who mixed the first record for us, was the perfect choice for engineer/coproducer. I wanted someone who knew me and how I worked. That decision not to have any other outside influence turned out to be the best thing because we really clicked on this second record. It turned out to be a remarkable group of sessions.

Sammy Hagar: I loved working with Mike Fraser on *Chickenfoot III*. When you're tracking, he doesn't necessarily interrupt you, but rather he gives you all the space you need and allows you to get your thing together. Then he tries to get the best take from you that he can. That's a beautiful thing. It's more comfortable working with a guy like that, but I can't say Andy Johns didn't do a genius job with the first record. It turned out working with Fraser on the second record really did save our ass. We wouldn't have gotten *Chickenfoot III* made without Mike. Our comanager, John Carter, died in the two months it took us to make that record. That put a dark cloud over the thing, but a producer like Mike kept it together, kept it clean, kept it simple, didn't bring any extra drama. Whatever drama we had was coming from the four of us, which really wasn't any, so it was great, and having Mike really helped matters. He's a real pro.

We were looking to cut ten really tight songs and to be a heavier band. I think Mike was the right producer for the job. He's got a great personality that I thought fit in very well with the four of us nutcases. He was the perfect producer to keep us on track, and he's an awesome engineer.

Mike Fraser: One of my main ambitions with *III* was really wanting to get Michael's harmonies in there because that was the special part of the Van Halen vibe, having the high harmonies right up front.

Michael Anthony: In this band, Sammy and I talked about us having this really cool background stuff in Van Halen and how we really wanted to get into that a lot deeper in Chickenfoot. For instance, on the first album, the song "Turnin' Left," the lead vocal is actually a harmony where we're both singing lead and harmony. On *Chickenfoot III*, Sam and I worked a lot with Joe on structure for some of the vocal harmonies that we did, what notes we're going to sing. Sometimes, you'll just do the basic thing that works all the time, and Joe will go, "Hey, why don't we try this?" and spin a different note in there, which is really cool and really expanded our sound a lot more.

My guitar had never sounded so good. I just couldn't believe the sound Mike captured. It was very thick and full of energy and soul, and so "rock 'n' roll band" sounding. I thought *Chickenfoot III* was the best I'd ever played and the best I'd ever been recorded. I couldn't wait for people to hear it.

Chad Smith: Really the best song that Sammy didn't want to sing because he said it was too fast is a song called "FRYDAY." It's never been released. Joe, Mike, and I knocked it out one morning. We cut it in two takes and it was done. Sammy didn't want to sing it, so sometimes the best shit is left on the floor. That happens with the Chili Peppers all the time, where we come up with this great music, and Anthony's like, "Naw, I don't really hear anything for it," and you're like,

"Nooo." If you can't get a vocal and melody to it, it just gets left in the bin. I was excited about the new album but I wasn't able to tour.

Kenny Aronoff: I was up playing with John Fogerty at a winery and Mick Brigden came up to me. He told me John Carter, who managed Sammy Hagar, sadly had died the week before. The news caught me off guard and I was devastated. He said, "Chickenfoot have finished a record and they're going on tour, but Chad has to go out on tour with the Red Hot Chili Peppers for a year and a half. Would you be interested in getting together and jamming to see if it's a fit?" It's a hard thing to replace Chad. He's an integral member and personality, but I jumped at the chance just to go up and play with the guys! The next thing I knew I got a phone call from Sammy, who was the nicest guy in the world. He's so direct and so present. "Everybody says you're the guy. Chad says you're the guy. I don't want to do it without Chad, but you will be able to keep this thing going. You hit hard and you've got the crazy energy of Chad." I headed up to jam with them for the first time. I had five projects going on at the time but I said, "I'll cancel them to play in this band!" This was the supergroup I'd always dreamed about being in.

Michael Anthony: I was excited to play with Kenny because he's played with everybody under the sun! At first, when he came to jam with us in the studio when we were thinking about going out and touring, he'd come in and written out all the drum parts. That's what he does when he comes in for a session. I remember him and me sitting there before Joe and Sam came in, and I was looking at him, and he had his music stand and was putting all the charts up, and I said, "Kenny, you know as soon as you know all that, you're tearing all that shit up and throwing it out, right? Because that isn't what this band's about. We want Kenny Aronoff; we don't want a Chad clone. You gotta be you. That's why we wanted you to come in and jam with us." So as he became more comfortable with us three and hanging out. We made him feel like we wanted him to be part of the band instead of a hired gun on drums. Once he got really comfortable with that, he probably got almost as close to being as crazy as Chad as you can get. It was great then, because it was like, "Alright, Kenny, do your own thing!"

Kenny Aronoff: We must have sounded pretty good by the end of that first jam because the next day we did the "Big Foot" video and it all just worked. They made me feel so comfortable and they were all the easiest guys to get along with. Sammy decided, "Yeah, let's go for it," and we hit the road. I've played in great bands, but every single player in Chickenfoot is a virtuoso. Chickenfoot is one of the top three bands I've ever played live with in my life. With Joe, what shocked me when he started playing was his rhythmic feel, which was un-fucking-real! To me, one of the greatest assets of a guitar player is how they play rhythm guitar, and a lot of them don't get it. He gets it. The placement of his 8th notes is so outstanding to me because I try to line my hi-hat up with the rhythm guitar player. If the rhythm guitar player is sitting in the pocket, I put my hi-hat right where his guitar rhythm is and decide then where to put my kick and snare. In that band, Michael was the perfect bass player, but it was Joe who I focused on. It's not the most typical approach.

I loved the fact that Kenny was a great drummer with super energy. Like Chad, he loves to pick up on the energy of a band and just drive it into the stratosphere, which is a really important part of what Chickenfoot is. Kenny's a bit different from Chad when it comes to where he places his groove. Kenny lays the snare and propels the band with his hi-hat like nobody else. That's different from Chad, who propels the band with his kick and brings the band back with the snare, but sort of dances around with the hat. Kenny's style of drumming is quite unique, actually, and he definitely goes a little bit crazy with us. When he's playing with John Fogerty, he's got a very strict set of guidelines that he's got to stick to, but with us, we've told him, "Go crazy!"

With Chickenfoot, I'd like to think that we'll be doing the exact same thing ten years from now. I know Sam's always going to write and record music because that's just part of who he is. He's so creative, he's always writing, he always has energy to sing, and he likes communicating with people.

Michael Anthony: We need to keep Chickenfoot on more of the front burner or close to the front of one of the rear burners. When I practice at home, I'll put on old Van Halen songs and jam to a lot of the songs. The other day, I actually put the first Chickenfoot record on and jammed to a couple of the songs. I put my bass down and just cranked it up and sat there listening to it, thinking, "Fuck, what a great album!" As long as everybody in the band does that every once in a while, listens to the music, and then remembers just how great it is, and how much fun we have together, I'm sure they'll remember what a great time we all have when we're all jamming together and we'll do another album.

Chad Smith: Chickenfoot is something I would love to keep doing. I know I'm the guy who's been holding it up doing the Chili Peppers the last couple of years. The band started out as me having a break and wanting to go play—then all of a sudden, everybody liked it and we made a second record, and I had to go back out on the road with the Chilis. I'm not going to have another window where I have two years off and can go do another Chickenfoot tour like we did for that first record, but I know we really enjoy playing music with each other, and really love creating music together. To me, even if it was just for that—just to make records, even if I couldn't tour—I would just love to get together and have fun and make new music. I would love to. We are friends and we have a good time together. At this late stage in the game of rock 'n' roll, if you can put that together and have people enjoy each other—not only musically but personally—then I'll look forward to hanging out with them. It's fun, and if you keep it fun it stays that way!

CHAPTER 23 ★★

Unstoppable Momentum—2013

> *"When it comes to giving every last drop of blood, sweat, tears and soul to your music, Satriani has few equals. He is relentlessly hardworking . . . His 14th studio album to date, it is also one of his most wildly imaginative and stylistically diverse."*
>
> —*Guitar World* magazine

My musical life has been like a huge snowball rolling down a hill—it just keeps getting bigger and going faster as time goes on, and the more records I put out and the more live performances I do, the more exciting the whole experience becomes. That's what the song "Unstoppable Momentum" is really about: It's the soundtrack to that realization. When I start to write a new song, it's as if time stands still. It's a uniquely private moment, when I'm alone in my studio and all of a sudden this feeling inside me blossoms and I express it musically. At that point there's no responsibility to turn it into a full song or a recording, to create an arrangement, to play it in front of anybody, or to see how it does on the radio. The music is still mine—it's free. It's pure art, and nothing beats that feeling. As soon as that music leaves the studio, there are expectations.

With those expectations come hard choices. If you are going to record that music, who's going to play it? What gear will you use? Which studio are you going to use for tracking? Who is going to help you produce it? How will it do on the radio? Will it be suitable for live performance? How will critics review it? You're no longer in that moment where you've just written something for yourself. During those moments, I sometimes imagine I'm engaging in a pure, solitary pursuit, much like surfing, where it's just you and Mother Nature. You're not really sharing what you do with anybody. It's not being diluted by market concerns or any professional expectations. It's a pure moment in life. I can identify with what painters feel when they finish that last stroke and stand back to look at their painting before anyone else has seen it. It's a fantastic moment. I feel the same way when I've written something that captures exactly what I'm feeling and crystallizes that moment in musical form.

In the old days, when I was getting ready to make a new record, I would listen to the demos endlessly. This time around, I kept telling myself I had to get away from that approach. So when I toured with Chickenfoot and then went on the subsequent G3 tours in 2012, I never brought any demos with me. There was a good month or two where I didn't listen to any demos at all. I just kept that music in my head and if I wanted to hear it, I would play it on the guitar. It would be a skeletal version of the song, without any set arrangement. It didn't have the trappings of a demo. This is an important point, because eventually you like what you keep hearing over and over again. They call it "demo-itis"!

After I got back from the last G3 tour at the end of October 2012, I knew I had to get things together. I didn't know who was going to play on the record, or which songs I was going to record, and I also hadn't yet decided on what kind of album it would be. This was a very different way for me to work, but in the end, it all came together. I wound up using quite a lot of guitar and synth tracks recorded at my home studio from the year's writing sessions.

I'm happily blessed with being prolific, so I write constantly. Sometimes they're full pieces, sometimes just little bits. I've got lots of those bits on my phone, on my laptop and my desktop, on scraps of paper, and in my notebooks. At the start of every recording project, the task is to assemble all these bits, see where I'm heading creatively, and make sure there isn't a diamond in the rough that I've forgotten about. Sometimes you come across a complete song, like "Jumpin' Out," or sometimes it's a little piece of something, like with "Can't Go Back." That was just a little riff I'd recorded on my phone. It came to me one day when there were a bunch of guys doing construction in the house, and the kitchen was the only place for me to hang out. I was sitting there with an acoustic guitar and I wrote that song while thinking about a friend of mine. I wrote maybe six to ten songs that day just sitting in the kitchen, exiled with my guitar. A week later when all the construction was finished, I brought all my notes down to the studio and came across that song. I'd forgotten what it was, but when I played it I instantly remembered the feeling I had when I wrote it, and the rest of the song just flowed. It seems like there's a constant flow of music in my head.

When I started writing "A Door into Summer," it had that wonderful feel-good vibe, like summer's coming and school is ending. It was that same kind of vibe that inspired me to write "Summer Song" back in late 1990. When someone hears a song that resonates with them and some part of their life, that song then becomes a key that unlocks their emotions and memories. I started to think about a new kind of summer song, twenty years later. This time around, I went deeper.

I brought the first demo into the *Chickenfoot III* sessions and told Sam, "You don't have to *sing* the verse. You can *talk* it." I thought it would be cool to do a song where Sam talked the verses, then sang the choruses. We played it for about fifteen minutes and the band looked at me like I was crazy! I said to myself, "All right, wrong time, wrong band for this song," but I remember going home that day thinking that song had a future with me. I just didn't know how to play it yet. Over the next two years, I would listen to the song over and over again and would sing a kind of guitar melody that I thought would work really well. I kept the melody in my head, vibing on it internally, so that when I finally was ready to record it, the melody would sound natural and relaxed. Ultimately, I wanted it to be about my memories, growing up on the East Coast when winter was over and spring was giving way to summer. School was ending and there were going to be the sort of crazy adventures and new experiences that are so important when you're a young kid. I was celebrating all of those memories.

I went through a similar experience, on a different emotional level, while writing "Shine On American Dreamer." The imagery I had in my head was that of a battered Cadillac, which is quintessentially American, driving down a road. I could see it just being a great rock 'n' roll rally song, but the song was truthfully about me coming to grips with the economic turmoil that had culminated in market crashes and economic devastation for millions of people around the world in 2008. That really was part of the failure of the American Dream. My grandparents came from Italy, believed in that American Dream, and worked so hard to accomplish it. It wasn't lost on me after reading several books about that economic collapse that a small group of people driven totally by greed would misuse the American Dream and completely destroy the lives of so many people, not only in the U.S.A. but all around the world. In part, what they did was taint that dream for future generations. What I hope the song inspires is a feeling that what we need to do is to keep working and tweaking and fixing our own individual goals and actions to make the American Dream a reality again.

That's a really tough subject to write a rock song about, and it's even tougher without lyrics, but that subject is what got me to play with the emotion I put into it. That's why the guitar solo is so expressive. It's not just a straight-electric, hyper–Chuck Berry solo; it's got a wild, emotional, yet classical sound to it. I wanted to express something heartbreaking during this solo. I also used elements of repetition in the arrangement. It's the only song on the record that has that kind of intense repetition, the playing of a melodic riff over and over again, and that represented to me how difficult it is to keep a country on course. If you look at the history of the world, nothing lasts. Every country just dissolves and civilizations crumble.

Keeping the American Dream going will require effort from every American. I asked myself at one point, "Are you crazy, Joe? Can you actually represent this in a song? Will people get it?" Eventually, I get to a point where I just do whatever I have to do to get the music to sound truthful to me. If someone decides later they want to play that song while they're working out, snowboarding, or driving in their car, that's cool. It's not my job to force people to think of the song the way I thought of it. Eventually, the artist has to give it away and move on and create more art.

"Jumpin' In" and "Jumpin' Out" were two songs I wrote and recorded on the same day and then stored in my "Possible Recording Project" folder on my computer. Apparently, after I recorded the demo to "Jumpin' In," I had written an alternate version, "Jumpin' Out." I'd recorded the whole song and totally forgotten about it. I'd even forgotten how to play it! It was in A Hungarian minor and had this kind of swinging guitar-as-tenor-sax kind of thing with the band playing as an ensemble behind me. Upon rediscovering it, I realized that it was a really cool song and that both of these pieces could go together in a yin and yang kind of way—one song about not being afraid to take chances, the other about knowing when *not* to take chances.

As the session dates were approaching, I sent Mike Fraser all the songs I was working on and asked, "Which ones do you like, which ones do you think suck, and which ones do you think I'm crazy to even attempt?" because I was at that point where I needed some feedback.

I hadn't really decided who was going to play on the record until the last minute. I had to go with my gut on which group of guys would be the best to record the album with. It wasn't clear-cut to me this time around because my whole system of not bringing the demos out on the road kind of worked against me in this respect.

Had I done so, a lot of that work of deciding who would play on the record would have been figured out. Then, by the time I arrived home, I could have told Mike exactly whom I wanted. It's dangerous to wait until the last minute because sometimes the players you want aren't available. I can't really explain why I felt that Chris Chaney, Vinnie Colaiuta, and Mike Keneally would work well together. I took a big chance that there would be some unusual chemistry between them. It really did turn out to be a very fruitful decision, because those guys clicked, played so well together, and injected so much life into the material.

Vinnie Colaiuta and Chris Chaney writing charts at Skywalker in '13

PHOTO BY ARTHUR ROSATO

Vinnie Colaiuta has such a different personality and groove from any drummer I've ever played with. His musicianship is awesome, and his timing is the most natural thing you've ever heard in your life. It's uncanny. My digital editor, Mike Boden, had first suggested Jane's Addiction's Chris Chaney on bass. We didn't know if we could get him, but we did, and he wound up being the perfect bassist for the sessions. He was fun, artistic, and had a huge bass sound. Mike Keneally was the last guy I chose. He was quite busy with his producing gigs and his work with Dethklok, and although he plays guitar most of the time, I was hiring him just to play keyboards. He's a brilliant guitarist and keyboardist, and he can flow between the two. He can *see* the guitar in his head when he's playing piano and vice versa. Mike seems to be free of any kind of methodical or didactic keyboard approach. He's an amazingly pure musician, and extremely creative.

Vinnie Colaiuta at Skywalker in '13
Photo by Arthur Rosato

The level of professionalism with all these guys was really amazing. They came prepared, could change direction at the drop of a hat, and always gave tremendous performances.

Mike Fraser: These guys had amazing musicianship. I don't believe they had even heard the songs we were doing until

> probably an hour before we tracked the song. They'd sit there with their little earbuds on listening to Joe's demo. Chris would chart the song out, and Vinnie would listen to the song once or twice, and then say, "Okay, let's try this," and on almost every take, he'd take a different groove until he'd figured out in his mind what he wanted to play. By the time we'd hit take six or seven, he'd know exactly what he wanted to do and nail it. So again, it was a very quick process, and nobody got bogged down and tired of doing the same song all day long. It was a really fresh venture, and they all interplayed off each other, and there was just all this intuitive stuff that was amazing to watch! To see Joe off in his little guitar corner with a big grin on his face the whole time—it was a magical record!

When you make a record, there's all sorts of things that you're trying to manage: production, the musicians, choosing the right gear, and then there's your playing and the songs themselves. Then you try to pull everything together and hope that it has that *je ne sais quoi* that makes it sparkle. What was fun about making this album was that all the elements fell into place in an exciting and natural way. The two weeks we spent in Vancouver mixing the album were emotionally thrilling because I knew I was moving forward into a new creative phase, and I had a great record as proof!

Conclusion: 2013 and Beyond

Once a new record is mixed, I don't spend a lot of time listening to it. I really need to focus on the live performance versions. Just looking at 2012 alone, I had to play "Satch Boogie," "Flying in a Blue Dream," "Crowd Chant," and many other fan favorites hundreds of times. What keeps things interesting is finding new ways to be expressive every night onstage. I try to find ways to apply who I am today to the songs I recorded ten, fifteen, or twenty-five years ago. When I listen to my older material, it's more confusing than illuminating because it's not how I experience those songs every night on stage. I do know those versions are what my fans relate to. The studio versions are in their playlists, so that's what they're relating to day after day. That's the total opposite of how I experience those songs. I'm living the "live" versions and hardly ever listen to the studio versions once they're done.

It's very difficult to say whether I prefer the studio or live versions of songs. One time in 2004, we were playing an outdoor gig in a town square in Wrocław, which is in southwestern Poland. It was on this weekend where they have live music for almost twenty-four hours straight, all the way until sunrise, in this beautiful square that looks like it must have been built eight hundred years ago. We didn't really know what to expect when we went on. We started doing "Crowd Chant," which was making its first appearance on tour that year, and all of a sudden this crowd of twenty thousand people was synched up with the band and singing this song with us. It was just amazing. I couldn't believe that this little idea I had in my studio was now being chanted by twenty thousand people on this beautiful summer night in Poland! There have been so many nights like that all around the world, where an audience has come to the party with one particular song in their heads, or where they sing the melodies I'm playing on every song. When an audience is with you like that, it's a very powerful experience.

Throughout my career, all of my records have been cathartic to a large degree, because I made an unconscious decision way back during my first album that I would concentrate on material that was an expression of my feelings, experiences, and memories. I didn't turn on the radio, listen to the Top 20, and say, "Okay, now write your version of that." I know people who do that and are very good at it, but at the time, I knew this was such a long shot. I was not going to try to break down the door of the music business doing the trendy thing; I knew I had to follow my own path. Whether it sold well or not, I needed to be happy with it artistically. I still feel that way.

Leonardo da Vinci said, "Art is never finished, only abandoned." I believe this to be true. It's the letting go of a record, a song, or even a solo that still remains so very difficult for me, and the act is so very cathartic, even after all these years. I still, however, find the process completely exhilarating. I was born to make music in a time when musicianship and originality were celebrated, and they still are—that's good fortune.

I wish I could go back and rewrite, rerecord, and replay so much of my music, but I've learned to respect the gift of time over the years. One's early recordings are like outrageous candid photos taken at a crazy party you wish you could forget, but there they are, reminders of who you were at a specific place and time. They reveal things about yourself that perhaps you missed the first go-round.

Writing this book has been cathartic enough for me, but not nearly as intense as reviewing John Cuniberti's wonderful remastering of my studio catalog. He has injected new life into the albums and made them sound more alive and exciting. Even though it's quite thrilling to undertake such a sweeping retrospective, I still prefer moving forward and not looking back. As I write this passage, I'm only halfway through the *Unstoppable Momentum* tour, and my fingers are still itching to reinterpret the new material onstage. I want to wrestle with the complexity of "Lies and Truths." And I look forward to being immersed in the emotion of "I'll Put a Stone on Your Cairn" night after night.

Looking back on almost thirty years of being a "solo artist," I am humbled by and grateful for all the love and support granted me by my fans, fellow musicians, managers, agents, promoters, record companies, press agents, and, most of all, my family. To be able to follow one's heart and pursue one's passion in life is truly a gift to be thankful for. Thank you!

The Gear: Album by Album

The Joe Satriani EP 1984: '54 Fender Stratocaster, '83 Kramer Pacer, homemade Boogie Body and Rubina-painted Strat-type electrics, '67 Marshall Super Lead, '78 Marshall MKII 100 watt-head, Roland JC-120, Boss DS-1, OD-1, and CE-1 pedals, EH Big Muff Pi pedal, Echoplex Tape Delay, MXR Flanger, Maxon Digital Delay

Not of This Earth 1986: '83 Kramer Pacer, Boogie Body and Rubina-painted Strat-type electrics, '67 Marshall Super Lead, '78 Marshall MKII 100-watt head, Roland JC-120, Scholz Rockman, silverface Fender Princeton Reverb amp, Boss DS-1, OD-1, BF-2, and CE-2 pedals

Surfing with the Alien 1987: two '83 Kramer Pacers, Boogie Body and Rubina-painted Strat-type electrics, vintage Coral Sitar, '67 Marshall Super Lead, '78 Marshall MKII 100-watt head, Roland JC-120, Gorilla practice amp, Scholz Rockman, original Chandler Tube Drivers, Cry Baby wahs, Boss DS-1, DD-2, OD-1, and CE-2 pedals

Dreaming #11 EP 1988: Ibanez JS1 Prototype "Black Dog," Scholz Rockman, '64 Fender P-Bass; live rig: Ibanez JS1;

'67 Marshall Super Lead, '78 Marshall MKII 100-watt head, Cry Baby wahs, Boss DS-1, DD-2, and CE-1 pedals

★ ★

Flying in a Blue Dream 1989: Ibanez JS1 Prototype "Black Dog," white Ibanez JS1, '83 Kramer Pacer, Boogie Body Strat-type electric, Fender '63 reissue Stratocaster, '64 Fender P-Bass, '71 Marshall Super Lead, '78 Marshall MKII 100-watt head, Roland JC-120, Gorilla practice amp, Scholz Rockman, Mesa Boogie Mark llc 100-watt head, Deering 6-string banjo, Cry Baby wahs, Boss DS-1, OD-1, and CE-2 pedals

★ ★

The Extremist 1992: Ibanez JS6, JS1, and "Black Dog" guitars, '83 Kramer Pacer, Boogie Body Strat-type electric, Gibson Chet Atkins Nylon String Electric, '69 Marshall full stack, Marshall 6100, Roland JC-120, '64 Fender Vibrolux Reverb, Soldano 100-watt head, Mesa Boogie Dual Rectifier head, Deering 6-string banjo, vintage National dobro, Gibson mandolin, Zoom headphone amp, '65 Gibson Hummingbird, Cry Baby wahs, Boss DS-1, OD-1, and CE-2 pedals

★ ★

Time Machine 1993: Ibanez JS guitars and Marshall 6100s for '90s live rig; '88 live rig: '67 Marshall Super Lead; studio tracks: Boogie Body Strat-type electric, Wells amp, Soldano, Marshall 6100, Roland JC-120, 5150 head, '58 Fender Esquire, Fender custom shop Stratocasters, Cry Baby wahs, Boss DS-1, DD-2, and CE-2 pedals

Joe Satriani 1995: Ibanez JS guitars, '58 Fender Esquire, Deering 6-string banjo, vintage National dobro, '58 Gibson Les Paul Jr., '84 Gibson Flying V, Wells amp, Marshall 6100, Roland JC-120, Peavey 5150 head, Peavey Classic combo, vintage Gibson Discover Tremolo amp, '53 Fender Deluxe, vintage Rickenbacker lap steel, Chandler Baritone guitar, Cry Baby wahs, Boss DS-1, OC-2, BF-2, and CE-2 pedals, Fulltone Ultimate Octave, Digitech Whammy

Crystal Planet 1998: Ibanez JS guitars, '58 Fender Esquire, '58 Fender Stratocaster, '58 Gibson Les Paul Jr., '84 Gibson Flying V, '83 Kramer Pacer, Wells amp, Marshall 6100, Roland JC-120, Peavey 5150 head, Gibson Lab Series combo, SansAmp rack and plug-in, Cry Baby wahs, Boss DS-1, DD-2, and CE-2 pedals, Fulltone Ultimate Octave, Digitech Whammy

Engines of Creation 2000: Ibanez JS guitars, '58 Fender Stratocaster, '64 Fender P-Bass, Wells amp, Marshall 6100, SansAmp rack and plug-in amp, '64 Fender Bassman, Hafler Triple Giant rack-mount head, Cry Baby wahs, Boss DS-1, and CE-2 pedals, Fulltone Ultimate Octave, Digitech Whammy, Moogerfooger pedals, EH Micro Synth

Strange Beautiful Music 2002: Ibanez JS guitars, Boogie Body Strat-type electric, '58 Fender Esquire, '58, '60,

'61, and '69 Fender Stratocasters, '64 Fender P-Bass, '58 Gibson Les Paul Jr., Martin '48 000-18 acoustic, Deering 6-string banjo, '84 Kramer Pacer, '95 Gibson Les Paul, Wells amp, Marshall 6100, Roland JC-120, Peavey 5150 head, Jerry Jones, Coral Sitar, Chandler Baritone guitar, Cornford prototype heads, Mesa Boogie Dual Rectifier head, Cry Baby wahs, Boss DS-1 and CE-2 pedals, Fulltone Ultimate Octave, Digitech Whammy, Echoplex Tape Delay, RMC wah pedals

Is There Love in Space 2004: Ibanez JS guitars, Ibanez JS 7-string prototypes, '66 Fender Electric XII, Rickenbacker 360 12-string electric, '58 Fender Esquire, Fender custom shop Stratocaster, '64 Fender P-Bass, '48 Martin 000-18 acoustic, '50 Martin D-28, Wells amp, Marshall 6100 and '71 Super Lead heads, Roland JC-120, Peavey 5150 head, Peavey JSX head and cabinets, Vox AC30, Chandler Baritone guitar, Peavey Mini Colossal, Cornford prototype heads, Mesa Boogie Dual Rectifier head, Cry Baby wahs, Boss DS-1, DM-2, DD-2, and CE-2 pedals, Fulltone Ultimate Octave, Digitech Whammy, Roger Mayer Deja Vibe

Super Colossal 2006: Ibanez JS guitars, '58 Fender Esquire, '66 Fender Electric XII, Rickenbacker 360 12-string electric, Fender custom shop Stratocaster, '64 Fender P-Bass, '73 Fender P-Bass, '48 Martin 000-18 acoustic, Wells amp, Marshall 6100, Peavey 5150 head, Wizard 100-watt head, Peavey Mini Colossal, Doctor Z Mini Z, Cry Baby wahs, Boss DS-1 and CE-2 pedals, Fulltone Ultimate Octave, Digitech Whammy, EH POG pedal

★ ★

Professor Satchafunkilus and the Musterion of Rock 2008: Ibanez JS guitars, '58 Fender Esquire, Fender custom shop Stratocaster, '64 Fender P-Bass, '73 Fender P-Bass, '48 Martin 000-18 acoustic, '06 Gibson Gold Top Les Paul, Wells amp, Marshall 6100, JMP, and 800 heads, Roland JC-120, Peavey 5150 head, Wizard 100-watt head, Ben Fargen JS prototype head, Peavey Mini Colossal, Cry Baby wahs, Vox Big Bad Wah and Satchurator prototypes, Fulltone Ultimate Octave, Digitech Whammy, Boss OC-2 pedal, Roger Mayer Octavia

Chickenfoot 2009: Ibanez JS guitars, '58 Fender Esquire, Fender custom shop Stratocaster, '48 Martin 000-18 acoustic, Rickenbacker 360 12-string electric, '06 Gibson gold top Les Paul, '06 Gibson JJP #1, Wells amp, Marshall 6100, Peavey 5150 head, Peavey JSX head and cabinets, Peavey JS prototype 100-watt head, Jerry Jones, Coral Sitar, Peavey Mini Colossal, Vox Big Bad Wah and Satchurator, Fulltone Ultimate Octave, Digitech Whammy, Roger Mayer Deja Vibe, Way Huge pedals

Black Swans and Wormhole Wizards 2010: Ibanez JS guitars, '58 Fender Esquire, '69 Fender Stratocaster, '64 Fender P-Bass, '73 Fender P-Bass, '48 Martin 000-18 acoustic, '06 Gibson JPP #1, Jerry Jones Coral Sitar, '59 Gibson L-5, Wells amp, Marshall 6100 and '73 Super Lead, Peavey 5150 head, Wizard 100-watt head, Marshall JVM410HJS head prototype, '64 Fender Bassman, Two Rock Classic Reverb amp, Vox Big Bad Wah and Satchurator, Fulltone

Ultimate Octave, Digitech Whammy, Roger Mayer Deja Vibe, Way Huge pedals, Sustainiac pickup system

Chickenfoot III 2011: Ibanez JS guitars, '58 Fender Esquire, '06 Gibson JPP #1, '59 Gibson 335, '55 Gibson Les Paul gold top, Rickenbacker 360 12-string electric, Marshall JVM410HJS amps, '59 Fender Twin amp, '53 Fender Deluxe amp, Two Rock Classic Reverb amp, Vox Big Bad Wah and Time Machine pedals, EH POG pedal

Unstoppable Momentum 2013: Ibanez JS guitars, Boogie Body Strat-type electric, '58 Fender Esquire, '06 Gibson JPP #1, '83 Gibson 335, '61 Fender Stratocaster, Marshall JVM410HJS amps, '59 Fender Twin amp and assorted '50s Fender amps, Peavey 5150 head, Wizard 100-watt head, Roland JC-120, Fargen Retro Classic, '64 Fender Bassman, Two Rock Classic Reverb and 10th Anniversary amps, Vox Big Bad Wah and Time Machine pedals, Boss DM-2 and OC-2 pedals, Digitech Whammy, Sustainiac pickup system

Acknowledgments

This book started out as a crazy idea from the mind of author Jake Brown. He felt that even after fourteen studio albums much about my creative process was still a mystery to my fans and that they would love to have me shed some light on that process. As we brainstormed the project it blossomed into something much bigger and more comprehensive than I could have imagined. I'm glad it did, and I thank Jake for coming to me with his idea.

I actually tried writing an autobiography a few years ago, but found the whole thing to be too cathartic. I felt it was a bit too early in my life to be looking back on everything with such scrutiny, and so it fell by the wayside. This time around, Jake's idea made more sense to me. We would concentrate on the studio albums, the work that goes into making a record, the creative process, the gear, and the colorful cast of characters who joined me along the way. Jake tirelessly interviewed not only me, but also everyone else who played a major role in helping me record my studio albums. He spoke with the musicians, engineers, producers, record company executives, etc. I must admit, I learned a thing or two about myself reading through the transcripts of those interviews.

However streamlined Jake's idea was, I found the whole process cathartic anyway. There was no escaping it in the end. The photographs alone brought back vivid memories both good and bad. Writing this book has proven to be hard work, too, but worthwhile and artistically reaffirming. It seems I've spent my whole life with a guitar strapped around my neck, trying to move forward, not looking back, always jumping into new musical territory. It's been immensely interesting, artistically satisfying, and fun! Music helps me make sense of the world. I guess it always has. It's taken a bit of brooding to sort things out along the way, but that process of digging deep into my soul everyday has defined a large part of my life, and has been the method behind my creativity.

I would like to thank Jake Brown; Glenn Yeffeth and all the good people at BenBella Books; my manager, Mick Brigden; my agent, Wayne Forte; and all my friends and musical cohorts who contributed their precious time and effort into making this book truthful, accurate, and fun to read.

My parents John and Katherine Satriani must have seen very early in my life that I was crazy about music, and they supported and nurtured me through it all. There is no way to thank them enough. My siblings deserve an apology for all the noise I made growing up, and a big thank-you as well, as they too helped and guided me on my musical adventures.

Special thanks to my wife, Rubina, and my son, ZZ, for everything they are, the lights of my life.

—Joe Satriani

First and foremost, I would like to thank the great Joe Satriani for granting me this once-in-a-lifetime opportunity as a biographer to collaborate on the writing of a book that factually kept me from retiring in 2011 after thirty-three books, took me to another level as a writer creatively, and gave my career a second life. I'll be forever grateful as a fan and author for the honor.

A million thanks to the indespensible Mick Brigden, the greatest music manager I've ever had the privilege of working with in fifteen years in the business. This book would *not* have been completed without your steady hand helping to guide the process, from arranging interviews with players and producers to acting as point person with our publisher once the deal was done. It has been a true privilege.

Thank you to the colorful cast of talented souls who contributed their time and interview commentary to help tell this amazing story, including the awesome Steve Vai, John Cuniberti, Mike Fraser, Glyn Johns, Andy Johns (R.I.P.), Sammy Hagar, Chad Smith, Michael Anthony, Larry LaLonde, Bongo Bob Smith, Jeff Holt, Jeff Campitelli, Gregg and Matt Bissonette, Eric Caudieux, Kenny Aronoff, Brian May, Billy Gibbons, Robert Fripp, and Stu Hamm.

Many thanks to our amazing publisher, BenBella Books, for giving this book a home, specifically publisher Glenn Yeffeth for first believing in the project, and all of the gifted staff who worked so hard on this book, including our awesome editor Erin Kelley, Adrienne Lang, Alicia Kania, Jennifer Canzoneri, Sarah Dombrowsky, Lindsay Marshall, Jenna Sampson, Monica Lowry, Debbie Harmsen, Adia Herrera, et al.

On the personal side, first and foremost, a thousand thank-yous to my Carriedoll for giving up two years of Sundays to my workaholism/tolerating my six-day work weeks necessary to undertake the writing of this opus and for inspiring me tirelessly along the way, I love you beyond all words and songs; our devoted pets, Scooter and Hannie; to my wonderful parents, James and Christina Brown, thank you for all your tireless support and love throughout my creative life as a musician and writer; my brother, Josh; the extended Thieme and Brown families. Thank you to my lifelong cast of amazing friends: Alex, Ellen, Jackson, and Willamena Schuchard; Andrew and Sarah McDermott; Sean Fillinich and Lisa Wood; Cris Ellauri; Adam and Shannon Perri; Alexandra Federov and Larry Jiminez; Paul and Helen Watts; Bob and Cyenne O'Brien; Richard,

Lisa, and Regan Kendrick; Joe Viers; Aaron C. Harmon; Tony and Yvonne Rose; John Cerullo; Kenny Aronoff; and anyone and everyone else whom I've had the chance to share this wild ride called life with over the past thirty-eight years!

—Jake Brown

Index

D

E

F

S

T

U